في ذكرى

مارك لينز

Environmental Challenges in the MENA Region

The Long Road from Conflict to Cooperation

Edited by Hamid Pouran and Hassan Hakimian

First published in 2019 by
Gingko
4 Molasses Row
London SW11 3UX

A CIP catalogue record for the book is available from the British Library.

ISBN 978-1-909942-21-9
eISBN 978-1-909942-22-6

Typeset in Times by MacGuru Ltd
Printed in the United Kingdom

www.gingko.org.uk
@GingkoLibrary

Contents

Foreword

Tony Allan

The Middle East region has endured a century of challenges marked by external interventions, accelerating climate change and population increase. The result has been growing political and social instability. The region's political systems have been overstretched with recurrent uncertainty, ongoing political conflict and bouts of intense armed conflict. As a result, regional and international media have enough bad news from the Middle East to regularly fill in television screens and pages of the print media.

In these circumstances it comes as no surprise that the environment does not make it on to front pages, as bad environmental news generally tends to be under-reported. Sadly, this pattern is not limited to the Middle East alone as under-reporting is also common in major economies such as the United States, the EU and other advanced and diverse economies.

The experience of trying to have sound environmental science considered in international negotiations has everywhere proven to be a very disorderly proce-dure. Short-term interests at both national and global levels, blind to the need for environmental stewardship, have determined problematic outcomes. The classic case is the battle being waged by those calling for precautionary policies on green-house gas emissions. Climate change politics has become an endless, toxic, frus-trating international political process.

The challenge taken up by the editors and authors of this volume is to fore-ground very effectively the need in the Middle East for the adoption of environ-mental policies, informed by science. The sustainable security of the peoples and governments of the region depends on the reversal of the evident, but generally ignored, degradation of the region's natural ecosystems. These dangerous trends are identified by the authors in this volume, but they regret that they have not yet found a way to get them effectively reported and discussed by legislators.

A number of very important messages are highlighted by the authors. In a world in which it is possible to manage public awareness by under-reporting politically destabilising bad news, the chapters in this book provide examples of how ecosystem crises can be made worse. One of the important contributions of the book is the reminder that invisible elements of the global political economy make it possible for governments to enjoy a version of water and food security that is vital but whose lack must remain politically invisible.

No one is aware – certainly not the peoples and legislators of Middle Eastern economies – that they have enjoyed a version of water and food security that has been invisible, and therefore politically feasible. This invisible system has, at no cost to the region's economies, also protected its environmental capital such as its water ecosystems.

The global food system has provided the solution of water security and some costless environmental protection. The Middle East economies have depended more than any other region in the world on the global food system, which has for the past century provided food, more importantly underpriced food, for any economy in the world that has not had enough water to ensure its food self-sufficiency.

By about 1970, the region as a whole could no longer feed itself and became a net food importer. If international food prices had reflected the true costs of production, as well as the costs of water consumed in producing it and the costs of water stewardship in the exporting economy, the global food market would have suffered an existential threat. In practice, internationally traded staple foods have been underpriced and the exporting economies have borne the environmental costs of production. As a consequence, water-scarce economies have been able – without any political stress – to import themselves out of their otherwise impossible predicaments of water and food insecurity.

The authors in this volume have made a very significant contribution by providing the scientific fundamentals on the status of the Middle Eastern environmental capital shared by the economies of the region. More importantly, they have drawn attention to and critiqued the character and capacity of the region's governance systems. They have many important things to say about the necessary and feasible social and environmental policies. They show how they are needed to reshape the expectations of society and create strong and diverse economies that protect the region's environmental resources and manage the atmosphere, water and biodiversity sustainably.

Tony Allan
SOAS, University of London and King's College London
July 2018

1

Introduction

Hamid Pouran and Hassan Hakimian

The Middle East and North Africa (MENA) region is well-known for its abundant fossil fuel resources and important geostrategic position. The region's popular image is, however, over-shadowed by violence and transboundary conflicts that threaten its stability with huge global implications. This perception has inevitably overshadowed the region's other pressing challenges.

In recent years, a combination of the impact of climate change and growing environmental fragility has preoccupied policymakers in the MENA countries. Yet ongoing conflict and rivalries have thwarted initiatives and collaborative action to address these challenges. Recurrent environmental setbacks and rapid depletion of the region's natural resources hence continue to pose major threats to the long-term economic, political and social stability of the region. This is despite the fact that the challenges from MENA's environmental insecurity in the 21st century may have potentially more adverse consequences for the region than the toll afflicted by conflict and violence. This book is an attempt at highlighting some of these challenges and exploring ways in which they can be addressed on a collective scale.

Environmental challenges arise in, and make their impact on, the specific contexts in which they operate. In the MENA context, demographic factors have contributed to the urgency with which environmental issues have presented themselves. Over the past five decades, the region has experienced some of the highest rates of population growth in the world. According to the World Bank,[1] the average population of the MENA region has increased almost 400% during this

---

1 World Bank, 'The World Bank Data', https://data.worldbank.org/country.

period with some parts – notably, the UAE and Qatar – experiencing growth rates exceeding 1,000%. Such high growth rates inevitably pose major environmental challenges including water shortages, land degradation and pollution. Despite their vast fossil fuel resources and the potential benefits of extensive solar irradiation, the region's arid and semi-arid climate has imposed major risks and limitations on these countries. For instance, rapid urbanisation throughout the region, the absence of adequate legal frameworks in addition to failure to implement national and international environmental protection guidelines have exacerbated environmental fragility in many parts of the region. Future forecasts and climate change projections troublingly suggest this condition is expected to get worse with further deterioration in the pipeline unless action is taken to stem the tide.

Since the start of the new millennium there has been an unprecedented level of temperature increases on a global scale.[2] We have already passed the 1°C increase in global mean temperatures and are on a fast track to experiencing 2°C mean temperature rises in the coming years (compared to the pre-industrial era). Viewed at a local level, this development may not seem drastic (i.e. microclimate); however, such an increase is broadly considered to pose a point of no return for climate change as it is capable of unleashing global changes which can pose existential threats for many countries and regions. More frequent and extreme heatwaves, droughts and floods may be expected with irreversible and devastating impacts of such climate change.

Despite the relatively small contribution of MENA countries to global warming, they are among the countries that would be most affected by climate change. Their arid and semi-arid climates have already put water resources under stress, and anticipated prolonged and hotter summers will make the region suffer disproportionally compared to others.

New studies, for instance, suggest that towards the end of the century severe heatwaves combined with humidity in the Persian Gulf region will make staying outdoors for more than a few hours at a time quite challenging for people.[3] The

2 S. J. Smith, J. Edmonds, C. A. Hartin, A. Mundra and K. Calvin, 'Near-Term Acceleration in the Rate of Temperature Change', *Nature Climate Change* 5.4, 2015, pp. 333–6, doi:10.1038/nclimate2552; S. M. Papalexiou, A. Agha-Kouchak, K. E. Trenberth and E. Foufoula-Georgiou, 'Global, Regional, and Megacity Trends in the Highest Temperature of the Year: Diagnostics and Evidence for Accelerating Trends', *Earth's Future* 6.1, 2018, pp. 71–9, doi:10.1002/2017EF000709.
3 J. S. Pal and E. A. B. Eltahir, 'Future Temperature in Southwest Asia Projected to Exceed a Threshold for Human Adaptability', *Nature Climate Change* 6.2, 2016, pp. 197–200, doi:10.1038/nclimate2833.

harsh conditions will be beyond the human adaptability threshold to tolerate; sweating and ventilation would not be enough to mitigate the heat. This means that some professions would face major restrictions and that the required infrastructure and the built environment need to undergo significant adaptation to cope with such radical climatic changes. The main question thus is not whether the MENA region will be affected by climate change, but how severe the impacts will be. The current urgency can however be mitigated by the fact that some of the countries are prosperous enough to be able to invest in new industries, diversify their economies and better adapt to the inevitable risks imposed by climate change before it is too late.

Despite the critical nature of these challenges, attention devoted to this subject is a relatively new phenomenon and there has generally been a dearth of academic studies dedicated to MENA's environmental sustainability in recent years. This book is an attempt at addressing this gap, aiming to explore some of the most important environmental issues that MENA countries currently face. It brings together a wide range of perspectives and contributions from specialists with multidisciplinary backgrounds including climate scientists, environmental engineers, social scientists and policymakers.

The book is predicated upon two critical premises. First, that expertise and awareness from a wide range of disciplines is required to understand and address these challenges. Second, to have a real chance of success, MENA countries need to be aware of their common environmental threats and the necessity to confront them through regional cooperation and coordination.

Environmental Challenges in the MENA Region originated in a conference organised by the London Middle East Institute (LMEI) in October 2016 on the occasion of the SOAS Centenary during 2016/17. Hosted at a leading institution for the study of the Middle East over the past hundred years, it was fitting that the conference recognised and highlighted the region's future challenges inasmuch as it shed light on its current and past problems and opportunities. The choice to focus on environment as a centenary theme was an appropriate way to do this.

The contributions in the book came from the conference's call for papers and were subject to rigorous peer-review selections. They have also benefited from feedback and discussions during and after the conference.

The opening chapter by Iyad Abumoghli and Matthew Broughton presents the big picture based on the UN Environment's latest Regional Assessment for West Asia. It provides an in-depth look at the state of the environment in the region and examines its future trends. The assessment brings to light the complexity of interlinked priorities contributing to human health and well-being and offers possible policy-relevant options for decision-makers in transitioning towards a sustainable future. Abumoghli and Broughton argue that peace and improved environmental governance, along with the water-energy-food nexus are the overriding factors that need to be addressed holistically to achieve sustainable development in the region. Several remedies are proposed to address the current environmental issues. Environmental policies need to be integrated into national and regional planning, implementation and regulatory frameworks. The capacity of, and cooperation among, public institutions and civil society need to be strengthened to better manage natural resources. Joint research, information sharing and collaboration between the countries of the region are also crucial for developing solutions for better conservation and the sustainable use of transboundary resources. Their assessment concludes by presenting a positive scenario of how the region may look if West Asia's core priorities are all addressed and provides insights into the course of actions that governments would need to take to reach this vision.

After this preliminary chapter, the next part of the book consists of three chapters dedicated to different aspects of climate change and its implications for the countries in the region.

Chapter 3 – by Nathalie Hilmi, Alain Safa, Victor Planas-Bielsa and Mine Cinar – exemplifies the role of climate change on ocean acidification and its subsequent effects on the region, highlighting the importance of including both macroeconomic and microeconomic analyses when environmental issues are discussed. After examining the ecological risks in MENA countries, Hilmi *et al* model the socio-economic impacts of disasters, ocean acidification and ecological risks. They use Extreme Value Theory and Peak-Over-Threshold concepts to define the critical threshold point for ocean pH value. They define the benchmark pH based on time series observations which exhibit moderate to large variations and use Monte Carlo simulations to examine the probability of disasters. This approach places the issue of ocean acidification at the heart of adaptation and environmental risk reduction strategies, with their findings pointing to the need for including ocean acidification in global climate change negotiations in addition to such factors as increasing temperatures, pollution, sea level rise, overexploitation of resources and invasive species introduction.

In Chapter 4, Tobias Zumbrägel turns to a critical examination of environmental protection and climate policy as 'one of the most important governance fields of this century'. His case study focuses on Qatar's ambitious efforts to be considered an environmentally responsible country. He argues that the recent 'green revolution' in Qatar (as well as several other Gulf monarchies like the UAE and to some extent Saudi Arabia) should be understood as a strategy of incumbents' hold on power rather than an authentic pledge to sustainability. In other words, by posing questions about the ways in which the fossil-rich Qatar has adopted climate policy and its reasons for doing so, he analyses the interconnections between environmental policy-making and regime resilience. In this analysis, what Zumbrägel calls *eco regime resilience* stands in sharp contrast to the existing literature, which is preoccupied with how to achieve a more sustainable development in the region.

In Chapter 5, Nancy Lindisfarne and Jonathan Neale discuss the interconnection between the MENA countries' oil resources, the importance of adaptation and transition to renewable energies to mitigate the impacts of climate change, and how these changes can create new job opportunities. They explain how the presence of vast oil resources creates both challenges and opportunities within the context of climate change.

The succeeding part of the book consists of another three chapters, focused on water scarcity and food security issues and their implications for the region.

In Chapter 6, Marta Antonelli and Tony Allan draw attention to the ways in which the political economies of the region have adapted to water scarcity in the face of a dramatic decrease in the region's per capita renewable water availability. These strategies have included reliance on virtual water 'imports', that is the inflow of water originating outside the region 'embedded' in food imports. The increase in virtual water 'imports' over the past 25 years has been mainly driven by the rise in population. Antonelli and Allan's analysis aims to identify and contrast the two enduring parallel narratives on how water and food security are achieved in the region. The dominant narrative, believed by citizens and legislators, is that supplies of water and food are secure, that serious water and food supply problems are not immediate but belong 'in the future'. The other narrative recognises that the region has a very serious water scarcity problem. Water scientists and professionals have identified how the region has been able to address its water and food needs via international trade. This narrative has been effectively backgrounded because it is politically destabilising. The second narrative also highlights the role that economic diversification has played in providing easy access to food imports that have in turn provided an effective version of water and food security. The authors show that while the adaptation strategy has been very effective it has not been part of public discourse, which remains very poorly informed.

In Chapter 7, Helen Lackner discusses Yemen's urgent environmental challenges, such as water scarcity, rising sea levels, changes in rainfall patterns and their relevance for Yemeni society, culture, politics and the economy. Lackner reminds us that in addition to the devastating, ongoing war in Yemen, the country suffers from depleted water resources and unless the environmental challenges are urgently addressed, the current war and the political debates to end it will become irrelevant as within approximately one generation most of the country will be uninhabitable. Yemen, which is already facing ruined infrastructures, conflicts and major social and health challenges, desperately needs international help not only to mitigate the current issues but to be able to deal with water scarcity and climate change impacts. Although Yemen faces some unique challenges, other countries in the region as well need to address similar challenges, hence many lessons should be learnt from Yemen's experience.

The latter study is followed by Chapter 8, where María Jesus Beltrán reflects on the complexities and political ecology of virtual water in Palestine, exploring how the link between water, agriculture and trade is central to understanding the contemporary social and environmental challenges in the occupied Palestinian Territories. The concept of virtual water makes the water-agriculture-trade relationship discernable, shedding light on agricultural trade flows in terms of water. Combining the agricultural flows of virtual water to and from Palestine in the Post-Oslo period with an examination of the power relations that governed these flows, this chapter shows how virtual water flows evolve within the (geo)political-economic context in which they are embedded, bringing to light Israel's control over the flow of Palestinian agricultural virtual water.

The final four chapters in the last part of the book are devoted to an examination of renewable energies in the MENA region and prospects for their development.

In Chapter 9, Philipp Dees and Georgeta Vidican Auktor tell us about the growing presence of renewable energies in the MENA energy generation portfolio and its impact on economic growth in these countries. Using panel estimation methods, they assess the impact of electricity generation from renewable energy sources on economic growth in the region and identify variables explaining differences in renewable electricity deployment. Their study shows that the effect of increasing renewable electricity generation is positive in economic terms, while capacity expansion has no significant effect on economic growth. Renewable electricity deployment is mainly explained by differences in oil and gas reserves, with a higher usage of renewables in those countries with lower oil reserves, and by stronger property rights. They conclude by suggesting that for MENA countries to capture a larger share of benefits associated with renewable energy deployment, policymakers should enhance investments in this emerging sector.

Chapter 10 by Safia Saouli and Kaveh Madani is a case study of renewable energies in Algeria. They explain that while Algeria benefits from its vast oil, natural and shale gas reserves it cannot achieve its desired economic growth if

renewable energies do not become an important part of the country's power industry. Over the past few years oil production has continued to decrease, causing
much concern since oil and gas make up 62% of government revenue and 97%
of export revenue. This has prompted the government to make the decision to
exploit shale gas resources in 2014 to widen their hydrocarbon portfolio. The situation is compounded on the demand side by soaring domestic energy consumption
induced by a growing population, economic growth and urbanisation and aided
by generous subsidies, hence the need to upscale the power generation capacity and electric grids. The chapter makes a strong case for the development and
integration of renewable energy in the national mix. If the government expects to
not only maintain its hydrocarbon exports and revenues, but also cope with rising
domestic consumption and take action to mitigate climate change, it has to place
renewable power generation as a top priority on its agenda.

In Chapter 11, Maral Mahlooji, Ludovic Gaudard and Kaveh Madani focus on
renewable energy alternatives for the fossil fuel dominated energy sector in Persian
Gulf countries. In their move toward sustainability, these countries are aiming to
increase the deployment of renewable energies. Policies intend to promote the
transition away from the incumbent fossil fuel in order to limit greenhouse gas
emission. However, it is equally important to ensure the unintended impacts of
such policies on other valuable resources are minimised. This chapter identifies
the most desirable energy alternatives for the Persian Gulf countries. A System of
Systems (SoS) approach is used to develop a holistic understanding of the sustainability of eleven energy technologies with respect to country-specific resources.
Results show how the inclusion of other factors makes some of the most popular
renewable resources unattractive. Differences in water stress, land availability and
economic resources among nations, as well as carbon emissions, lead to variable
relative desirability of energy alternatives. The findings thus suggest that the most
viable clean energy options are context-specific.

Finally, in Chapter 12, Juman Al-Saqlawi, Niall Mac Dowell and Kaveh
Madani shed light on the prospect of relying on solar energy in Oman. Given the
potential of solar energy as an alternative fuel and the lack of renewable-based
policies in Oman, identifying the opportunities for its successful implementation
can only be achieved through an initial understanding of the energy sector. To this
end, the chapter provides a review of the energy sector in Oman, from home production and import of primary fuels to eventual final uses. The major stakeholders
involved are identified and alternative primary fuels are discussed. The approach
divides Oman's energy sector into three main sectors: the primary (supply) sector,
the intermediary sector and the demand (end-use) sector. The contribution of these

sectors to CO_2 emissions are analysed in detail to identify the challenges for this fossil fuel dependent country to make significant reductions in its carbon emission and provide alternative clean energies as a viable option for households and firms.

The contributions in this book underscore the important point that MENA's environmental challenges are of a transboundary nature and affect all countries within the region. A prime example is the dust storms. Dust particles often stem from conflict zones and are contaminated with war remnants. Such pollutants do not stay beyond border check points, they can potentially damage the health of millions of people thousands of miles away from where they originate. Apart from their extensive health hazards, they also cover the surface of solar panels and significantly drop their efficiencies. Even if MENA moves towards renewable energies and deploys solar farms extensively, it needs to find a way to step up its land conservation methods and minimise dust storm formations and its impact across the region through cooperation. It is thus evident how interconnected the environmental challenges are: we cannot isolate one single environmental issue and try to address it without a proper understanding of its formation, functions, connections and the role that it plays within the entire ecosystem.

Without this recognition, billions of dollars spent on solar energy power generation in the Gulf states will be doomed to failure. The fate of Masdar City, which was supposed to become a green and zero carbon city is a good reminder in this context. Masdar City (in the UAE) is now considered a green ghost town and a failed dream in sustainable planning.[4] This costly attempt shows that while investment and financial support are essential, they are not enough for sustainable development. Social responsibility, cultural awareness, collective efforts and regional cooperation are also needed to achieve environmental sustainability.

Air, water and soil pollution, climate change, water shortage, sustainable agriculture, energy security, land degradation, deforestation, biodiversity, waste management and weak environmental institutes are now common challenges for all MENA countries. Each of these issues is becoming increasingly important as we see rapid economic growth and urbanisations in these nations and as the impacts of climate change becomes more apparent. Collaboration between the divided MENA countries is not easy but it is achievable and would reinforce and

---

4 J. Evans, A. Karvonen and R. Raven, eds., *The Experimental City*, Abingdon 2016; 'Masdar's Zero-Carbon Dream Could Become World's First Green Ghost Town', *The Guardian* 16 February 2016, https://www.theguardian.com/environment/2016/feb/16/masdars-zero-carbon-dream-could-become-worlds-first-green-ghost-town.

accelerate the results of currently isolated efforts in response to environmental problems.

This book provides an interdisciplinary approach elaborating on some of the major environmental concerns in the region. Its aim is to provide a tangible image of some of the main problems, from climate change to water shortage and renewable energies. This is only a small step towards a long journey in addressing a subject that not only affects the environmental quality and the health and well-being of the region's people but also potentially affects the security of the entire region and its long-term stability.

Finding solutions depends on understanding the problems correctly as a first step. To that effect, this book aims to highlight some of the most urgent environmental concerns in the MENA region and explores ways in which they can be addressed.

Bibliography

'Masdar's Zero-Carbon Dream Could Become World's First Green Ghost Town', *The Guardian*, 16 February 2016, https://www.theguardian.com/environment/2016/feb/16/masdars-zero-carbon-dream-could-become-worlds-first-green-ghost-town.

Evans, J., A. Karvonen and R. Raven, eds., *The Experimental City*, Abingdon 2016.

Pal, S. J., and E. A. B. Eltahir, 'Future Temperature in Southwest Asia Projected to Exceed a Threshold for Human Adaptability', *Nature Climate Change* 6.2, 2016, pp. 197–200, doi:10.1038/nclimate2833.

Papalexiou, S. M., A. Agha-Kouchak, K. E. Trenberth and E. Foufoula-Georgiou, 'Global, Regional, and Megacity Trends in the Highest Temperature of the Year: Diagnostics and Evidence for Accelerating Trends', *Earth's Future* 6.1, 2018, pp. 71–9, doi:10.1002/2017EF000709.

Smith, S. J., J. Edmonds, C. A. Hartin, A. Mundra and K. Calvin, 'Near-Term Acceleration in the Rate of Temperature Change', *Nature Climate Change* 5.4, 2015, pp. 333–6, doi:10.1038/nclimate2552.

World Bank, 'The World Bank Data', https://data.worldbank.org/country.

2

Environmental Outlook for the West Asia Region

Iyad Abumoghli and Matthew Broughton

The West Asia region

The West Asia region is comprised of two geographic sub-regions – the Mashriq: Iraq, Jordan, Lebanon, Palestine, Syria; and Yemen and the Gulf Cooperation Council (GCC) countries: Bahrain, Kuwait, Oman, Qatar, Saudi Arabia and United Arab Emirates (UAE). The GCC economies are predominantly oil based, with a relatively advanced stage of development, and the Mashriq countries have more diversified economies, with industry, tourism, services and agriculture being the predominant sectors. Yemen is the only country that can be categorised as a Least Developed Country (LDC).

Despite its relatively small surface area, environmental pressures are tremendous in the region and are exacerbated by drought, rapid population growth, conflicts, strife and human migration. In addition to their devastating impacts on human lives, conflicts can destroy infrastructure, degrade the environment and tear apart the fabric of sustainable development. Their impacts are often unfairly endured by the most vulnerable sectors of society, affecting health, livelihoods and compounding poverty.

The complex, mutually reinforcing relationship between peace, security and the environment means that the latter plays a pivotal role in human well-being. Just as conflict can be a driver of environmental damage, degraded or poorly managed ecosystems can become a source of conflict over access to natural resources. On the other hand, healthy ecosystems and sustainably managed resources can help to minimise the threats of disasters and conflicts, providing a platform for post-crisis recovery, progress and peace.

The GEO-6 regional assessment for West Asia

UN Environment, also known as United Nations Environment Programme (UNEP), is the voice of the United Nations on environmental issues and the leading global environmental authority that sets the global environmental agenda. Its work encompasses assessing global, regional and national environmental conditions and trends, developing environmental instruments and strengthening institutions. In West Asia there is somewhat limited progress in terms of placing the environment at the top of national agendas, therefore UN Environment focuses on mainstreaming environment across development planning in the region to achieve this goal.

As part of its mandate, UN Environment works to understand and reduce the impacts of environmental degradation on human health, livelihoods and security in the aftermath of disasters and conflicts. It also emphasises the role of healthy ecosystems and sustainably-managed resources in reducing the risk of conflicts. UN Environment has responded to several crisis situations in West Asia, delivering environmental expertise to national governments and partners in response to various disasters, wars and political conflicts. More recently, it made 'Peace, Security and the Environment' the basis for the main narrative of the West Asia component of the sixth edition of the Global Environment Outlook (GEO) report. GEO is UN Environment's flagship report that aims to keep the environment under review. The sixth edition of the global report, launched in 2018, built upon regional assessment processes and aimed to assess the state of the global environment, review policies and options and chart the outlook on priority environmental issues while also identifying emerging challenges.

Between April and May 2015, six GEO conferences were convened in each of the UN Environment regions to consult with relevant stakeholders. The conferences saw the participation of more than 400 experts and representatives from 85 countries. During these conferences, regional outlooks were drafted, priority issues and trends were agreed upon, and emerging concerns were identified.

The inaugural West Asia conference was held from 10–14 May 2015 in Amman and was attended by 53 stakeholders, including representatives of governments, regional partners and experts. At this meeting, it was agreed that the assessment should be guided by seven regional priorities: water, land, marine resources, biodiversity, air, climate change and waste management. Along with the identified regional priorities, two umbrella themes were chosen to govern the West Asia assessment: 1) peace, security and environment, and 2) the water-energy-food nexus.

The publication, launched in May 2016, involved various levels of participation, starting with grassroots involvement and concluding with high-level government oversight. The key achievements lie not only in the process of developing the report but also in the method used to obtain the results. In full, 20 chapters were produced by lead authors, assisted by 36 thematic authors and 63 reviewers. The impact of the approach was hailed to be the first in the region to extend stake-holder engagement to the wider part of society in order to include academics and non-profit organisations, as well as the private sector.

The report's methodology followed the Driver-Pressure-State-Impact-Response (DPSIR) causal framework to inform decision-making by describing the interplay between man and the environment. As such, as well as reporting on the state and trends of the environment in West Asia, the report also offers an analysis of policy-relevant responses for decision-makers in achieving environ-mental goals and objectives. This policy analysis is intended to help countries position themselves on the most effective pathways for transitioning towards a more peaceful, secure and sustainable future.

Peace, security and the environment

With the understanding that environmental issues cannot be addressed in isola-tion, the GEO-6 Regional Assessment for West Asia[1] took a holistic approach in creating a comprehensive picture of the interdependent factors contributing to human well-being. The assessment is unique as it is the only GEO regional assessment that highlights the subject of conflict and human migration as a major contributing factor affecting the environment. In fact, the assessment shows that just as the environment is threatened by a lack of peace and security and increas-ing levels of conflict in the region, the latter crises can be caused by environmen-tal issues.

West Asia has long suffered from ongoing wars and political conflicts, the results of which have had devastating impacts not only on the environment, but also on social structures and human health. For example, the Palestinian-Israeli conflict has resulted in the overexploitation of groundwater in the West Bank and Gaza due to water scarcity.[2] This in turn has led to seawater intrusion into many of Gaza's wells.[3] Added to this is the unsafe disposal of wastewater and nitrate

---

1 UNEP, *GEO-6 Regional Assessment for West Asia*, Nairobi 2016.
2 PWA, *Palestine: The Right to Water*, Palestinian Water Authority 2012, http://www.pwa. ps/userfiles/file/marselya.pdf.
3 M. Zeitoun, *The Hidden Politics of the Palestinian-Israeli Water Conflict*, London 2008.

contamination from agriculture, resulting in poor water quality and the spread of many diseases.[4]

The ongoing war in Syria and fighting terrorism in Iraq have also created a heavy toxic footprint and significant environmental health concerns now exist, including radioactive health impacts from missiles, major respiratory issues from burning sulphur and oil fields, and soil and water contamination due to hazardous chemical residues from explosives.[5] Large swathes of Syria's forests have been destroyed by shelling and woodcutting and several wildlife reserves have been destroyed during the conflict. The region has also witnessed mass displacement of people across the Middle East, leading to severe environmental stresses to which refugees themselves are the most vulnerable. The impact of the influx of refugees is greatly intensified by the refusal of governments to acknowledge informal settlements and, subsequently, to provide adequate stabilisation solutions.[6] In addition, most refugees will not be able to return home before minefields are cleared and unexploded weaponry eradicated, a process which can take many years.

According to the United Nations High Commissioner for Refugees, 4.8 million Syrians have fled to neighbouring countries, overwhelming governmental institutions and natural resources and creating profound environmental and health-related challenges.[7] For instance, poor waste management increases the likelihood of disease outbreaks. At the start of July 2015 there were an estimated 2.97 million refugees in Lebanon, Jordan, Yemen and Iraq, generating an estimated total of about 1,440 tonnes of waste per day. In Lebanon alone, which has the highest per person concentration of refugees in the world, refugees generate about 15.7 per cent of the country's total municipal solid waste per day.[8]

GEO-6 also demonstrates that efforts to secure access to natural resources can be a driver of conflict in the region. A clear example of this is the military conflict

---

4 UNCTAD, *Report on UNCTAD Assistance to the Palestinian People: Developments in the economy of the occupied Palestinian territory*, Geneva 2015, http://reliefweb.int/sites/ reliefweb.int/files/resources/tdb62d3_en-1.pdf.
5 United Nations High Commission for Refugees, *Syria regional refugee response: Inter-agency information sharing portal*, UNHCR 2015, http://data.unhcr.org/syrianrefugees/ country.php?id=107.
6 United Nations Office for the Coordination of Humanitarian Affairs, Government of Lebanon, *Lebanon crisis response plan 2015–2016*, https://docs.unocha.org/sites/dms/ CAP/2015-2016_Lebanon_CRP_EN.pdf.
7 United Nations High Commission for Refugees, *Syria regional refugee response: Inter-agency information sharing portal*, 2015, http://data.unhcr.org/syrianrefugees/country. php?id=107.
8 Sweepnet, *The regional solid waste exchange of information and expertise network in Mashriq and Maghreb countries*, 2014, http://www.sweep-net.org/countries.

in Iraq, spanning several decades and leading to levels of environmental degradation unprecedented in the region. In recent years, Iraq has experienced significant
droughts, aggravating an underlying water crisis. With studies predicting that the
Tigris and Euphrates may dry up by 2040,[9] Iraq is now witnessing displacement
of farming communities who are seeking access to safe drinking water. Water
scarcity in Yemen has likewise led to power struggles for control of resources and
internal displacement of people and increased numbers of refugees and migrants.[10]

Failures to manage such environmental challenges can be a further source of
conflict. In mid-July 2015, a waste crisis erupted in Lebanon following the closure
of the country's main sanitary landfill due to overcapacity. For nearly a year,
the city streets of Beirut were clogged with huge piles of rubbish, causing an
environmental and public health disaster and leading to social unrest and mass
street protests. It is therefore quite apparent that just as conflict results in environmental degradation, environmental challenges can also be a source of conflict in
the region. The result is a vicious cycle of poverty-reinforcing overexploitation
and environmental degradation, which in turn exacerbates social stratification and
conflict.[11] Further compounding these concerns are the underlying environmental
priorities identified in the GEO-6 assessment.

Water resources

No doubt, freshwater scarcity is one of the most critical challenges facing the
region. West Asia's renewable water resources vary considerably from country to
country. Iraq, for example, possesses a large internal renewable water resource,
while GCC countries are highly dependent on non-conventional sources such
as desalinated water and treated wastewater, producing about 60 per cent of the
world's desalinated water.

Rapid population growth and urbanisation, increased frequency of drought and
extreme events, and improved standards of living have contributed to a widening
gap between supply and demand, exerting pressure on groundwater extraction

9 M. Rowling, 'Iraq's Environment, Water Supply in Severe Decline', *Thomson Reuters
Foundation News* 2014,
http://news.trust.org//item/20140127121610-cdrqu/.
10 United States Agency for International Development, *Yemen: country development
cooperation strategy 2014–2016*, https://www.usaid.gov/sites/default/files/documents/1860/
CDCS_Yemen_Public%20Version.pdf.
11 S. Sipkin, 'Water Conflict in Yemen', *ICE Case Studies* 235, 2012, http://www1.american.
edu/ted/ice/Yemen-Water.htm.

rates. The region has already surpassed its natural capacity to meet its own water demand and only four out of twelve countries are above the water scarcity limit of 1,000 cubic metres per person per year.[12] This has been further exacerbated by the political unrest that has arisen in Iraq, Syria and Yemen and the recent influx of refugees impacting water supply and sanitation services.

The resulting overexploitation of groundwater resources throughout West Asia has had considerable environmental impacts and has resulted in a deterioration of water quality, seawater intrusion and the depletion and salinisation of aquifers. Moreover, GEO-6 indicates that the effects of climate change on temperature, rainfall and sea level may significantly reduce existing water resources, leading to decreases in the flow of major rivers and groundwater recharge rates, increased water demand – especially for irrigated agriculture – and an increase in the variability and frequency of extreme events.[13] The degree of expected impacts will also vary between countries, with the GCC countries particularly affected.

Clearly such impacts need to be addressed and governments have been paying more attention in recent years to developing holistic policies in line with the integrated water resources management approach called for in the Johannesburg Plan of Implementation and encouraged by the Sustainable Development Goals (SDGs). Water management should be considered across a wide range of sectors, including agriculture, tourism and industry, the latter which uses most of the water. Several countries, such as Jordan, Palestine, the UAE and Yemen have already developed integrated plans which are at an implementation stage. The lessons learned from these experiences can be invaluable in informing the planning process in the region, which currently lacks appropriate governance due to inadequate institutional and legal frameworks. Subsequently, water policies are often fragmented, confined to national development plans and focus on increasing water supply with little demand management practices. Thus, comprehensive water sector reform and good governance conducive to inter- and cross-sectoral coordination is essential for the success of the integrated approach. Decisionmakers and stakeholders must define the mandate of their water sectors, obligate the required financial and human resources, enable a free flow of information and enforce coordination mechanisms.

---

12 K. Abu-Zeid, *An Arab Perspective on the Applicability of the Water Convention in the Arab Region: Key Aspects and Opportunities for the Arab Countries*, Workshop on Legal Frameworks for Cooperation on Transboundary Waters, Tunis, 11–12 June 2014, http://www.gwp.org/Global/GWP-Med%20Files/News%20and%20Activities/MENA/Tunis%20Workshop_June2014/5.2.K.Abuzeid_WaterConvention_Arab_Region.pdf.
13 Sipkin, 'Water Conflict in Yemen'.

The lack of regional cooperation and absence of agreements on shared water resources complicates water management in the region. Shared water remains a sensitive topic, particularly in areas overshadowed by political conflicts, such as in the Jordan River basin. As a result, data sharing between countries is also very limited and there exists no common understanding of the state and development of water availability, use and trends. This impedes the development of a common vision on shared water resource management. However, there are promising signs of cooperation efforts surfacing in the region, including the development of regional water strategies, such as the 2030 Arab Water Security Strategy and a GCC Unified Water Strategy.

Land resources

Water scarcity is also a significant limiting factor in another priority issue in the region; namely, land degradation. With deserts and drylands occupying around two thirds of West Asia, the natural aridity of the region, combined with high population growth, increasing rates of consumption and continuous conflicts and wars, means that the region is highly vulnerable to the spread of land degradation and desertification.

In Iraq, which is 97 per cent arid, desertification affects 39 per cent of the country's surface area, with a further 54 per cent under threat. Despite the fact that it has the largest area of farmlands in the region, Iraq suffers the most from soil salinity and wind erosion and loses an estimated 250 square kilometres of arable land each year.[14] In contrast, human impacts are possibly the main cause of land degradation in Jordan, which is covered by more than 80 per cent in rangelands. Rainfed agriculture is one of the most vulnerable sectors in Jordan and land-use conflict and mismanagement have led to livestock overgrazing, increased pressure on land resources and ultimately soil erosion.[15]

The spread of land degradation and desertification and its economic and

---

14 Food and Agriculture Organization, *Iraq country profile 2011*, http://www.fao.org/ag/agp/agpc/doc/counprof/iraq/iraq.html.
15 Jordan Ministry of Agriculture, *Updated Rangeland Strategy for Jordan*, Directorate of rangeland and Badia in collaboration with the IUCN, Jordan 2014, http://www.moa.gov.jo/Portals/0/pdf/English_Strategy.pdf; AOAD, *First Meeting for National Focal Points of Arab Network for Rangelands Sustainable Development*, Jordan 2015, http://www.aoad.org/frstFPMeetPastRes.pdf; IFAD, *Syrian Arab Republic: Thematic Study on Participatory Rangeland Management in the Badia*, International Fund for Agricultural Development, Rome 2012, http://www.ifad.org/pub/pn/badia.pdf.

environmental consequences are among the most critical challenges facing West Asian countries. With the carrying capacity of the land too low to support people with freshwater and food, the continuous shrinkage of agricultural lands will jeopardise food security in the region. Unfortunately, the most severe impacts will be felt in countries where the share of agriculture in gross domestic product (GDP) is high, such as in the Mashriq and Yemen.

The climate change projections presented in GEO-6 are very much a cause for concern. The predicted changes in the region's temperature, rainfall and sea level are all expected to exacerbate the extent of land degradation in West Asia. This, of course, will have devastating impacts on rangelands and rain-fed cropland and will likely contribute to loss of biodiversity, the spread of desertification and a greater intensity and frequency of droughts and dust storms. In fact, the effects of climate change are already being felt in several countries, where higher temperatures and lower precipitation levels have led to salinisation of water and soil. This can be seen in Iraq and Oman, where extensive salt crusts have formed on the surface of large areas of agricultural land due to increased surface temperatures and reduced mobility of near-surface groundwater.

Forests and rangelands are vital for the conservation of biodiversity and reducing vulnerability to climate change. Increasing the resilience of these ecosystems requires sound planning and integrated management strategies to develop rangelands and combat desertification, achieve food security and improve land and water use. Comprehensive and synergistic policy responses are needed that consider all the multiple drivers and pressures of land degradation.

Unfortunately, the management of land resources in West Asia is fragmented among different national institutions, leading to inefficient policies. For sustainable management to be successful, appropriate policy frameworks are needed, including organisational, institutional, legal and political structures that promote programme planning and implementation. Again, environmental governance should be incorporated into the activities of social, economic and administrative institutions, with environmental and land-use policies mainstreamed into national planning processes. Cooperation among countries is another key factor, as is local community participation, which not only capitalises on traditional knowledge but promotes ownership and effective collective action by the whole community.

Coastal and marine resources

Land deterioration is also occurring along the region's coastlines. Most coastal ecosystems have been classified as vulnerable, having lost significant portions of their original extent, and are in need of further representation in the protected area network. West Asia is host to some of the world's most important coastal and marine environments. Its rich biodiversity includes habitats such as mangrove stands, coral reefs, wetlands and seagrass and algal beds. It is also home to several endangered species, including dugongs, turtles, dolphins and cormorants. With West Asia's social, cultural and economic links to the sea, these precious ecosystems also provide essential goods and services, and support a rapidly growing tourism industry.

Unfortunately, these ecosystems are facing a number of pressures, perhaps most notably from the rapid coastal zone development and construction of ports and artificial islands. Although a relatively recent phenomenon, intensive dredging and reclamation activities have significantly changed the geography of many coasts in the region. By the early 1990s, over 40 per cent of the coasts of the GCC countries had been modified.[16] These artificial coastlines have caused alterations in tidal currents and sediment transport pathways and resulted in substantial loss of biodiversity. Dugongs, in particular, have been severely affected by marine construction activities that have devastated the seagrass beds on which they feed.

Pollution is another major impact of the increasing pressure on coastal areas and poses a threat to both marine biota and public health. Discharges of sewage, processing waste and drainage from urban, agricultural and industrial activities are the main culprits. Desalination and power plants, in particular, constitute 48 per cent of the total industrial effluent flowing directly into the marine environment of the ROPME (Regional Organization for the Protection of the Marine Environment) Sea Area.[17] The outflow of warm water from desalination plants also causes significant changes to the temperature and salinity of seawater, severely affecting marine organisms.

Oil exploration, production and transportation is another contributor to pollution. The Strait of Hormuz, the Bab Al-Mandab Strait and the Suez Canal are all strategically important oil shipping routes, with around 25,000 to 30,000 ships transiting through the Red Sea and Gulf of Aden each year. Chronic oil pollution is being observed near the major ports in these areas due to operations at oil terminals, and it is estimated that over 5,000 tonnes of oil have been spilled in the Red Sea. As the coastlines of the region are becoming increasingly urbanised, the rate

---

16 W. Hamza and M. Munawar, 'Protecting and Managing the Arabian Gulf: Past, Present and Future', *Aquatic Ecosystem Health & Management* 12.4, 2009, 429–39, doi: 10.1080/14634980903361580.
17 ROPME, *State of the Marine Environment Report*, Kuwait 2013.

of exploitation of living marine resources is also rising. Several species, such as finfish, lobsters, scombroids and cuttlefish are overexploited, and according to the IUCN Red List of Threatened Species, 22 per cent of West Asian fishes are now considered threatened species.[18] Overfishing is a major threat to fishing industries in West Asia and is considered to be responsible for the decrease in landings of major commercial species in recent years.

GEO-6 recommends various policies for the management of coastal and marine resources, including integrated coastal zone management, the establishment of marine protected areas and fish stock enhancement. Integrated and ecosystem-based marine planning and management promotes holistic and adaptive approaches to natural resource management that contribute to sustainable development in coastal areas. Countries in the region are increasingly incorporating policies into their strategic plans and visions that enable an integrated approach, with several updating their biodiversity strategies and action plans in accordance with the Aichi Targets of the Convention on Biological Diversity (CBD). In fact, 11 countries have developed and are in the process of updating their policy instruments in order to implement this and other international agreements, such as the Nagoya and Cartagena Protocols. Nonetheless, the pace remains slow, owing to the overwhelming nature of the task for government officials and the lack of effective implementation mechanisms. Capacity building and institutional strengthening is clearly required in some West Asia countries to ensure a basis for good governance of biodiversity conservation.

The Strategic Plan for Biodiversity 2011–2020 provides the region with numerous opportunities to conserve and restore both marine and terrestrial ecosystems, which are also under threat. Results from country preparations for their fifth national reports to the CBD showed that biodiversity across West Asia is experiencing a rapid decline in both habitat cover and species populations. GEO-6 expects this trend to continue, driven by urban encroachment on natural habitats, illegal hunting and trade, and overgrazing and overconsumption surpassing the carrying capacity of ecosystems. All these contribute to degrading the region's habitats and driving species towards extinction.

A collaborative and regional approach that includes joint research and information sharing is needed for developing effective solutions. The Regional Organization for the Protection of the Marine Environment (ROPME) and the Regional Organization for the Conservation of the Environment of the Red Sea and Gulf of Aden (PERSGA) are playing important roles in coordinating such efforts. In

---

18 IUCN, *The IUCN Red List of Threatened Species*, 2015, http://www.iucnredlist.org.

addition, the Mediterranean Action Plan and the protocols of the Barcelona Convention form a central legal and institutional framework for cooperation between the Mediterranean countries.

Climate change

Any discussion about the region's coastlines cannot fail to mention the anticipated impacts of climate change, with increases in temperature, salinity and acidification expected to have serious consequences on marine biodiversity in the region. The coral reefs in the ROPME sea area and the Red Sea are particularly vulnerable, as was witnessed in 1998 when maximum sea-surface temperatures reached 38°C and led to massive coral bleaching and mortality.

By 2100, average temperatures are predicted to increase by 1–3°C in a medium emissions scenario, and by 2–5°C in a high emissions scenario.[19] Rainfall will exhibit larger variability than temperature, with a general reduction in average monthly precipitation projected, particularly for the upper Euphrates and Tigris river catchment. The projections are indeed alarming and such declines in freshwater resources available for agricultural production will threaten both water and food security in the region and result in failure to implement adopted agricultural policies. There is therefore an urgent need to improve the understanding of climate change in the region, as well as the vulnerability of society, economy and the environment to the impact of climate change.

Possibly one of the most serious threats climate change poses is that of sea level rise. It is expected that a one metre rise in sea level would directly affect 41,500 square kilometres of coastal area, mostly in Kuwait, Qatar, UAE and Bahrain, reducing agricultural land and destroying economic and population centres.[20] In fact, 83 square kilometres, or 11 per cent, of Bahrain's land area would be lost by 2050 as a result of a 0.3 metre increase in sea level.[21]

---

19 UNFCCC, *Country GHG Emission Reports for Bahrain, Jordan KSA, Kuwait, Lebanon, Oman, Syria, Qatar, UAE, Yemen*, 2015, http://unfccc.int/national_reports/non-annex_i_ natcom/items/2979.php.
20 M. K. Tolba and N. W. Saab, *Arab Environment: Climate Change: Impact of Climate Change on Arab Countries: 2009 Report of the Arab Forum for Environment and Development*, Arab Forum for Environment and Development, 2009, http://www.afedonline. org/afedreport09.
21 S. Al-Jeneid S., M. Bahnassy, S. Nasr and M. El Raey, 'Vulnerability Assessment and Adaptation to the Impacts of Sea Level Rise on the Kingdom of Bahrain', *Mitigation and Adaptation Strategies for Global Change* 13.1, 2008, pp. 87–104, doi: 10.1007/ s11027-007-9083-8.

Owing to a steadily growing population and economic activity, total energy consumption in West Asia has risen in recent decades, leading to increases in carbon dioxide (CO_2) emissions. These vary greatly across the region, with Qatar emitting 43.89 tonnes of CO_2 per person in 2011, while Palestine emitted only 0.57 tonnes.[22] Actions aimed at mitigating greenhouse gas emissions (GHG) are becoming more prominent. Most countries in West Asia have submitted an Intended Nationally-Determined Contribution (INDC) as part of the United Nations Framework Convention on Climate Change (UNFCCC) process, demonstrating a commitment on the part of each country to periodically report actions to limit emissions.

The climate change mitigation processes most commonly presented include the review of policies and policy instruments to build a low-carbon economy, such as promoting the efficient use of water and energy, increasing the share of renewable sources in the energy mix, and the use of public transport and cleaner vehicles and fuels. The impacts of climate change will likely have complex synergetic interactions with other ecosystem stressors, amplifying potential effects. It is therefore imperative that effective regional and national adaptation strategies are developed that identify vulnerable systems and consider the cumulative impacts of multiple stressors, rather than considering the potential impacts from climate change alone.

Air quality

Climate change is closely related to another regional priority, which is the issue of air quality. Greenhouse gas emissions are not only key drivers of climate change, but also major sources of air pollutants that are harmful to human health and ecosystems. The level of particulate matter in the countries of West Asia is considered to be very high and GEO-6 demonstrates that this has progressively increased over the past two decades as a result of increased activities in power and water production, industry, transportation and construction. In fact, air pollution is now considered one of the top environmental risk factors for human health in the region and it is estimated that it was responsible for more than 70,000 premature deaths in West Asia in 2010.[23]

Natural driving forces can also contribute to air quality issues, particularly sand and dust storms. These events are a global environmental problem that have an immense impact on health and livelihoods, forcing airports and schools to close,

---

22 World Bank, *GDP and Population Data*, 2015, http://data.worldbank.org/country.
23 IHME, *Global burden of disease (GBD)*, 2013, http://www.healthdata.org/gbd.

interrupting supply chains, destroying crops and causing road accidents. Although a natural feature of this arid region, their frequency and intensity have escalated in the last 30 years due to unsustainable use of land and water resources, desertification, drought and climate change. In March and May 2012, the region was hit with probably the worst dust storms in history. The impacts were severe and almost all aspects of people's daily lives were disrupted, with schools and airports closed, road traffic paralysed and hospitals congested with cases of respiratory diseases.

Iraq is especially vulnerable to sand and dust storms and much of the country's fertile land has been literally blown away as desertification has intensified. The Iraqi government recorded 122 dust storms and 283 dusty days in one single year, and within the next ten years Iraq could witness up to 300 dust events per year.[24] As such, the government of Iraq, with the support of UN Environment, has developed a national strategy to combat sand and dust storms which can serve as an example to other countries in the region. Indeed, international cooperation and joint research are needed in tackling the issue, addressing the root causes and better understanding the relationship between the storms, climate change and land degradation.

Despite the fact that most West Asian countries have ambient air quality and emission standards, the particulate matter concentrations still exceed legal standards and World Health Organization (WHO) guidelines. Efforts are being made by countries to improve air quality monitoring and reporting capabilities and considerable progress has been made in internationally agreed goals related to the removal of lead from petrol and the phasing out of substances that deplete the ozone layer. However, further controls and long-term monitoring of pollutants are still required, in addition to introducing cleaner fuels and pollution-reducing technologies.

Waste management

Exposure to hazardous chemicals and waste is an increasing concern in West Asia and GEO-6 has identified waste management as a priority issue for the region. Population growth, urbanisation, rapid industrial development and improved standards of living have all contributed to a sharp rise in waste generation in recent years. Regional municipal solid waste generation is increasing at about

---

24 M. Kobler, *Dust Storms of Iraq*, UN Secretary General for Iraq, A ministerial meeting in Nairobi, Kenya 2013, http://www.term123.com/dust-storms-of-iraq/ #mh32BcOB4S6cRkIG.99.

3 per cent per year, with nearly 90 per cent disposed of in unlined landfill sites contaminating groundwater resources.[25]

Although waste management efforts are largely localised ad hoc initiatives, strategies aimed at supporting integrated waste management are being considered on a regional scale. The Gulf Cooperation Council has produced guidelines for the management of municipal solid waste, as well as a Common System for the Management of Hazardous Chemicals, establishing minimum legislation for the member states in dealing with hazardous chemicals. Integrated waste management provides a significant opportunity for the whole of West Asia, however, different approaches are required across the region. Many countries have developed waste policies and legal frameworks, as well as national strategies and action plans. However, these have seen varying degrees of effectiveness and their implementation has often been hampered by technical, administrative and financial shortcomings.

The integrated management of waste needs to be approached in a comprehensive manner, with stakeholder engagement and extended producer responsibility in key industries, importers and their supply chains. Modernisation of waste management data systems is also important for effective management and control. An example is the Nadafa programme in Abu Dhabi, which has established a live data management system based on geographic information technology to track the generation, collection and movement of waste. The solid waste management plant at Mesaieed in Qatar is another example of a successful initiative in the region and combines recycling, composting and incineration with energy recovery.

Moving away from the traditional linear economic model of make, use and dispose and transitioning towards a circular economy is an approach gaining momentum internationally, and one that is suggested by GEO-6. The benefits of building such a regenerative system in West Asia, whereby products and materials are increasingly recovered and regenerated, are clear. More effective use of materials would help lower costs, reduce waste and provide valuable goods and services to economies in the region. Of course, this would first require addressing any potential barriers to the use of recycled materials.

The integrated approach

Maintaining nexus priorities is a challenge complicating these environmental

---

25 D. P. Dumble, *West Asia MSW Treatment and Disposal Technology Report, Options for Reducing GHG Emissions*, 2015, https://wedocs.unep.org/handle/20.500.11822/15646.

issues in the region. Unsustainable consumption patterns threaten water, energy and food security. High population and urban growth rates combined with current consumption patterns compound pressure on the region's limited land and water resources. West Asia countries in conflict or affected by sudden large influxes of displaced people face challenges to satisfy their energy requirements. This need increases deforestation and the exposure to air pollutants due to burning of materials such as plastics, tyres and other waste in uncontrolled conditions for heating purposes. The harsh climate in the Gulf countries causes high cooling demand throughout the year, and this is compounded by huge energy waste caused by a mixture of low efficiency appliances, high living standards and an energy intensive lifestyle. In fact, the GCC countries are ranked among the highest ranked countries in terms of energy consumption per capita.

Examining the interconnecting aspects of regional priorities offers a platform for the discussion of synergies and coordinated efforts, providing the first step towards integrated resource management and a potential roadmap to economic and social sustainability. For instance, GEO-6 shows that if the region is unable to achieve sustainability in the water, energy and food nexus then it is unlikely it will be able to do so in terms of peace, security and the environment. This linkage presents certain challenges to the region, which will need to attach equal weight to each element of the nexus if security and sustainability are to be realised.

Integrated solutions for water, energy and food shortages will be essential in achieving the Sustainable Development Goals (SDGs). SDG 6, in particular, focuses on ensuring available and sustainable management of water and sanitation, as such it has strong linkages to the accomplishment of all other goals. Regional policies are therefore required that support a holistic and synchronised approach to addressing priorities and the mapping of interdependencies to the SDGs. With these targets representing major components of the future environmental setting, West Asia needs to clarify how future planning regarding the SDGs should unfold. Jordan through its 2025 vision, Bahrain and Qatar in their 2030 visions, and UAE in its vision 2021 have taken steps towards integrating the principles and objectives of the SDGs into their national development plans and strategies. Saudi Arabia has also considered achieving the SDGs in its 10th development plan.

The 2030 Agenda for Sustainable Development commits the global community to achieving sustainable development in its three dimensions – economic, social and environmental – in a balanced and integrated manner. The integrated approach implies that these dimensions are interconnected, interdependent, and multi-sectoral. Streamlining the integrated approach into development planning at the country level is therefore essential and economic, social and environmental spheres must be integrated into a multi-sectoral policy design within the goals of sustainable development.

As GEO-6 demonstrates, West Asia faces increasingly complex issues that defy traditional categorisation and are difficult to resolve. Development efforts are also often uncoordinated and encumbered with numerous independent policy processes, stakeholders and resource burdens that often result in outcomes that are inefficient and ineffective. Therefore, in order to find viable solutions that may have impacts across priorities, a preferred mechanism is to institutionalise integrated environmental assessments that investigate the different aspects of social and economic development that are affected by environmental impacts. Such assessments can then be linked to social and economic development goals and targets. Moving away from single issue interventions to an integrated approach that develops entire systems will ensure that the region's complex issues are tackled in a holistic way – crucial for the successful implementation of the 2030 Agenda.

Environmental governance

Environmental governance has always been a critical part of sustainable development and is the overarching element that needs to be strengthened in implementing the 2030 Agenda. However, as GEO-6 shows, the ability to act remains limited due to institutional weakness and a lack of adequate resources and appropriate legal frameworks. In many West Asian countries, environmental governance is government-led, centred and regulated with little participation from local authorities except to enforce or implement decisions. Environmental issues are typically addressed through multiple plans, such as those related to climate change, ecosystem management and chemicals and hazardous waste. However, with matters such as security and the economy often perceived to be more pressing, and with low public awareness and participation in environmental governance processes, governments are not compelled to direct additional resources towards streamlining environmental issues into national planning.

Proper allocation of authority within environmental governance needs to be enhanced and environmental institutions empowered and decentralised. GEO-6 also emphasises the importance of strengthening the participation and involvement of stakeholders in environmental decision-making processes, including non-governmental organisations, the private sector and local communities. It suggests that good environmental governance can be achieved if a policy and legislative framework that puts emphasis on rights, inclusiveness and fairness is adopted.

Appropriate and fair policies that take into account societies' common goals are undeniably crucial to support social equity and equality, and can only be achieved through the inclusion of all stakeholders. Improving access to environmental data and information will also help improve public engagement.

Environmental governance is cross-cutting and is the mechanism through which peace and resilience can be realised in West Asia. Of course, effective environmental governance requires the enforcement of environmental legislation. The capacity to do so is dependent on the availability of technical capacities, human and financial resources, as well as the political consensus necessary to mobilise such resources in favour of environmental goals. Despite considerable gains in these areas in recent decades, constraints still remain and can hamper the ability to implement effective and comprehensive environmental policies.

Transformational finance for sustainable development

There is a need for clear, integrated policies aimed at shifting the region from current long-established economic systems towards a green economy that is low-carbon, resource efficient and socially inclusive. The concept of the green economy, which was a major focus of the Rio+20 conference in 2012, has emerged in recent years as a strategic priority for many governments and inter-governmental organisations. In West Asia, countries are beginning to pursue economic policy reforms in order to facilitate the channelling of capital into green areas and stimulate the transition to a green economy. Examples include UAE, Jordan, Lebanon and Palestine, which are now taking steps to develop national visions and roadmaps on mainstreaming sustainable consumption and production and green economy into national planning.

Momentum is also growing to align at a more fundamental level the financial system with sustainable development. The 2030 Agenda for Sustainable Development and the Paris Agreement represent the most ambitious multilateral goals ever set. Achieving these goals requires an unprecedented mobilisation of both public and private finance, some US$90 trillion over the next 15 years.[26] Clearly, innovation in financial mechanisms will be needed, as well as building the confidence of external funding sources to support public and private sector procurement processes. Such confidence can be strengthened if governments share liabilities and risks with private sector partners in a fair and equitable manner, and adopt

---

26 UNEP, *The Financial System We Need: Aligning the Financial System with Sustainable Development*, Nairobi 2015.

regulations and standards to remove market barriers, such as those preventing the reuse of recyclable waste. Countries can also seek to work on strengthening revenue collection systems to improve domestic capacity through environmental taxes and revenue collection, such as pollution penalties and fines. Such tariff schemes can already be found in Jordan, Oman and the UAE.

Financial centres have a key role to play in unlocking transformational levels of financing and the private sector is showing increased leadership. Through the innovative UN Environment Programme Finance Initiative, efforts are now being made to promote sustainable finance in the region. Financial institutions, including central banks, are beginning to engage in a constructive dialogue around investing in environmental sound technologies, as well as integrating environmental considerations into all aspects of the financial sector's operations and services. UN Environment's ongoing research on the potential of financial technology (FinTech) to drive green as well as inclusive finance, particularly in developing countries, is likewise a promising sign. FinTech has the potential to break new ground in the transformation towards green financing by reducing the costs for payments, providing better access to capital and supporting the alignment of the financial system with sustainable development.

A sustainable outlook

The GEO-6 Regional Assessment for West Asia identifies peace, security and the environment, and the water, energy and food nexus as its overarching themes. As the assessment demonstrates, these themes and their aligned priorities cannot be addressed in isolation, and policymakers will need to assess the impacts of their policy options in relation to other priorities in a holistic framework. As such, when planning for water security in the region, it is necessary to take groundwater extraction rates into consideration, along with its impact on the agricultural sector and food security. Similarly, policy options that encourage water desalination cannot ignore the issue of energy resources or disregard the impact on biodiversity and the subsequent social and economic consequences of reduced fish catches. Failure to introduce sectoral policy integration, policy mixes and regional integration will result in priorities being treated in isolation with potentially grave outcomes. An integrated approach in decision-making processes is necessary in order to understand synergies and find sustainable solutions to the challenges that exist across sectors and priority areas. Such an approach paves the way for addressing the complexity of the interlinked environmental, social and economic challenges confronting decision-makers in the region.

West Asia is currently at a crossroads with a variety of potential conclusions. In this regard, GEO-6 offers a visionary outlook for the next 25 years, 10 years after the target date for achieving the Sustainable Development Goals. It analyses the policy pathways that countries in the region could follow to achieve the SDGs and provides a basis for how the region might look like after successful implementation of measures to reach the SDG milestones. This vision of environmental sustainability assumes fulfilment of the core priorities in West Asia. Adopting this positive outlook, several outcomes can be achieved including: healthy citizens, clean water and good hygiene, green affordable energy, responsible consumption and production, mitigation of climate change impacts, protection of marine life and conservation of land resources, and a level of regional cooperation working towards peace, justice and security for all.

To achieve this scenario systemic adjustments and appropriate policies are needed that stress good governance, regional cooperation, data availability and sharing, capacity development and the transition to an inclusive green economy. Addressing these interconnected vulnerabilities in effective, sustainable, socio-economic and environmental policies will reduce the impact of major environmental threats, such as climate change and natural hazards, and help maintain environmental health. Institutionalising these types of policies and regulatory frameworks will cause ripple effects across many different sectors, leading to greater well-being and prosperity in West Asian societies and help put the region on the right track to achieving the ambitious goals of the 2030 Agenda for Sustainable Development.

Bibliography

Abu-Zeid, K., *An Arab Perspective on the Applicability of the Water Convention in the Arab Region: Key Aspects and Opportunities for the Arab Countries*, Workshop on Legal Frameworks for Cooperation on Transboundary Waters, Tunis, 11–12 June 2014, http://www.gwp.org/Global/GWP-Med%20 Files/News%20and%20Activities/MENA/Tunis%20Workshop_ June2014/5.2.K.Abuzeid_WaterConvention_Arab_Region.pdf.

Al-Jeneid, S., Bahnassy, M., Nasr, S. and El Raey, M., 'Vulnerability Assessment and Adaptation to the Impacts of Sea Level Rise on the Kingdom of Bahrain', *Mitigation and Adaptation Strategies for Global Change* 13.1, 2008, pp. 87–104, doi: 10.1007/s11027-007-9083-8.

AOAD, *First Meeting for National Focal Points of Arab Network for Rangelands Sustainable Development*, Jordan 2015, http://www.aoad.org/frstFPMeetPastRes.pdf.

Dumble, D. P., *West Asia MSW Treatment and Disposal Technology Report, Options for Reducing GHG Emissions*, 2015, https://wedocs.unep.org/handle/20.500.11822/15646.

Food and Agriculture Organization, *Iraq Country Profile 2011*, http://www.fao.org/ag/agp/agpc/doc/counprof/iraq/iraq.html.

Hamza, W. and Munawar, M., 'Protecting and Managing the Arabian Gulf: Past, Present and Future', *Aquatic Ecosystem Health & Management* 12.4, 2009, pp. 429–39, doi: 10.1080/14634980903361580.

IFAD, *Syrian Arab Republic: Thematic Study on Participatory Rangeland Management in the Badia*, International Fund for Agricultural Development, Rome 2012, http://www.ifad.org/pub/pn/badia.pdf.

IHME, *Global Burden of Disease (GBD)*, 2013, http://www.healthdata.org/gbd.

IUCN, *The IUCN Red List of Threatened Species*, 2015, http://www.iucnredlist.org.

Jordan Ministry of Agriculture, *Updated Rangeland Strategy for Jordan*, Directorate of rangeland and Badia in collaboration with the IUCN, Jordan 2014, http://www.moa.gov.jo/Portals/0/pdf/English_Strategy.pdf.

Kobler, M., *Dust Storms of Iraq*, UN Secretary General for Iraq, A ministerial meeting in Nairobi, Kenya 2013, http://www.term123.com/dust-storms-of-iraq/#mh32BcOB4S6cRkIG.99.

United Nations Office for the Coordination of Humanitarian Affairs, Government of Lebanon, *Lebanon Crisis Response Plan 2015–2016*, https://docs.unocha.org/sites/dms/CAP/2015-2016_Lebanon_CRP_EN.pdf.

PWA, *Palestine: The Right to Water*, Palestinian Water Authority 2012, http://www.pwa.ps/userfiles/file/marselya.pdf.

ROPME, *State of the Marine Environment Report*, Kuwait 2013.

Rowling, M., 'Iraq's Environment, Water Supply in Severe Decline', *Thomson Reuters Foundation News* 2014, http://news.trust.org//item/20140127121610-cdrqu.

Sipkin, S., 'Water Conflict in Yemen', *ICE Case Studies* 235, 2012, http://www1.american.edu/ted/ice/Yemen-Water.htm.

Sweepnet, *The Regional Solid Waste Exchange of Information and Expertise Network in Mashriq and Maghreb Countries*, 2014, http://www.sweep-net.org/countries.

Tolba, M. K. and Saab, N. W., *Arab Environment: Climate Change: Impact of Climate Change on Arab Countries: 2009 Report of the Arab Forum for Environment and Development*, Arab Forum for Environment and Development 2009, http://www.afedonline.org/afedreport09.

UNCTAD, *Report on UNCTAD Assistance to the Palestinian People: Developments in the Economy of the Occupied Palestinian Territory*, Geneva 2015, http://reliefweb.int/sites/reliefweb.int/files/resources/tdb62d3_en-1.pdf.

UNEP, *The Financial System We Need: Aligning the Financial System with Sustainable Development*, Nairobi 2015.

UNEP, *GEO-6 Regional Assessment for West Asia*, Nairobi, Kenya 2016.

UNFCCC, *Country GHG Emission Reports for Bahrain, Jordan KSA, Kuwait, Lebanon, Oman, Syria, Qatar, UAE, Yemen*, UNFCCC 2015, http://unfccc.int/national_reports/non-annex_i_natcom/items/2979.php.

United Nations High Commission for Refugees, *Syria Regional Refugee Response: Inter-Agency Information Sharing Portal*, UNHCR 2015, http://data.unhcr.org/syrianrefugees/country.php?id=107.

United Nations Office for the Coordination of Humanitarian Affairs, Government of Lebanon, *Lebanon Crisis Response Plan 2015–2016*, https://docs.unocha.org/sites/dms/CAP/2015-2016_Lebanon_CRP_EN.pdf.

United States Agency for International Development, *Yemen: Country Development Cooperation Strategy 2014–2016*, https://www.usaid.gov/sites/default/files/documents/1860/CDCS_Yemen_Public%20Version.pdf.

World Bank, *GDP and Population Data*, 2015, http://data.worldbank.org/country.

Zeitoun, M., *The Hidden Politics of the Palestinian-Israeli Water Conflict*, London 2008.

3

Environmental Risks and Ocean Acidification in the MENA Region

Nathalie Hilmi, Alain Safa, Victor Planas-Bielsa and Mine Cinar

Introduction

In a world with local and global instability in economic, social and financial policies, an environmental disaster can have particularly devastating effects at economic and human levels. We are also witnessing an increasing 'legalisation' of
the causes and consequences of environmental degradation. The issue of predic-
tion which includes anticipation and evaluation of natural and anthropogenic risk
is posed in terms of moral and sometimes criminal, political responsibility. In
this context, researchers themselves might be tempted to 'hedge' legal risks by
considering the most 'extreme' assumptions in their forecasts. In this research,
we describe the ecological risk and disasters in Middle East and North African
(MENA) countries and examine the probability of future disasters. The first
section of this chapter lists the history and the present state of disasters and ocean
warming in MENA, while the second section builds a Gaussian and non-Gaussian
model of disaster threshold levels of pH in oceans, and the last section outlines
policy actions as conclusions.

Ecological risks in MENA countries

This section seeks to establish an assessment of the attitude of the region's countries towards management of environmental risks, whether occurred naturally or
caused by climate change.

Standard economic theory considers that there is no limitation for the possible growth of the production of goods and services (these include environmental goods, 'public goods', and non-renewable natural resources). The degradation of nature is taken into account in these theories only if it induces quantifiable negative externalities in terms of costs or decreases in welfare. Standard economic theory, characterised by the belief in spontaneously self-regulating market, treats nature as 'natural capital' and its degradation is analysed through the conventional theory of public goods and incentives.

Other scholars, breaking with the liberal vision, prefer the context of 'social choice' to suggest 'operational' proposals for sustainable development that would preserve intergenerational equity without interrupting the process of economic growth.[1]

Some researchers, although aware of the vague and often ideological concept of global public goods, admit that it makes sense to do public debate on environmental issues[2] and re-legitimise the use of public aid in development (ODA), not through ethics and solidarity,[3] but by putting pressure on policymakers of both national governments and international organisations that can impose responsible environmental management solutions worldwide. Achieving this goal requires not only better preparation policies capable of dealing with inevitable environmental hazards, such as earthquakes, but also prevention mechanisms to avoid the damage caused by hazards such as flooding, storms and drought, some with resulting fires.

At the international level, environmental risks, including climate change, are priority issues for international organisations. Environmental summits such as the agreement in Warsaw in 2013 and the new protocol at the 2015 summit in Paris involve a large number of countries. During these talks, policy recommendations about sustainable development have become a key concept. Human and material damage due to environmental calamities are becoming increasingly important throughout the world. Material losses in 2011 are estimated at 370 billion dollars, three times the amount estimated for the year 2009. Human losses are estimated

---

1 Such as the environmentalist movement authors who are in line with previous recommendations of the Club of Rome in a global think tank that deals with a variety of international political issues. Founded in 1968 at Accademia dei Lincei in Rome, Italy, the Club of Rome describes itself as 'a group of world citizens, sharing a common concern for the future of humanity'.
2 F. Constantin, *Les biens publics mondiaux. Un mythe légitimateur pour l'action collective?*, Paris 2002.
3 J-J. Gabas and P. Hugon, 'Les biens publics mondiaux et la coopération internationale', *Economie Politique* 4.12, 2001, pp. 19–31.

at nearly 304,000 deaths in 2010, and nearly 3.3 million in the 40 years from 1970 to 2010. Countries in the Middle East and North African (MENA) region are facing profound changes in social, political and economic structures since the beginning of the Arab Spring. Most of these countries are also living in political-socio-economic crisis.

Figure 1 indicates the environmental risks encountered by countries in the MENA region. Middle East and North Africa is considered a particularly hazardous area. The number of environmental disasters in this region has tripled since 1980, while the figure has only doubled worldwide. The large number of disasters is mainly due to rapid urbanisation and water scarcity in the region, as well as climate change. Floods have caused the most damage in terms of the decrease in the percentage of gross domestic product (GDP). In 2008, flooding in the governorates of Hadramout and Al-Mahrah (Yemen) cost $1.6 billion, equivalent to 6 per cent of the GDP. Droughts were the second largest environmental disaster and hit vast areas recurrently. Economic losses and social consequences represent an increasingly important weight. Of the environmental disasters that occurred in the MENA region between 1980 and 2010, 81% of disasters were concentrated in just six countries: Algeria, Djibouti, the Arab Republic of Egypt, the Islamic Republic of Iran, Morocco and the Republic of Yemen.

Rapid urbanisation in the MENA region is among the most likely causes for the increase in exposure of persons and economic assets to environmental disasters. The urban population already makes up 62% of the total population and is expected to double in the next three decades. In addition, 92% of the population lives in 3% of the area. There also exists alarming figures in terms of the efficiency of infrastructure such as drainage, and the amount of illegal and therefore unregulated construction.

At the same time, according to the Intergovernmental Panel on Climate Change (IPCC),[4] rising sea levels could affect millions of people in the MENA region. In Egypt, a rise of 1 metre of sea level will affect 12 per cent of agricultural land and 3.2 per cent of the population.[5]

According to projections made by climate scientists and experts of the United Nations, the MENA region is the second most area affected by climate change in the world. In 2050, the region will likely face a decrease of 50% of its fresh water

4 IPCC, Special Report, *The Regional Impacts of Climate Change, Chapter 7: Middle East and Arid Asia*, http://www.ipcc.ch/ipccreports/sres/regional/index.php?idp=153.
5 M. K. Tolba and N. W. Saab, *Report of the Arab Forum for Environment and Development, VIII*, 2009.

supply. Therefore, water must be imported or desalinated, at an estimated cost equivalent to 1% of total GDP in the region. As a result of the rising sea levels the region will become one of the areas most exposed to water stress globally. Although this may become the most problematic environmental disaster, the risk of flooding currently is the most frequent problem for countries in the region, as shown in Figures 2 and 3.

As we identify the nature of environmental disasters in the MENA region, we find that the risks are significant, increasing and can harm the well-being of populations. We focus now on two major risks: climate change and ocean acidification.

Global climate change

Although the socio-economic impacts of climate change are uncertain, recent estimates are increasingly worrying:

- Significant areas of extreme and high risks of climate change show that the Maghreb region is particularly exposed.
- The region as a whole will face a decrease in precipitation and water stress. IPCC experts expect that global warming will cause more extreme weather events such as droughts and torrential rains.
- Desertification will increase, especially in the Maghreb countries of Morocco, Algeria, Tunisia and Libya. This phenomenon is associated with water shortages and threatens food security and increases poverty.
- Deterioration of agricultural systems mainly applies to Tunisia and Algeria on the eastern shore of the Mediterranean. According to the IPCC, the major crop yields could decrease an average of 2% per decade if no real effort to adapt is implemented.[6] Meanwhile, in response to global demand, production will be required to increase by 14% per decade. Fisheries will also be affected by a loss of marine biodiversity.
- The threat of rising water levels particularly affects Egypt. Rising sea levels, one of the major consequences of global warming, are now expected to be higher than past estimates. Scientists now expect an average increase of 26 centimetres to 98 centimetres by 2100 against 2007 report estimates of 18 centimetres to 59 centimetres.[7] Climatologists now have to seriously consider the ice melting phenomena in

---

6 IPCC, Climate Change 2007.
7 Ibid.

Greenland and Antarctica. Between 1901 and 2010, ocean levels already rose by 19 centimetres. The coastal communities will be impacted by more frequent flooding and increased coastal erosion, two phenomena aggravated by the massive urbanisation of seashores.

All these elements related to climate change reinforce the rise of environmental risks previously identified.

As they already did in 2007, experts warn against the economic costs of inaction. All studies confirm that the more governments delay, the heavier the cost will be for future generations. An increase in global temperature of 2°C could thus result in a loss of between 0.2% and 2% of global annual revenues. The IPCC has compiled modelling work for the past seven years, but has not produced solid results for the 'costs and benefits' of the fight against climate change. The only cost figures put forward are on the third part of the 2014 report[8] and point to an economic loss of 0.06% on projected growth of 1.6% to 3% per year through 2100.

Studies by the World Bank show that long-term climate change is likely to lead to a cumulative decrease in household income in Tunisia of about $1.8 billion (6.8 per cent of the GDP) and $5.7 billion (23.9 per cent of the GDP) in the Republic of Yemen in the next thirty to forty years.

Ocean acidification: the other CO_2 issue

Ocean acidification is identified as a major threat to marine species and ecosystems in one of the United Nations Sustainable Development Goals: Goal 14.3 which aims to minimise and address the impacts of ocean acidification through enhanced scientific cooperation at all levels (United Nations, 2015).

Ocean acidification is the process through which the balance of the global ocean chemistry is changing. It consists of a decrease in ocean pH resulting from the dissolution of additional CO_2 (primarily due to mankind's increasing need for energy and its subsequent production by burning fossil fuel) in seawater from the atmosphere. This process becomes significantly relevant in the context of biology and its impact on living organisms. Some areas, such as upwelling waters, polar and sub-polar regions, some coastal and estuarine waters, are natural 'hot spots' for ocean acidification.

Ocean acidification may alter shell growth in molluscs and coral skeleton

---

8 IPCC, Climate Change 2014: Mitigation of Climate Change.

structure. Concerning fish species, shellfish are deeply affected by ocean acidi-fication, while the fate of some species like finfish is still uncertain. It is not known whether fishes will have psychological (due to neurotransmitter effects of exposure to high CO_2 waters) or physiological issues compromising their natural process of reproduction. The study of the impacts of ocean acidification needs to likewise include issues pertaining to altered food-webs. For example, key trophic links such as shelled pteropods are sensitive to CO_2 levels in the highly productive Southern Ocean where there are upwelling zones naturally rich in CO_2.

Ocean acidification will result in adverse economic impacts on employment, income level, food security, trade and profits, and social and cultural impacts on well-being, poverty alleviation, social conflicts and population migration. Amongst the sectors that might endure dramatic social and economic downsides are tourism, fisheries and aquaculture.

Research on ocean acidification is still in its early days. If the chemical effects are now recognised, the biological and ecological impacts have to be identified and documented. Modelling may help to acquire relevant missing data, create adequate results, initiate the investigation of strategies and policies to mitigate the effects of ocean acidification. Yet the knowledge is still limited, especially the biological uncertainties that need to be explained, so the socio-economic assessment is rela-tively undetermined. Case studies and best practices examples can serve as lessons, and interaction between natural and social sciences is crucial not only in develop-ing existing research, but also in proposing relevant strategies to decision-makers.

Studies on greenhouse gases and global warming in Turkey

In this section we review the literature on the environment and global warming in Turkey – a special case in the region – looking at studies conducted by the Ministry of Meteorology, and by university departments of forestry, agriculture, geography and meteorology.

Turkes et al (2000)[9] argue that Turkey is in serious risk of becoming subject to the following effects of global warming: decreased water supplies in urban areas, more frequent forest fires over larger areas, decreased agricultural production, warmer climate, more use of air conditioning and therefore of energy, increased sea levels, increased dry lands and increased number of tropical weather days.

---

9 M. Turkes and H. İklim, 'Şiddetli Hava Olayları ve Küresel Isınma' [Weather, Climate, Extreme Events and Global Warming], *TC Başbakanlık Devlet Meteoroloji İşleri Genel Müdürlüğü*, 2000, pp. 187–205.

Karakaya and Ozcag (2001)[10] consider the case of rising CO_2 emissions by studying the effects of a carbon tax imposed on all CO_2 emissions and of the allocation of tradable emission permits.

Oluk and Oluk (2007)[11] have sampled third year university students for awareness of greenhouse effect, climate change, and global warming in Manisa, Turkey. The authors discovered that even though the students were aware of the three concepts, there were serious misconceptions about the cause and effect chains and they needed to be educated on these topics.

Studying the average temperatures in Turkey between 1971–2000, Kayhan (2007)[12] concludes that as a consequence of global warming and increased greenhouse gases there will be more flash floods, higher death rates, decreased agricultural production, forest fires, ultraviolet exposures and air pollution, and more use of energy related to extreme weather conditions.

Onder et al (2009),[13] in their study of the impact of climate change on aridity in Turkey, use data from the 1990s utlising a regional climate change (RCM) model to forecast weather conditions in 2070s:

> The RCM, which was developed in Japan, is based on the MRI model. The potential impacts of climate change were estimated according to the A2 scenario of Special Report on Emissions Scenarios (SRES). Aridity index, the ratio of precipitation to potential evapotranspiration, was computed by using measured data for the present condition and estimated data by the RCM for the future years. [...] In the southern regions of Turkey, especially along Mediterranean coasts, projected precipitation for 2070s will be 29.6% less than the present. On the contrary, an increase (by 22.0%) in precipitation was projected along the coast of Black Sea. The model predicted that the temperature might increase by 2.8–5.5°C in the different regions of the

10 E. Karakaya and A. G. M. Ozcag, 'Surdurulebilir Kalkinma ve Iklim Degisikligi: Uygulanabilecek Iktisadi Araclarin Analizi' [Sustainable Development and Climate Change: Analysis of Applicable Economic Instruments], First conference in fiscal policy and transition economies, University of Manas, 2001.
11 E. A. Oluk and S. Oluk, 'Yüksek Öğretim Öğrencilerinin Sera Etkisi, Küresel Isınma ve İklim Değişikliği Algılarının Analizi' [Analysis of opinions of higher education Buca Eğitim Fakültesi Dergisi], 2010, p. 22.
12 M. Kayhan, 'Küresel iklim değişikliği ve Türkiye' [Global Climate Change and Turkey], Türkiye İklim Değişikliği Kongresi Bildiri Kitapçığı, 2007, pp. 81–3.
13 D. Onder, M. Aydin, S. Berberoglu, S. Onder and T. Yano, 'The use of aridity index to assess implications of climatic change for land cover in Turkey', Turkish Journal of Agriculture and Forestry 33.3, 2009, pp. 305–14.

country. This increase in temperature could result in higher evaporative demand of the atmosphere in the future (on the average 18.4 and 22.2% in the Mediterranean and Black Sea coastal regions, respectively, and 17.8% in the whole country). Thus, an increase in aridity was foreseen for the whole Turkey except the north-eastern part.

And Sağlam *et al* (2008)[14] project:

> [Global] warming and climatic changes [will introduce] important changes in fish populations living in the seas. Some fish species will have to migrate to other regions. In addition, it is expected that especially lessepsian fish species will increase in the our [Turkish] seas which will migrate from the Red Sea and Atlantic Ocean to the Mediterranean Sea by The Suez Channel and Gibraltar.

Öztürk (2002)[15] notes that Turkey is listed among the countries which will be affected by greenhouse gases which in turn cause increased forest fires, decreased rainfall, dry urban areas and agricultural lands. He notes that the effects of lack of rainfall will result in reduced and diseased crops, bug infestation, reduced animal husbandry, reduced tourism due to higher temperatures (economic effects), as well as soil erosion, poorer quality of animals and crops and damaged environment (environmental effects), and increased internal migration (social effects).

Ergünay (2007)[16] lists extreme disasters in Turkey and mentions that 1,235 people have lost their lives due to flash floods in Turkey between the years 1955–2007 and 61,000 units of housing have been destroyed.

In general, the studies tend to support the Hyogo Framework for Action 2005–2015, that is, building the resilience of nations and communities in face of disasters, and endorse its strategic goals and five priorities for action, which are:

1. Make disaster risk reduction (DRR) a priority.

---

14 N. E. Sağlam, E. Düzgüneş and İ. Balık, 'Küresel Isınma ve İklim Değişikliği' [Global Warming and Climate Change], *Ege Universty Journal of Fisheries and Aquatic Sciences* 25, 2008, pp. 89–94.
15 K. Öztürk, 'Küresel İklim Değişikliği ve Türkiyeye Olası Etkileri' [Global Climate Change and its Possible Effects on Turkey], *Gazi Eğitim Fakültesi Dergisi* 22.1, 2002, pp 47–65.
16 O. Ergünay, 'Türkiye'nin afet profili' [Disaster Profile of Turkey], *TMMOB Afet Sempozyumu Bildiriler Kitabı*, 2007, pp. 5–7.

2. Know the risks and take action.
3. Build understanding and awareness.
4. Reduce risk.
5. Be prepared and ready to act.

The studies also back policies for implementing disaster risk reduction at state, regional and international levels.

Modellisation of the impacts of ocean acidification

Ocean acidification is primarily caused by the burning of fossil fuels, which emits carbon dioxide into the air and builds in the atmosphere; about a third of all that CO_2 dissolves into the ocean. CO_2 absorption decreases the pH of the ocean, changes the chemistry of the water and has negative effects on the organisms living in it. The process is chemically well understood and there is no doubt that human-emitted CO_2 has caused an increase of 30% in the acidification of the ocean (at a pH value of about 8.1 in average).

The pH values are typically monitored as world averages and the global slow decrease of pH has been well documented. However, ocean pH is a local measure with a high degree of variability across the globe, and local pH variations can reach several orders of magnitude. There have already been localised episodes of temporary extreme acidification in coastal areas, producing an equilibrium crisis and affecting both the biodiversity and the economic environment.

The purpose of our model is to qualify the effect of the slow decline in global pH mean in the magnitude and frequency of the extreme events at the local level.

Figure 4 shows the evolution of reported disasters. The increase may be explained in part by increased exposure due to population growth, and also by an increased number of weather-related disasters caused by global warming.

Global vs. local impact of ocean acidification

Today, global average value of ocean pH is 8.1, decreasing from a value of 8.3 during the last glacial era, and it is expected to reach 7.8 in the year 2100 due to the current level of CO_2 absoprtion.[17] However, when considering consequences of acidification on specific ecosystems it is not the global average that we must

---

17 J. C. Orr, 'Recent and future changes in ocean carbonate chemistry', *Ocean Acidification*, eds. J.-P. Gatusso and L. Hanson, Oxford 2001, pp. 41–66.

look at, but the possible pH peak that can be reached in a determined time horizon. High frequency data for localised areas reveal that pH is a dynamic quantity whose range and variability depends greatly on local conditions, and in some areas one can undergo variations of more than 1 unit of pH.[18]

One of the reasons for this variability is that pH is determined by many other variables such as temperature, salinity, or aragonite saturations among others. As an example, the pH changes through the water column, and is typically lower at deep points (Rios 2015), and thus upwelling areas are more exposed to variability and temporal high acidification episodes at very localised areas.

Upwelling areas are not the only locales that can be labelled as 'at risk' areas; some specific locations may also have coincidental factors that make them more exposed to raises in CO_2 partial pressure (pCO_2), resulting in a higher sensitivty to acidification. For instance, areas exposed to intakes of fresh water, such as the Arctic Ocean, are potentially at risk since these intakes reduce responsiveness to chemically neutralising pCO_2's acidifying effects (AMAP 2013).

High temporal variability at the local level implies that pH levels that are only expected to be attained at the global level in 2100 could be effectively reached at in a very near future in certain at-risk areas. Extreme events can be defined as localised (temporally and geographically) quantifiable events that pass a given threshold. Some well-known cases are excessive rainfall, temperature extremes, annual frequency of typhoons in a given region, etc.

Rahmstorf and colleagues[19] maintain that the number of extreme events linked to climate change have escalated in the past decades, and there is strong evidence that at least part of this increase is linked to human influence. The growth in the number of extremes in a dynamical system can always be explained by either a shift on the mean, or by a change in the shape of the probability density function that governs the underlying process.[20]

Extreme Value Theory (EVT) is the statistical tool that is used to model and describe the behaviour of extreme events.[21] Using EVT we describe and make

18 G. E. Hofmann, J. E. Smith, K. S. Johnson, U. Send and L. A. Levin, 'High-Frequency Dynamicsof Ocean pH: A Multi-Ecosystem Comparison', *PLoS ONE* 6.12, 2011, p. e28983, doi:10.1371/journal.pone.0028983.

19 S. Rahmstorf and D. Coumou, 'Increase of extreme events in a warming world', *PNAS* 108.44, 2011, pp. 17905–9.

20 D. Coumou and S. Rahmstorf, 'A decade of weather extremes Nature climate change', *Nature Climate Change* 2.7, 2012, pp. 491–6.

21 E. J. Gumbel, *Statistics of Extremes*, New York 1958; S. Coles, *An Introduction to Statistical Modeling of Extreme Values*, London 2001; J. Beirlant, Y. Goegeburg, J. Teugels and J. Segers, *Statistics of Extremes: Theory and Applications*, London 2004.

inferences about the tail of the distribution and, in particular, we fix a threshold and only consider events that are beyond the treshhold value. It has been proved[22] that for very general class of systems, the resulting tail distribution follows a Generalised Pareto Distribution (GPD) that can be parametrised as follows:

$$P\left(x - t > y \mid x > t\right) = \left(1 + \frac{\eta y}{\sigma_u}\right)^{\frac{-1}{\eta}}$$

In the formula above, 't' is the threshold, 'σ' is a scale parameter, and 'η' is a shape parameter than gives information about how fat the tails are. The theory is very general and quite independent of the field of application. It has been successfully applied, for instance, to physical and meteorological processes, but also to large financial and economic losses.[23]

Montecarlo simulation of POT statistics for shapeshifting pH dynamics

We model variations of the underlying probability distribution of coastal areas as an Ornstein-Uhlenbeck process with Gaussian noise:

$$dX_t = -\beta\left(X_t - \mu_t\right)dt + \sigma_t dW_t$$

Here, 'X_t' is the pH, 'μ' is the mean reverting parameter. 'σ' is the standard deviation of the Gaussian process, and 'β' is a parameter that refers to how strongly the process reverts to its mean. The solution to stochastic equations where parameters are stationary is well known, and the asymptotic probability distribution of future values is again a Gaussian distribution with mean 'μ' and variance '$\sigma_X = \sigma^2/2\beta$', and the process '$X_t$' has an exponentially decaying autocorrelation with exponent '−β'.[24]

Calibration of the Ornstein-Uhlenbeck process is location dependent. Thus, modelling open ocean sites will have a stable mean reverting parameter and a low volatility, while coastal locations may fit better with a time dependent mean reverting parameter to account for daily oscillations that may be caused

22 A. Belkama and L. De Haan, 'Residual life time at great age', *Annals of Probability* 2, 1974, pp. 792–804; J. Pickands, 'Statistical inference using extreme order statistics', *The Annals of Statistics* 3, 1975, pp. 119–31.
23 M. Gilli and E. Këllezi, 'An application of extreme value theory for measuring financial risk', *Computational Economics* 27.2, 2006, pp. 207–28.
24 B. Oksendal, *Stochastic Differential Equations: An Introduction with Applications*, London 2003.

by physical changes, like temperature, but also by changes in CO_2 levels due to natural biological activity.

However, our goal is not to calibrate our model to a specific site, but to illustrate the effect that the variation of the model parameters may have in the probability that an acidification disaster occurs, and point out that this risk may be underestimated when we do not consider three important factors: 1) the long-term acidification trend; 2) the increase in the volatility of the pH variation; and 3) the effect of non-Gaussian variations, in particular with positive excess of kurtosis, which is an indicator of the emergence of fat tails.

To perform our analysis, we fix a benchmark process with reasonable values for the parameters and calculate how the probability of a pH disaster may increase dramatically, even through small variations in parameters.

The definition of *disaster*, or the level at which we can consider the pH to have reached an extreme value, is itself a parameter that will depend on location. Not all species react or are impacted in the same way by acidification,[25] and depending on the ecosystem, the critical pH level may be different. To attain an objective measure, we consider an *extreme episode* as a moment in which the pH decreases by 4 standard deviations from its mean value. (We consider 4 standard deviations of the asymptotic solution for the Ornstein-Uhlenbeck process, that is, the threshold 't' is defined as $pH_{threshold} = \mu - 4 \div \sigma_x$). Whether an extreme episode leads to a biological or economical disaster is something that needs to be considered on a case by case basis.

Consistent with the order of magnitude that is found in pH time series for locations where variability is moderate to large,[26] we select the mean pH of $\mu = 8$, $\beta = 5$, and $\sigma_x = 0.2$ as parameters for our benchmark.

Downward trend for the mean pH

As a parameter variation, we first consider a linear decrease in mean pH value, which has been clearly documented in the literature.[27] The decrease is slow

25 K. J. Kroeker, R. L. Kordas, R. N. Crim and G. G. Singh, 'Meta-analysis reveals negative yet variable effects of ocean acidification on marine organisms', *Ecology Letters* 13, 2010, pp. 1419–34.
26 G. E. Hofmann, J. E. Smith, K. S. Johnson, U. Send and L. A. Levin, 'High-Frequency Dynamics of Ocean pH: A Multi-Ecosystem Comparison', *PLoS ONE* 6.12, 2011, p. e28983, doi:10.1371/journal.pone.0028983.
27 W. S. Broecker and T. Takahashi, 'Calcium carbonate precipitation on the Bahama Banks', *J. Geophys. Res* 71.6, 1966, pp. 1575–602; R. A. Feely, S. C. Doney and S.

enough to allow us to consider the characteristic time-scale of the process stationary, and this time-scale depends on the mean reverting parameter β. The stronger
the mean reverting component, the faster the system converges to its stationary
solution.

Figure 5 shows a simulation of the benchmark process in which the mean
decreases from 8 to 7.85 pH units. The green line indicates the initial mean value μ
= 8. The red line indicates the threshold value $pH_{threshold}$ =7.747 – a disaster occurs
if the pH stays below that point long enough.

Something that we can easily compute in the Gaussian case is the percentage of
days that the process remains over the threshold, as a function of the mean value
μ(t), and the pH volatility, σX(t).

$$P\left(X_t < pH_{\text{threshold}} \mid \mu(t), \sigma_X(t)\right)$$

The highly nonlinear effect of the downward drift in the mean pH value can be
seen in Figure 6. A decrease in pH value by 2.5% increases the chances of an
acidification extreme event by forty times.

Changes in the volatility of the process have a nonlinear impact on the probability of reaching the critical point. We can put together the two effects in a *risk
map* as in Figure 7. Each point in the 2D map corresponds to a pair of values (μ,
σ_X). The bottom left corner corresponds to the benchmark process, and points
toward the upper right corner which corresponds to the process in which the mean
value μ has decreased (increase of global acidification) and the variability has
increased. The map's colours correspond to different values for the acidification
disaster risk, with warmer colours indicating higher risk levels. The scale of the
colour bar refers directly to the probability of transcending the threshold limit, and
therefore the probability of the occurrence of an extreme event.

Departure for normal case

If the Gaussian noise condition is removed from the model, we are no longer able
to easily calculate the effect of parameter shifts. One option would be to substitute
Gaussian noise for a more general Levy-driven stochastic term, for which some
theoretical results exist. A simpler, although more practical, direction that we have
taken here is to study a discretised version of the Ornstein-Uhlenbeck process

---

Cooley, 'Ocean acidification: present conditions and future changes in high-CO_2', *World:
Oceanography* 22, 2009, pp. 1490–2.

numerically, and then to modify the noise term from a distribution with different kurtosis values.

We generate a random variable whose distribution is a small deformation of the normal distribution. In particular, we generate the random variables as $z=F^{-1} \circ (D \circ F(w))$, where 'w' is a normal random variable, 'F' is the cumulative distribution function, and 'D' is a small polynomial deformation that does not modify the mean or the variance of the distribution, but adds a small kurtosis.

We simulate a number of discrete Ornstein-Uhlenbeck processes (setting dt=0.01) to calculate the asymptotic probability distribution of X_t, from which we can easily calculate the probability of such values that are beyond the threshold.

By modifying the deformation parameter, we obtain different sample probability values that we plot against the asymptotic probability distribution kurtosis, which is smaller than the kurtosis for the underlying stochastic process. The result in Figure 8 shows that deviations from the Gaussian hypothesis have a significant effect on the disaster risk, which should be a parameter to consider in all statistical analysis of pH time series.

We can hence conclude that as pH levels decrease, environmental risks become a greater probility.

General conclusion

The international community signed a definitive agreement on GHG emissions in 2015 in Paris. The final aim is to keep global temperatures 'well below' 2.0°C above pre-industrial times and to 'endeavour to limit' the increase in temperature to 1.5°C. The first step is to limit the amount of greenhouse gases produced by human activity to levels that trees, soil and oceans can absorb naturally, beginning at some point between 2050 and 2100. Therefore, a zero CO_2 emission is still a panacea and not economically viable on a worldwide scale. We believe that environmental issues and environmental risks will continue to be major problems for the international community and especially in developing countries, including MENA countries.

Although a global mitigation approach is always valid and would most likely lead to sustainable outcomes, special efforts should be made on a regional level, based on scientific data pertaining to the economy, culture or available natural resources. All the countries of the MENA region are at the heart of the issue of sustainable development. The prospects for economic growth must integrate social and environmental dimensions. Environmental risks are natural or due to human activities, and economic actors have an incentive to avoid them or find ways to adapt.

First, economic actors will have to develop the ability to limit social cost for unavoidable scenarios, and then they must boost their efforts in adapting their behaviour and work to a less risky environment, at a local level but also at national and regional levels.

Second, as economies are mostly driven by the private sector, the latter must be considered an important stakeholder throughout the process of determining adaptive solutions in a very long-term sustainable development approach and not just when short-term financial gains are concerned. The integration of the private sector should be taken into consideration also at national and international levels. The private sector should be involved in environmental actions too, where firms can be encouraged to become environment-friendly.

Third, ocean acidification should be included in global climate change negotiations in addition to increasing temperatures, pollution, sea level rise, overexploitation of resources and invasive species introduction. Preventing ocean acidification must be at the heart of adaptation and environmental risk reduction strategies. Such a move enables both raising awareness of a collaborative approach by the international community in the face of a global risk, and allows us to measure the consequences of human activity on ecosystems in order to propose the most appropriate solutions. Scientists can distinguish spicies which are most tolerant to ocean acidification in order to develop their culture, thus using biodiversity as a natural capital, not to mention the non-monetary values of ecosystem services. The protection and preservation of biodiversity in a healthy planet is a legacy that should be transmitted to new generations.

Fourth, to achieve rapid results in protecting the oceans, all the stakeholders should be involved. As we have noticed, developing countries are the most vulnerable to climate change and ocean acidification but also more than 85% of population are living in these countries. No solution can be found without their participation as countries but also as households and especially indigenous populations who should be involved in the international negotiations because they are likely to be the most impacted communities and the most determing population. We understand that the hierarchy of needs may place environmental quality in the back burners due to more pressing problems of famine, extreme poverty and disease. Yet efforts should be made to develop local mitigative actions, such as marine protected areas, in addition to human adaptation solutions.

Fifth, the gap of 'environmental' awareness between the global North and South has been bridged thanks to the establishment of an international climate green fund financed by countries with historical responsibility for carbon dioxide emission. This fund will support the developing countries' efforts from 2020 onward. The MENA countries should be ready if they want to face the challenges set by Green Climate Fund. This international fund would help to improve eco-system and community resilience through offering better management options and reducing the negative effects of other stressors (overfishing, destruction caused by divers, bad water quality). In addition to the Green Climate Fund, a Blue Ocean Fund could be raised.

Sixth, environmental risks, including ocean acidification, are considered long-term factors which impact countries, their economies and all the components of the GDP: consumption, investment, government spending and trade. Therefore, environment policies should be completely integrated not only in cyclical and structural policies, but also in all governmental decisions, including fiscal, mon-etary and social policies. Evironmental issues should be considered in both mac-reconomic and microeconomic capacities.

Seventh, as taking action implies investment, it appears more and more clear to the civil society movement that finance can be reformed vis-à-vis the climate issue. 'Making finance flows consistent with a pathway towards low greenhouse gas emissions and climate resilient development' is now an official objective in the Paris Agreement (Article Two), at the same legal level as the goals relating to global average temperature increase and the adaptation objective. Epitomised by the larger 'divestment movement', which calls for the end of fossil-fuel subsidies around the world, financial instruments should be implemented like taxes, insur-ances, loans and bonds, equities and derivatives, etc. The biobanking scheme can complement the credit-trading scheme with biodiversity credits. In the Ecosystem Marketplace, natural capital is considered as important as other forms of capital. Industries and financial markets should be part of the solution at the same level as international organisations, governments and NGOs. Greening the financial system and business, and including ocean-related issues should be part of mitiga-tion and adaptation strategies.

Finaly, communication between different stakeholders is crucial: scientists, policymakers, CEOs, businessmen, traders, bankers, international organisations and NGOs. As economists are common components to all those parties, their language can be understood by most stakeholders. Through education and train-ing, populations can be informed and included in adaptative capacities. Scientific facts along with recent advances and remaining questions should be presented in everyday language to people to convince them about about climate change and ocean acidification risks.

Bibliography

Beirlant, J., Y. Goegeburg, J. Teugels and J. Segers, *Statistics of Extremes: Theory and Applications*, London 2004.

Belkama, A. and L. De Haan, 'Residual life time at great age', *Annals of Probability* 2, 1974, pp. 792–804.

Broecker, W. S. and T. Takahashi, 'Calcium carbonate precipitation on the Bahama Banks', *J. Geophys. Res* 71.6, 1966, pp. 1575–602.

Coles, S., *An Introduction to Statistical Modeling of Extreme Values*, London 2001.

Constantin, F., *Les biens publics mondiaux. Un mythe légitimateur pour l'action collective?*, Paris 2002.

Coumou, D. and S. Rahmstorf, 'A decade of weather extremes Nature climate change', *Nature Climate Change* 2.7, 2012, pp. 491–6.

Ergünay, O., 'Türkiye'nin afet profili' [Disaster Profile of Turkey], *TMMOB Afet Sempozyumu Bildiriler Kitabı*, 2007, pp. 5–7.

Feely, R. A., S. C. Doney and S. Cooley, 'Ocean acidification: present conditions and future changes in high-CO_2', *World: Oceanography* 22, 2009, pp. 1490–2.

Gabas, J-J. and P. Hugon, 'Les biens publics mondiaux et la coopération internationale', *Economie Politique* 4.12, 2001, pp. 19–31.

Gilli, M. and E. Këllezi, 'An application of extreme value theory for measuring financial risk', *Computational Economics* 27.2, 2006, pp. 207–28.

Gumbel, E. J., *Statistics of Extremes*, New York 1958.

Hofmann, G. E., J. E. Smith, K. S. Johnson, U. Send and L. A. Levin, 'High-Frequency Dynamicsof Ocean pH: A Multi-Ecosystem Comparison', *PLoS ONE* 6.12, 2011, p. e28983, doi:10.1371/journal.pone.0028983.

Hofmann, G. E., J. E. Smith, K. S. Johnson, U. Send and L. A. Levin, 'High-Frequency Dynamics of Ocean pH: A Multi-Ecosystem Comparison', *PLoS ONE* 6.12, 2011, p. e28983, doi:10.1371/journal.pone.0028983.

IPCC, Climate Change 2007.

IPCC, Climate Change 2014: Mitigation of Climate Change.

IPCC, Special Report, *The Regional Impacts of Climate Change, Chapter 7: Middle East and Arid Asia*, http://www.ipcc.ch/ipccreports/sres/regional/index.php?idp=153.

Karakaya, E. and A. G. M. Ozcag, 'Surdurulebilir Kalkinma ve Iklim Degisikligi: Uygulanabilecek Iktisadi Araclarin Analizi' [Sustainable Development and Climate Change: Analysis of Applicable Economic

Instruments], First conference in fiscal policy and transition economies, University of Manas, 2001.

Kayhan, M. 'Küresel iklim değişikliği ve Türkiye' [Global Climate Change and Turkey], *Türkiye İklim Değişikliği Kongresi Bildiri Kitapçığı*, 2007, pp. 81–3.

Kroeker, K. J., R. L. Kordas, R. N. Crim and G. G. Singh, 'Meta-analysis reveals negative yet variable effects of ocean acidification on marine organisms', *Ecology Letters* 13, 2010, pp. 1419–34.

Oksendal, B., *Stochastic Differential Equations: An Introduction with Applications*, London 2003.

Oluk, E. A. and S. Oluk, 'Yüksek Öğretim Öğrencilerinin Sera Etkisi, Küresel Isınma ve İklim Değişikliği Algılarının Analizi' [Analysis of opinions of higher education Buca Eğitim Fakültesi Dergisi], 2010, p. 22.

Onder, D., M. Aydin, S. Berberoglu, S. Onder and T. Yano, 'The use of aridity index to assess implications of climatic change for land cover in Turkey', *Turkish Journal of Agriculture and Forestry* 33.3, 2009, pp. 305–14.

Orr, J. C., 'Recent and future changes in ocean carbonate chemistry', *Ocean Acidification*, eds. J.-P. Gatusso and L. Hanson, Oxford 2001, pp. 41–66.

Öztürk, K., 'Küresel İklim Değişikliği ve Türkiyeye Olası Etkileri' [Global Climate Change and its Possible Effects on Turkey], *Gazi Eğitim Fakültesi Dergisi* 22.1, 2002, pp. 47–65.

Pickands, J., 'Statistical inference using extreme order statistics', *The Annals of Statistics* 3, 1975, pp. 119–31.

Rahmstorf, S. and D. Coumou, 'Increase of extreme events in a warming world', *PNAS* 108.44, 2011, pp. 17905–9.

Sağlam, N. E., E. Düzgüneş and İ. Balık, 'Küresel Isınma ve İklim Değişikliği' [Global Warming and Climate Change], *Ege Universty Journal of Fisheries and Aquatic Sciences* 25, 2008, pp. 89–94.

Tolba, M. K. and N. W. Saab, *Report of the Arab Forum for Environment and Development, VIII*, 2009.

Turkes, M. and H. İklim, 'Şiddetli Hava Olayları ve Küresel Isınma' [Weather, Climate, Extreme Events and Global Warming], *TC Başbakanlık Devlet Meteoroloji İşleri Genel Müdürlüğü*, 2000, pp. 187–205.

4

Being Green or Being Seen Green? Strategies of Eco Regime Resilience in Qatar

Tobias Zumbrägel

Rethinking the Gulf monarchies' 'environmental enthusiasm'

In recent years, studies on legitimacy and legitimation, as well as the interdependence of domestic and international dimensions, have gained greater attention in the research of authoritarian rule.[1] At the same time, environmental protection and climate policy have gained prominence as 'important governance fields of this century that cannot be put into the low-priority politics box'.[2] Combining these two fields of research, I argue that the recent 'green revolution'[3] in Qatar (as well as several other Gulf monarchies like the United Arab Emirates and to some extent Saudi Arabia) should be understood as a strategy of the incumbents' hold on power rather than an authentic pledge to improve sustainability. In other words, by asking how and why the fossil-rich emirate of Qatar has adopted climate policy, I intend

---

1 J. Gerschewski, 'The three pillars of stability: Legitimation, repression, and co-optation in autocratic regimes', *Democratization* 20.1, 2013, pp. 13–38, doi: http://dx.doi.org/10.1080/135 10347.2013.738860; and M. Kneuer and T. Demmelhuber, 'Gravity Centres of Authoritarian Rule: A Conceptual Framework', *Democratization* 23.5, 2016, pp. 775–96, doi: http://dx.doi. org/10.1080/13510347.2015.1018898.
2 B. Never, 'Regional Power Shifts and Climate Knowledge Systems: South Africa As a Climate Power?', *GIGA German Institute for Global and Area Studies* 125, 2010, p. 13, https://www.giga-hamburg.de/de/system/files/publications/wp125_never.pdf.
3 I. Quaile, 'Green energy revolution in the Gulf?', *Deutsche Welle* 21 February 2013, http://www.dw.com/en/green-energy-revolution-in-the-gulf/a-16608352.

to uncover the interconnection between environmental policymaking and regime resilience. I understand the latter as the dynamic, process-oriented and continual attempt of a regime, i.e. 'the formal and informal organisation of the centre of political power',[4] to survive.[5] Such an analysis of what I call *eco regime resilience* stands in sharp contrast to existing literature, which predominantly asks questions on how to achieve a more sustainable development[6] in the region.[7]

The chapter is structured as follows: having outlined a number of contradictions and pointed out why the Gulf royals' recent emphasis on sustainability should not solely be interpreted as an outstanding commitment to combat climate change, I propose the model of *eco regime resilience*, where I explain how regimes gain legitimation by engaging in a greener path that ultimately fosters the ruling elites' hold on power. Subsequently, this model will be applied to a case study on Qatar. By looking at the broader context of the emirate's decision to host the 18th session of the Conference of the Parties to the United Nations Framework Convention for Climate Change (UNFCCC) (COP18) and the 8th session of the Conference of the Parties serving as the Meeting of the Parties to the Kyoto Protocol (CMP8) in 2012, the aim is to identify how a newly adapted climate policy can boost and strengthen autocratic rule. Once Qatar's climate policy has been revisited in the light of the proposed conceptual model, an overall conclusion as well as further potential for future research will be provided.

The enigma of oil-wealthy Gulf monarchies turning green

The states of the Gulf Cooperation Council (GCC)[8] – like many other Arab countries – are especially vulnerable to climate threats such as sea level rise, air pollution or desertification. Moreover, most of them are also confronted with

4 R. Fishman, 'Rethinking State and Regime: Southern Europe's Transition to Democracy', *World Politics* 42.3, 1990, p. 428.
5 S. Heydemann and R. Leenders, eds., *Middle East Authoritarianisms: Governance, Contestation, and Regime Resilience in Syria and Iran*, Stanford 2013, p. 5.
6 Sustainability is generally described as 'meeting the needs of the present generation without compromising the needs of future generations'. M. P. Todaro and S. C. Smith, *Economic Development*, Boston 2011, p. 467. Adding the term 'development' underlines the idea that economic patterns can help to achieve this goal.
7 M. Raouf and M. Luomi, eds., *The Green Economy in the Gulf*, London 2016; and M. Luomi, *The Gulf Monarchies and Climate Change: Abu Dhabi and Qatar in an Era of Natural Unsustainability*, London 2012.
8 Consisting of Bahrain, Kuwait, Oman, Qatar, Saudi Arabia and the United Arab Emirates.

shrinking resources and a global decline of oil price.[9] From this perspective, the Gulf monarchies' striving for sustainability seems valid. Yet, what is puzzling is that they carry on following a path towards rapid modernisation and economic development embedded in an allocation character based on rentierism.[10] Examples include the ongoing (partial) provision of unlimited free electricity and water in some Gulf monarchies, as well as the establishment of unsustainable buildings, constructions and facilities, artificial islands that lead to biodiversity loss, and thousands of light buildings with their full glass fronts cooled down with air conditioners. Moreover, all resource-wealthy countries on the Arab Peninsula have increasingly expanded their hydrocarbon sector in the last few years, among which the Dolphin Gas Project constitutes only the most well-known example. The reasons why Gulf royals do not give up on fossil fuels despite socioeconomic challenges are manifold and include easy trading, established markets, growing demand from many developing countries – especially in Asia – and because 'solar and other potential renewables may not yet offer a cost-competitive solution'.[11] Finally, as a solution to future energy shortcuts the advanced nuclear research and development in many Gulf countries is rather a response to energy policy than environmental values.[12]

When turning to the international side of climate policy, further conundrums appear. There is an alleged contradiction between the GCC states' progressive eco-friendly development in contrast to the actual policy position in bodies of the global climate regime such as the UNFCCC, which most experts consider either passive or non-existent.[13] On the international platform, all Gulf countries, especially Saudi

---

9 Raouf and Luomi, eds., *The Green Economy in the Gulf*, p. 11.

10 H. Beblawi and G. Luciani, *The Rentier State*, New York 1987. The basic concept of the rentier state theory revolves around the central role of redistributing incoming wealth from external rents, such as oil, among the citizens.

11 M. Husaini and L. El-Katiri, 'Prospects for Renewable Energy in GCC States: Opportunities and the Need for Reform', *The Oxford Institute for Energy Studies (OIES)* 10, 2014, p. 4, https://www.oxfordenergy.org/wpcms/wp-content/uploads/2014/09/MEP-10.pdf; and S. Hertog and G. Luciani, 'Energy and Sustainability Policies in the Gulf States', *The Transformation of the Gulf: Politics, Economics and the Global Order*, eds. D. Held and K. Ulrichsen, New York 2012, pp. 236–57.

12 Luomi, *Gulf Monarchies*, pp. 49–51; M. Luomi, 'Mainstreaming Climate Policy in the Gulf Cooperation Council States', *Oxford Institute for Energy Studies (OIES)* 7, 2014, https://www.oxfordenergy.org/publications/mainstreaming-climate-policy-in-the-gulf-cooperation-council-states/; and C. Davidson, *After the Sheikhs: The Coming Collapse of the Gulf Monarchies*, London 2012, p. 173.

13 J. Althaus, 'COP 18 in Qatar: Between "Fossil of the Day" and "Best Green Practice". What the Gulf States can contribute to the success of the Climate Change Conference in

Arabia in its pivotal role within the Arab Peninsula, are perceived as laggards. Since the 1990s, together with other members of the Organization of the Petroleum Exporting Countries (OPEC) they have aimed to 'slow [...] down the climate protection and reduction target negotiations, and thus protect the status of petroleum in the global energy industry'.[14] Such an obstructionist policy only makes sense when the intention is to extent the hydrocarbon era as long as possible and to deny complying with the UNFCCC's goal towards a low-carbon development.[15]

In the light of all these contradictions, this chapter argues that the Gulf monarchies' latest focus on environment protection and climate policy is essentially an extension of their non-environmental goals. These policies should primarily be conceived as the adaptive capacity of regime resilience based on garnering legitimation on a national and international level.

Linking environmental policymaking and legitimation: a theoretical model for *eco regime resilience*

The perception that autocracies need to legitimise themselves just as democracies do in order to stay in power has become more and more accepted among scholars.[16] Building on this, I treat legitimacy as a multi-layered feature of political regimes and legitimation as the dynamic, process-oriented aspect of creating this specific form of political acceptance.[17] Due to the fact that measuring the compliance of citizens poses substantial challenges when it comes to operationalisation, especially in authoritarian contexts, for most scholars legitimation constitutes the more feasible category to study empirically. By focusing on legitimation, scholars investigate strategies and techniques (regardless of whether they are successful or not) applied by the ruling elite in order to gain support and consent.[18] Here,

Qatar', *Friedrich Ebert Foundation*, 2012, http://library.fes.de/pdf-files/iez/global/09464. pdf.

14 Althaus, 'COP 18 in Qatar', p. 2.

15 Luomi, 'Mainstreaming Climate Policy', p. 18.

16 Gerschewski, 'Pillars of Stability', p. 18; Kneuer and Demmelhuber, 'Gravity Centres', p. 785.

17 D. Beetham, *The Legitimation of Power*, Basingstoke 1991, p. 15; and O. Schlumberger, 'Opening Old Bottles in Search of New Wine: On Nondemocratic Legitimacy in the Middle East', *Middle East Critique* 19.3, 2010, pp. 237–9, doi: http://dx.doi.org/10.1080/19436149.20 10.514473.

18 Gerschewski, 'Pillars of Stability', pp. 18–21; and H. Albrecht and O. Schlumberger, 'Waiting for Godot: Regime Change without Democratization in the Middle East', *International Political Science Review* 25.4, 2004, p. 288.

a crucial aspect needs to be acknowledged: because of a lack of competitive, free and fair elections (that is, input-legitimation), autocratic rulers 'are forced to transmit legitimacy messages' more than ever, 'and thus are more dependent on legitimation strategies and popular support' than democracies.[19] That is to say, autocratic rulers compensate the missing input level by a greater focus on performance (that is, output-legitimation), which is manifested in different legitimation strategies.[20] The following attempt intends to conceptualise legitimation strategies along three key questions including: 1) the why (motives); 2) the who (target groups); and 3) the how (modes of influence).[21]

Starting with the first aspect, as noted by Alex Wang's case study on China and according to suggestions by other Gulf experts, there are various legitimising motives that explain why even regimes that are highly dependent on fossil fuels may benefit from implementing an eco-friendly agenda. These motives consist of: a) climate threats may lead to a growing dissatisfaction among the population or decreasing trust in the government and its crisis management due to a failure to fulfil responsibilities; b) bad performance in combating climate change, e.g. revealed by media or rankings, can harm the reputation and credibility of a country; c) environmental degradation such as a decrease in air quality often leads to increased investment in, for instance, the health sector or protecting the ecosystem, which may result in a poorer economic performance; d) a new policy field provides windows of opportunity for establishing new and strengthening already existing networks of collaborations, which helps to foster the patronage networks; and, lastly, e) installing renewable energy sources domestically not only assures energy security in the future in the face of continual population and economic growth, but also contributes to the internal sale and allows a hydrocarbon trade surplus for the exporting sector, which, at the same time, helps to uphold the incoming high revenues from oil and gas.[22]

I argue that these motives have been taken into consideration when transmitting specific legitimising effects and satisfying demands from different groups that play a crucial role for the regime to persist. Along these lines, three important target groups can be identified: while special focus has been exclusively laid on

---

19 Kneuer and Demmelhuber, 'Gravity Centres', p. 778.
20 F. W. Scharpf, 'Legitimacy in the Multilevel European Polity', *Max Planck Institute for the Study of Societies* 9.1, 2009, pp. 173–204 http://www.mpifg.de/pu/workpap/wp09-1.pdf.
21 Schlumberger, 'Opening Old Bottles', pp. 236–9.
22 A. Wang, 'The Search for Sustainable Legitimacy: Environmental Law and Bureaucracy in China', *Harvard Environmental Law Review* 37, 2013, 394–8; Luomi, 'Mainstreaming Climate Policy', p. 60; and Hertog and Luciani, 'Energy and Sustainability'.

the domestic population and the core elite (also called 'winning coalition') for a long time, previous studies have emphasised the importance of the international audience.[23] Particularly, the increasing scholarly attention paid to 'environmental security' by the end of the 1980s triggered the recognition of environmentalism as an international norm. Therefore, it is arguable that some GCC states have adopted a more sustainable agenda 'because they want others to think well of them, and they want to think well of themselves'.[24] Taking the demands of the various audiences seriously allows us to answer questions such as how a regime seeks support among its target groups, which, in turn, is linked to questions about modes of legitimation.

In answer to the question of how legitimation strategies are transmitted to the regime's addressees, I suggest a division of three modes of legitimation in accordance with other empirical findings, namely: 1) an organisational mode; 2) an ideational mode; and 3) a material mode.[25] The first mode refers to all formal and informal measures taken to build coalitions and networks and to tie strategically relevant actors closer to the regime. Indeed, there is a debate within scholarship whether mechanisms of patronage networks and cooperation should be rather seen as a distinctive pillar besides legitimation since they are more likely driven by loyalty and cost-benefit calculations than support.[26] Instead, and in line with previous works, I argue differently by understanding patronage networks as specific forms of political inclusion that can be viewed as a legitimation strategy.[27] In essence, there are two ways of fostering the patronage network by introducing new policies: either autocratic rulers include new individuals in the system by establishing new institutions and organisations (that is, through a widening strategy), or they bind already existing members closer to the regime by providing

---

23 Gerschewski, 'Pillars of Stability', p. 23; Kneuer and Demmelhuber, 'Gravity Centres', p. 781; and Albrecht and Schlumberger, 'Waiting for Godot', pp. 371–92.

24 M. Finnemore and K. Sikkink, 'International Norm Dynamics and Political Change', *International Organization* 52.2, 1998, p. 903.

25 Schlumberger, 'Opening Old Bottles', pp. 237–8; Albrecht and Schlumberger, 'Waiting for Godot', p. 376; and C. Derichs and T. Demmelhuber, 'Monarchies and Republics, State and Regime, Durability and Fragility in View of the Arab Spring', *Journal of Arabian Studies* 4.2, 2014, pp. 186, doi: http://dx.doi.org/10.1080/21534764.2014.974322; and Davidson, *After the Sheikhs*, p. 11.

26 Gerschewski, 'Pillars of Stability', pp. 22–3.

27 Albrecht and Schlumberger, 'Waiting for Godot', pp. 381–2; and A. Bank and T. Richter, 'Neopatrimonialism in the Middle East and North Africa: Overview, Critique and Alternative Conceptualization', paper presented at the workshop Neopatrimonialism in Various World Regions, GIGA German Institute for Global and Area Studies, Hamburg, 23 August 2010, p. 6.

new channels of interaction and collaboration (that is, through a strengthening strategy). The second mode describes all ideal forms of legitimation, which can both consist of rhetorical components applying a specific language that fosters a country's green credibility and/or justifying concrete decisions and non-verbal aspects like greenwashing techniques such as annual celebrations, environmental awareness days, green awards and other initiatives. Lastly, the material mode is characterised by all 'tangible' aspects of policymaking which is mainly based on mushrooming environmental projects to secure future water and energy consumption but also to attract attention at home and abroad.

Climate laggard Qatar catches up

The small peninsula in the Persian Gulf can be described as a typical microstate (small physical size, small national population, geopolitical 'sandwich position' between different regional powers), characterised by dynastic rule and strong authoritarian state structures.[28] Qatar's wealth is mainly based on revenues from exporting liquid natural gas (LNG), making it a classical example of a (late) rentier state.[29] These rents enable the ruling emir, Tamim bin Hamad Al Thani, to provide welfare gains such as free utility services to his population with the consequence that the emirate has the uppermost consumption of water and electricity per head, all the while counting among the driest countries worldwide.

Moreover, the wealth from the revenues of the LNG export has enabled the country to increase its international reach: inspired by the 'Dubai Model', from the 2000s onwards Qatar – like several other Gulf microstates – has sought to gain international attention and boost its international image for leveraging power 'through innovation, strategic investment, branding, and openness to globalisation'.[30] Many outsiders have observed lately how several fossil-rich GCC states are exploring environmentalism as a policy niche and have started using huge amounts of their sales proceeds from the hydrocarbon economy for

28 J. E. Peterson, 'Qatar and the World: Branding for a Micro-State', *Middle East Journal* 60.4, 2006, p. 741.
29 M. Gray, 'A Theory of "Late Rentierism" in the Arab States of the Gulf', *Center for International and Regional Studies* 7, 2011, https://repository.library.georgetown.edu/bitstream/handle/10822/558291/CIRS OccasionalPaper7MatthewGray2011.pdf.
30 M. Hvidt, 'Economic and Institutional Reforms in the Arab Gulf Countries', *Middle East Journal* 65.1, 2011, p. 87; Gray, 'Late Rentierism', p. 28; N. Scharfenort, 'Urban Development and Social Change in Qatar. The Qatar National Vision 2030 and the 2022 FIFA World Cup', *Journal of Arabian Studies* 2.2, 2012, pp. 209–30, doi: http://dx.doi.org/10.1080/21534764.2012.736204; and Davidson, *After the Sheikhs*, p. 44.

launching more eco-friendly and sustainable projects and initiatives. Christopher Davidson, for instance, notes how 'environment has recently become a high-profile policy in some Gulf monarchies' and that those states 'have transformed what was previously a liability for their regional and international reputations into something of a strength'.[31]

Yet, one is inclined to ask what gave the impetus for this environmental poli-cymaking? In fact, Gulf states like the UAE and Qatar turned green during a time of increasing internal pressure that originated from socioeconomic prob-lems such as population growth, energy shortages, dissatisfaction about corrup-tion and increased questioning of the Gulf's development paradigm. The general societal discontent was accompanied by a greater call for the acknowledgment of the importance of environmental issues.[32] Additionally, international rankings and indexes like the WWF Living Planet Report 2014 and the Germanwatch annual report of 2013 exposed the Gulf monarchies' unsustainable lifestyle and develop-ment for having the biggest environmental footprint and constituting a 'haven of ecocide'.[33] It was especially this international pressure and criticism for 'being the worst environmental polluters worldwide' that prompted some GCC states to include climate policy as a core task for receiving 'a better reputation in the inter-national policy arena'.[34] As Luomi has shown by an investigation of the UAE's climate policy, a 'low performance in international environmental rankings, and consequently in the views of the media' had a huge effect on the countries' 'image-conscious leaderships'.[35]

In fact, Qatar is a late starter with regards to implementing climate policies. At least until 2011, Qatar's international behaviour in environmental matters could be characterised as that of a laggard. Certainly, the major turning point began in autumn of 2011 when Doha was chosen to host the next COP18/CMP8. For many observers it came as a surprise when Qatar won the bid.[36] At first, many

---

31 Davidson, *After the Sheikhs*, p. 76.
32 W. Al Othman and S. F. Clarke, 'Charting the Emergence of Environmental Legislation in Qatar. A Step in the Right Direction or Too Little Too Late?', *Sustainable Development: An Appraisal of the Gulf Region*, ed. P. Sillitoe, New York 2014, pp. 120–1.
33 Luomi, *Gulf Monarchies*, p. 45; 'Living Planet Report: Species and Spaces, People and Places', *World Wide Fund WWF*, 2014, http://www.wwf.de/fileadmin/fm-wwf/Publikationen-PDF/WWF-LPR2014-EN-LowRes.pdf.
34 D. Reiche, 'Energy Policies of Gulf Cooperation Council (GCC) Countries – Possibilities and Limitations of Ecological Modernization in Rentier states', *Energy Policy* 38.5, 2010, p. 2397.
35 Luomi, *Gulf Monarchies*, p. 106.
36 Luomi, *Gulf Monarchies*, p. 218.

observers reacted with criticism to this decision and an article from *Al-Jazeera* on 25 November 2012 pointed to the fact that it was 'a little bit like McDonald's hosting a conference on obesity'. Similarly, in a *Yahoo News* article from 22 November 2012, Michael Casey criticised the decision by arguing that 'having one of the OPEC leaders in charge of climate talks is like asking Dracula to look after a blood bank'. In order to counter this criticism and to present itself as a reliable host, the country had to come up with an authentic climate action plan within a short period of time. Hence, Qatar provides an interesting case in how its ruling decision-makers have implemented a stronger environmental orientation in close accordance to legitimising pillars that secure the stability of the ruling Al-Khalifa family.

Qatar's green legitimation strategies

The organisational mode of legitimation

Not surprisingly, Qatar's Ministry of Environment, which was established in 2008, did not manage to fulfil its vision of becoming the leading institution for environmental protection, which is why by early 2011 Qatar's green promotion was pushed forward by individuals and agencies such as the General Secretariat for Development Planning. According to some observers, this failure is linked to the then minister, al-Midhadhi, who was an inexperienced and uninfluential figure, and the institution's activities were described to be 'still in their infancy'.[37] In contrast, the appointed chairman of the climate conference, Hamad bin Ali al-Attiyah, is a popular figure in Qatari politics, well-known for his outspokenness and as the 'mastermind of Qatar's LNG programme' in his positions as minister of energy and industry and deputy prime minister.[38] It seems conflicting that a person with decades of experience in the oil and gas industry became the chairman of the UNFCCC COP18/CMP8. The fact that he is now the president of the Administrative Control and Transparency Authority increases doubts whether his appointment was more about loyalty than professionalism.

Another event that occurred in the broader context of the climate conference was the fact that in 2013 Ahmed Amer Mohamed al-Humaidi replaced the minister of environment, al-Midhadhi. Al-Humaidi was instructed to improve

---

37 Al Othman and Clarke, 'Environmental Legislation in Qatar', p. 122; and Luomi, *Gulf Monarchies*, p. 160.
38 Luomi, *Gulf Monarchies*, pp. 159–60.

the performance of the environmental ministry, which was described as 'under-resourced in terms of staff and expertise' with a weak minister at its head since its creation in 2008.[39] What seems striking here, again, is the fact that the new minister was the former senior manager of Qatar Petroleum, one of the country's most important companies. As may be deduced, figures like al-Humaidi and al-Attiyah appear to be examples of co-optation, whose assignments reveal also the close relationship between environmental issues and the hydrocarbon industrial sector in Qatar. Moreover, both assignments disclose the fact that this mechanism of co-optation is not limited to the domestic arena but must be rather seen as a two-level game. For instance, as chief negotiator to the UNFCCC, al-Humaidi (like al-Midhadhi until 2013) is the mediator between the state of Qatar and the global climate regime with the aim of enhancing the emirate's eco-friendly image. Furthermore, al-Attiyah had a deep impact on conducting Qatar's accession talks towards becoming the 147th member of the International Renewable Energy Agency (IRENA). Another example may be seen in the greater role the Qatar Foundation has played in engaging in environmental topics. Under the leadership of the former 'first lady', Sheikha Moza bint Nasser, the foundation is perceived to be 'by far the most comprehensive and ambitious of the government-controlled NGOs',[40] which tends to 'play an instrumental role in Qatar's sustainability efforts'.[41]

From an international perspective, Qatar used the attention gained by hosting the climate conference to boost foreign alliances and networks. For instance, in 2012, Qatar agreed to become a member of the Global Green Growth Forum (3GF) in Denmark, which is a cooperation of seven states (Denmark, South Korea, Mexico, China, Kenya, Qatar, and Ethiopia) and various other actors from the business and civil society sector. At the same time, Qatar was one of the first countries to join the Global Green Growth Institute (GGGI) based in Seoul. This centre is known to promote sustainability in developing countries through expert and knowledge transfer and in 2013 Qatar gained attention because of its huge financial assistance to the institute.[42] Likewise, especially from 2012 onwards,

---

39 'Advancing Sustainable Development: Qatar National Vision 2030. Second Human Development Report', *General Secretariat for Development Planning (GSDP)*, 2009, p. 86, .
40 M. Kamrava, 'Royal Factionalism and Political Liberalization in Qatar', *The Middle East Journal* 63.3, 2009, p. 407, doi: https://doi.org/10.3751/63.3.13.
41 'Foundations for a Green Future', *Qatar Foundation*, 2015, http://www.qf.org.qa/content/the-foundation/issue-73/foundations-for-a-green-future.
42 M. Luomi, 'The International Relations of the Green Economy in the Gulf: Lessons from the UAE's State-led Energy Transition', *Oxford Institute for Energy Studies (OIES)* 12, 2015, https://www.oxfordenergy.org/publications/the-international-relations-of-the-green-economy-in-the-gulf-lessons-from-the-uaes-state-led-energy-transition/.

Doha has intensified bilateral negotiations with other states to discuss environmental matters. Examples include an exchange of experiences with Morocco,
agreements with Argentina and Romania in sectors such as trade, investment,
food/energy security and eco-friendly technology imports from Sweden. Having
said this, it may not be surprising that Doha hosted the Qatar Sustainability Expo
at the same time the climate summit took place within walking distance from
the conference centre. Additionally, knowledge-building plays a major role in
Qatar. In cooperation with the Potsdam Institute for Climate Impact Research,
the Centre for Climate Research was initiated during the UN climate summit in
2012.[43] Overall, the examples underline how Qatar fosters its cliental mentality
and accompanied mechanisms of co-optation such as elite rotation and mainte-
nance, either by creating new agencies (i.e. widening) or by consolidation already
existing networks within a specific policy niche (i.e. strengthening) to tie strategically relevant actors and agencies closer to the regime. The new policy field of
environmentalism has therefore opened the windows of opportunity to increased
international collaboration, particularly for technology transfer that can compensate the emirate's lack of human capital and sell the Qatar brand to the outside
world.

The ideational mode of legitimation

The conference was also used as a forum to advance Qatar's reputation on its
climate policy symbolically with the aim of seeking international recognition and
towards a reconfiguration of Qatar's image as an environmental polluter. Hereby,
the applied rhetoric by Qatari decision-makers includes at least two fundamental
points which deserve closer attention: 1) framing a certain discourse about a false
image of Qatar as the worst greenhouse gas emitter and placing an emphasis of
the small emirate's condition as a developing country (although it is one of the
wealthiest countries on earth); and 2) the even more striking focus on the emirate's
pioneering and leadership role in combating climate change.

   With regards to the first point, al-Attiyah used the conference inauguration
to mark that '[he] never believed in per-capita as a measure for distribution of
emissions. [That he] think[s] it's calculated to show the small countries as the bad
boys'.[44] Similarly, Emir Al Thani claimed during the opening that other countries

---

43 Luomi, *Gulf Monarchies*.
44 R. Doherty, 'Top polluter Qatar defends right to host climate talks', *Reuters* 4 November
2012, http://www.reuters.com/article/us-climate-qatar-idUSBRE8AP0V820121126.

should do more in contrast to his emirate that was considered a developing country. Noimot Olayiwola quoted the Emir's words in a *Gulf Times* article on 5 December 2012: 'the developed nations need to fulfil their commitments of finding solutions and reducing emissions as well as their obligations to help the developing countries in their efforts at energy and greenhouse gases reduction.' Moreover, during several occasions leading figures have pointed to the fact that, as the backbone of Qatar's wealth and economic growth, LNG is the cleanest of all fossil fuels. In this sense, LNG has been always the 'perfect excuse' to reduce any external pressure on the elite to combat the domestic greenhouse gas emissions.[45]

The second facet of representing Qatar's green leadership had been stressed several times during the COP18/CMP8 in 2012 and afterwards. It was often incorporated as one aspect of Qatar's National Vision (QNV) 2030, which can be described as the country's 'first strategic long-term planning document and its first sustainable development plan'.[46] Most references to Qatar's self-declared eco-friendly leadership role stem from the vision's goal of generating 20% of the country's total energy from renewable energy sources by 2024.[47] Although Qatar is far from fulfilling these goals, it has been reiterating that it 'is at the forefront of sustainable outreach plans in the region'.[48]

Essentially, one can detect a strong emphasis on a certain discourse that aims at promoting the emirate's environmental advancements. This rhetorical overestimation of Qatar's leadership role in green policies, for instance by referring to the QNV 2030, provides an alleged image of the country as an eco-friendly advocate without proving the existence of substantial efforts. At the same time, the rhetorical discourse has been strategically used to oppose erstwhile criticism. While the rhetorical component certainly plays an important role in justifying and adding credibility to principles on limiting environmental degradation on behalf of the global climate regime, it is not the only means used for garnering (ideational) legitimation. Even more interesting is the question of how climate policy can be used as an enhancing factor when it comes to imitative good governance structures like

---

45 Luomi, *Gulf Monarchies*, p. 186.
46 Luomi, *Gulf Monarchies*, p. 161.
47 J. Meltzer, N. Hultman and C. Langley, 'Low-Carbon Energy Transitions in Qatar and the Gulf Cooperation Council Region', *Global Economy and Development program at the Brookings Institution*, 2014, p. 13, https://www.brookings.edu/research/low-carbon-energy-transitions-in-qatar-and-the-gulf-cooperation-council-region/.
48 'Qatar Sustainability Network successfully launched to enhance research and sustainability', *Qatar Construction Guide*, 2012, http://qatarconstructionguide.com/index/index.php?id=3&art=221&lang=en.

political pluralism and participation. Qatar's purchased climate demonstration provides a good example of this practice during the climate conference COP18/CMP8 in Doha in 2012, when key decision-makers orchestrated a protest march through the capital raising awareness about climate change, with approximately 500 participants taking part. The demonstration was organised by a non-governmental environmental organisation established shortly before the conference thanks to huge financial funding from the Qatari government. Throughout the various media channels, it was labelled as the broadest form of political participation that has ever taken place in the small country, which has nearly no political freedom.[49]

The material mode of legitimation

Acknowledging what has been said so far, it is unsurprising that many incentives and projects were implemented while hosting the climate conference in 2012. Many vanity projects aimed at securing a high living standard in the future and finding solutions towards a low-emission use of fossil fuels. Domestically, water scarcity has been one of the most pressing threats to the emirate's stability. This is because Qatar is almost completely dependent on seawater that is desalinated through high-energy efforts, which, in turn, cause a high level of greenhouse gas emissions. As a result, Qatar's General Electricity and Water Corporation has planned to deploy a project to secure future demands on water as a first step. The project costs US$2.5 billion and comprises two desalination plants and five reservoirs driven by photovoltaic cells.[50]

Another future threat for the Al Thani ruling family is growing societal dissatisfaction over energy shortages, which is why a strong focus is placed on installing renewable energy sources. One of these projects is certainly the Solar Smart-Grid Project located in Qatar's Education City, which was labelled 'the solar flagship' by the Solar GCC Alliance in 2015. Established in 2012, with the Qatar Foundation as its main holder, the city has announced lately that the solar photovoltaic systems will produce 1.6800 megawatts by 2020. In 2013, Qatar Solar Technologies announced the first phase of the construction of several small-scale alternative energy projects in different locations in Qatar with the aim of constructing solar thermal module fabrication facilities and solar farms.[51] It is expected that the

---

49 J. Vidal, 'Doha climate conference diary', *The Guardian* 2 December 2012, https://www.theguardian.com/environment/blog/2012/dec/03/doha-climate-conference-diary.
50 Luomi, *Gulf Monarchies*, p. 176.
51 'New milestones make Qatar a hub for renewable energy and sustainability', *Arab Sustainability Association* 3 April 2013, http://www.ifpinfo.com/asa/asa-news.

building of solar panels will steadily increase in the next few years, since Qatar will be hosting the FIFA World Cup in 2022 and has pledged to provide all stadia with solar-powered cooling systems, making the tournament highly environmental friendly. Additionally, constructions on a metro system through Doha are being undertaken to improve transportation systems for the tourists but also to limit the pollution caused by ongoing traffic.[52]

Several mitigation projects are also being developed, including the Jetty Boil-off Gas Recovery project under the umbrella of Qatar Petroleum, Qatargas, and RasGas in the city of Ras Laffan that aims at reducing 90% of current flaring.[53] In 2012, Qatar announced the launching of the al-Shaheen Oilfield Gas Recovery and Utilisation Project in cooperation with Maersk Oil Denmark that aims at capturing the associated gas that was previously flared. It is labelled as another milestone since it is the first UNFCCC's project under the banner of the clean development mechanism in the Middle East.[54] Similarly, the development of the al-Karkara oil field was completed by 2012 and is promoted as being the first field to have zero gas flaring.[55] At the opening of the Qatar National Convention Centre in December 2011, in which the COP18/CMP8 took place, the official website of the Qatar Foundation labelled the centre as 'another milestone of sustainability'. The environmentally beneficial building supplied by solar cells on the roof is supposed to be 30% more efficient in water and energy consumption than usual meeting rooms.

The many proposed projects and campaigns clearly underline Qatar's involvement in striving towards improving sustainability with a special focus on preventing water and electricity shortages in the future and mitigation strategies to continue the expansion of the hydrocarbon sector. Moreover, this 'superlative performance' diverts attention from the lacking structure and legal framework conditions; many projects have been planned but not implemented and their status of construction is unknown.

php?news_id=2451.
52 Scharfenort, *Urban Development*, p. 220; and P. Alagos, 'Doha Metro will help cut emissions', *Gulf Times* 13 April 2015, http://www.gulf-times.com/qatar/178/details/434830/%E2%80%98doha-metro-will-help-cut-emissions%E2%80%99.
53 P. Alagos, '"Biggest" Environmental Project in the World Opens in Qatar', *Gulf Times* 29 April 2015, http://www.gulf-times.com/qatar/178/details/437040/%E2%80%98bigges t%E2%80%99-environmental-project-in-the-world-opens-in-qatar.
54 Luomi, 'Mainstreaming Climate Policy', pp. 41–3; and Hertog and Luciani, 'Energy and Sustainability', p. 253.
55 Meltzer, Hultman and Lanley, 'Low-Carbon Energy Transitions', p. 13.

Qatar's green turn revisited

Generally, it is noteworthy that the hosting of the climate summit was the result of a broader strategy to host various conferences in order to increase the country's international attraction.[56] This idea becomes even more persuasive when taking into account that the impetus for the bid appears to have emerged from the Ministry of Foreign Affairs instead of the Ministry of Environment.[57] Indeed, hosting the conference in the country with the highest ecological footprint led to the legitimacy of the host being questioned. In this light, the Qatari decision-makers set up a national task force for the UNFCCC meeting only a few months before its beginning in order not to end up empty-handed.[58] Nevertheless, it seems striking that there has been no observable evidence that Qatar is advancing its institutional setting or enforcing laws in the environmental sector. Moreover, the country's content-related input within the UNFCCC was rather limited or neutral. Only in collaboration with the UAE, Saudi Arabia and Bahrain, Qatar submitted a paper to stress their need for economic diversification that is related to national mitigation actions.[59]

Certainly, one can detect a progressive rhetoric and a potential willingness to combat climate change which, however, neglects to incorporate a substantial campaign or a legal dimension. For instance, relying on the QNV 2030 to present climate protection as a key issue seems puzzling when considering that environmental protection has been described very superficially in the document without clear strategies or aims. In fact, the paper mentions the need for environmental management only to such extent as is consistent with the country's general economic growth.[60] Moreover, surveys have pointed out that one-half of Qatar's population 'did not agree with the vision and the other half did not know the vision existed'.[61]

---

56 Peterson, 'Qatar and the World', pp. 746–8; and Hvidt, 'Economic and Institutional Reforms', p. 88.

57 K. C. Ulrichsen, email message to author, 21 May 2015.

58 Luomi, *Gulf Monarchies*.

59 'Conference of the Parties Eighteenth session doc. FCCC/CP/2012/MISC.2: Submission from Bahrain, Saudi Arabia, Qatar and United Arab Emirates', *United Nations Framework Convention for Climate Change (UNFCCC)*, 2013, http://unfccc.int/documentation/submissions_from_parties/items/5916.php.

60 'Qatar National Development Strategy 2011–2016', *General Secretariat for Development Planning (GSDP)*, 2011, http://www.mdps.gov.qa/en/knowledge/HomePagePublications/Qatar_NDS_reprint_complete_lowres_16May.pdf.

61 L. Khatib, 'Qatar and the Recalibration of Power in the Gulf', *Carnegie Middle East Center*, 2014, p. 13, http://carnegie-mec.org/2014/09/11/qatar-and-recalibration-of-power-in-gulf-pub-56582.

Furthermore, many projects and incentives reveal that they centre mainly around mitigation strategies to reduce emissions but overlook adaptation strategies to encounter threats of climate change *ex ante*. Such a one-dimensional approach appears to be a 'way to extend the era of fossil fuels' as long as possible.[62] All in all, there is great doubt whether Qatar feels committed to sustainability first and foremost, and whether there will be any real changes in Qatar's climate policy in the near or medium term. Quite the contrary, it is assumed that the emirate will further modernise its infrastructure and develop construction projects with severe consequences for the environment. Another assumption is that increasing budgetary constraints due to the falling price of fossil fuels and the embargo of other Arab states since 2017 will rather bring a quick end to the costly shift towards a more sustainable economy.[63]

Having this in mind, how else can we explain such environmental undertaking in the scope of hosting the climate conference? First, the emirate has shown signs of fostering networks and support bases through co-optation and cooperation as a legitimation strategy. Meanwhile, the appointment of al-Attiyah, who held several positions in the government previously, is an example of a strategy for *strengthening* the support base, and al-Humaidi's appointment is an example of a strategy for *widening* the support base since he comes from the private sector. Furthermore, the emirate used the opportunity for hosting the conference to build alliances, as various involvements in new environmental groups and organisations reveal. Qatar has been utilising a specific language aimed at triggering a discourse of moral justification on the one hand, and on the other hand has phrased foreign policy goals and a certain mission in the form of the QNV 2030 to divert attention from the local government's deficiencies. Lastly, the Qatari regime has reinforced its branding of modernisation and its 'narrative [...] of making the impossible possible'[64] by placing great emphasis on a performance embellished by several superlative and alleged best-practice projects and campaigns. In short, the small emirate has instrumentalised the recognition gained from the conference in implementing a new policy in order to garner support and gain credibility both from a national and international audience and to foster networks of patronage. It is worthy to note how many of the suggested strategies in the conceptual model tend to overlap in practice or reinforce each other, evident in the intensive involvement of the Qatar Foundation.

---

62 Luomi, *Gulf Monarchies*, p. 43.
63 K. C. Ulrichsen, email message to author, 21 May 2015.
64 Derichs and Demmelhuber, 'Monarchies and Republics', p. 189.

Legitimising policymaking: a final appraisal

The chapter's central points were to stress that Qatar's green turn should foremost be seen as a means to strengthen autocratic power structures. In this sense, I have argued that this does not happen through *ad hoc* decision-making but is rather coordinated in close accordance with already existing legitimation pillars that secure the resilience of the regime. The case study of environmental policymaking outlines the growing awareness of regimes to the need to appear legitimate, a fact which has gained greater attention in scholarship. Hence, it is insufficient to claim that in order 'to stay in power, an autocrat needs two things: money and loyalty'.[65] Instead, any regime, even the most autocratic one, needs an 'idea of legitimacy' that secures the support of the respective population and the international audience. Such an 'idea of legitimacy' is not static but dynamic and needs to be continually adjusted when a regime is confronted with new key tasks as shown by the example of increasing climate challenges. Not fulfilling these tasks leads to deteriorating statecraft which can directly influence the regime's legitimacy.

In the specific case analysed here, it has been illustrated that introducing new policy processes is a means to supplement the regime's idea of legitimacy. This theory has been based on rational motives like securing the welfare state by ensuring water and energy supply in future, cutting emissions by, for example, technology transfer and fostering networks. Additionally, constructivist motives play a certain role in branding Qatar as a country that is at the forefront in the sectors of modernisation, globalisation, economy and business.[66] Moreover, an interest in environmentalism underlines the ruler's image as an 'enlightened monarch' and a 'modernisation manager'.[67] Furthermore, the study has demonstrated that the Qatari ruling elites rely on mechanisms of input-legitimation only to such extent as required to bind strategically relevant actors – most of whom come from the private sector and the ruling family. In addition, the lack of an effective environmental governance in the form of an institution or agency with overall climate-related responsibility is compensated by a stronger focus on performance (output-legitimation). In this sense, vibrant superlative activities throughout many different sectors and fields are accompanied by a language specific to policymaking used to improve the emirate's perception abroad. Yet, the 'noise made by

---

65 J. Brownlee, T. Masoud and A. Reynolds, 'Tracking the "Arab Spring": Why the Modest Harvest', *Journal of Democracy* 24.4, 2013, p. 32, doi: https://doi.org/10.1353/jod.2013.0061.
66 T. Zumbrägel, 'Is Qatar really going green?', *Newsletter of the European Centre for Energy and Resource Security (EUCERS)* 55, 2016, .
67 Derichs and Demmelhuber, 'Monarchies and Republics', p. 89; and Hertog and Luciani, 'Energy and Sustainability', p. 248.

the numerous announcements on initiatives related to renewable energies' diverts attention from the fact that, in the end, the ambitious plan of becoming a green leader often lacks practical implementation or meaningful contribution.[68] These findings lead to another conclusion; Qatar's recent environmental output has been undertaken in order to satisfy predominantly the demands of three different target groups with different underlying motives, namely: 1) the international audience by portraying the country as a trustful ally with international leverage; 2) the domestic population by pursuing a high living standard in the future; and 3) the 'winning coalition' to strengthen the clientelist networks. All in all, this study has intended to be a first step towards better understanding what Sean Yom describes as how incumbents integrate, adjust and 'implement new policies in an effort to survive'.[69]

Future research and more in-depth investigations about other Gulf monarchies are needed to further test the conceptual model proposed here. For instance, a comparative study with Abu Dhabi's Masdar Initiative would be fruitful since Masdar seems to be a greenwashing campaign that is also driven by state interests in economic diversification, branding and mechanisms of co-optation.[70] Additionally, cooperation between the states, and particularly within the Gulf Cooperation Council (GCC), in the field of environmentalism seems an interesting concept to scrutinise in the scope of the given research question. While further in-depth inquiry is necessary, one can assume that most of the implemented green policy output aims at serving specific state interests. In other words, the Gulf rulers are acting rather 'as if' they are committed to pursue a path towards sustainability while they are utilising the new policy field in order to strengthen their regime resilience.

---

68 I. J. Bacherielle, 'Renewable Energy in the GCC Countries. Resources, Potential, and Prospects', *Gulf Research Centre*, 2012, p. 12, http://library.fes.de/pdf-files/bueros/amman/09008.pdf; and Luomi, 'Mainstreaming Climate Policy'.
69 S. Yom, 'Collaboration and Community amongst the Arab Monarchies', *Project on Middle East Politics (POMEPS)*, 2016, memo prepared for the workshop International Diffusion and Cooperation of Authoritarian Regimes, Hamburg, 8–9 June 2016, p. 1, http://pomeps.org/2016/07/15/collaboration-and-community-amongst-the-arab-monarchies/#_ftn1.
70 T. Zumbrägel, 'The Quest for Green Legitimation: Reconsidering the environmental enthusiasm of the Arab Gulf monarchies', *Orient* 85.1, 2017, p. 57.

Bibliography

Albrecht, H. and O. Schlumberger, 'Waiting for Godot: Regime Change without Democratization in the Middle East', *International Political Science Review* 25.4, 2004, pp. 371–92.

Alagos, P., '"Biggest" Environmental Project in the World Opens in Qatar', *Gulf Times* 29 April 2015, http://www.gulf-times.com/qatar/178/details/437040/%E2%80%98bigges t%E2%80%99-environmental-project-in-the-world-opens-in-qatar.

Alagos, P., 'Doha Metro will help cut emissions', *Gulf Times* 13 April 2015, http://www.gulf-times.com/qatar/178/details/434830/%E2%80%98doha-metro-will-help-cut-emissions%E2%80%99.

Althaus, J., 'COP 18 in Qatar: Between "Fossil of the Day" and "Best Green Practice". What the Gulf States can contribute to the success of the Climate Change Conference in Qatar', *Friedrich Ebert Foundation*, 2012, http://library.fes.de/pdf-files/iez/global/09464.pdf.

Bacherielle, I. J., 'Renewable Energy in the GCC Countries. Resources, Potential, and Prospects', *Gulf Research Centre*, 2012, http://library.fes.de/pdf-files/bueros/amman/09008.pdf.

Bank, A. and T. Richter, 'Neopatrimonialism in the Middle East and North Africa: Overview, Critique and Alternative Conceptualization', paper presented at the workshop Neopatrimonialism in Various World Regions, GIGA German Institute for Global and Area Studies, Hamburg, 23 August 2010.

Beblawi, H. and G. Luciani, *The Rentier State*, New York 1987.

Beetham, D., *The Legitimation of Power*, Basingstoke 1991.

Brownlee, J., T. Masoud and A. Reynolds, 'Tracking the "Arab Spring": Why the Modest Harvest', *Journal of Democracy* 24.4, 2013, pp. 29–44, doi: https://doi.org/10.1353/jod.2013.0061.

Casey, M., 'Qatar set to host major climate talks', *Yahoo News* 22 November 2012, https://www.yahoo.com/news/qatar-set-host-major-climate-talks-155020012.html?ref=gs.

Davidson, C., *After the Sheikhs: The Coming Collapse of the Gulf Monarchies*, London 2012.

Derichs, C. and T. Demmelhuber, 'Monarchies and Republics, State and Regime, Durability and Fragility in View of the Arab Spring', *Journal of Arabian Studies* 4.2, 2014, pp. 180–94, doi: http://dx.doi.org/10.1080/21534764.2014.974322.

Doherty, R., 'Top polluter Qatar defends right to host climate talks', *Reuters* 4 November 2012, http://www.reuters.com/article/us-climate-qatar-idUSBRE8AP0V820121126.

Finnemore, M. and K. Sikkink, 'International Norm Dynamics and Political Change', *International Organization* 52.2, 1998, pp. 887–917.

Fishman, R. M., 'Rethinking State and Regime: Southern Europe's Transition to Democracy', *World Politics* 42.3, 1990, pp. 422–40.

Gerschewski, J., 'The three pillars of stability: Legitimation, repression, and co-optation in autocratic regimes', *Democratization* 20.1, 2013, pp. 13–38, doi: http://dx.doi.org/10.1080/13510347.2013.738860.

General Secretariat for Development Planning (GSDP), 'Qatar National Development Strategy 2011–2016', 2011, http://www.mdps.gov.qa/en/knowledge/HomePagePublications/Qatar_NDS_reprint_complete_lowres_16May.pdf.

General Secretariat for Development Planning (GSDP), 'Advancing Sustainable Development: Qatar National Vision 2030. Second Human Development Report', 2009, http://hdr.undp.org/sites/default/files/qhdr_en_2009.pdf.

Germanwatch, 'The Climate Change Performance Index Results', 2013, https://germanwatch.org/de/download/7158.pdf.

Gray, M., 'A Theory of "Late Rentierism" in the Arab States of the Gulf', *Center for International and Regional Studies* 7, 2011, https://repository.library.georgetown.edu/bitstream/handle/10822/558291/CIRSOccasionalPaper7MatthewGray2011.pdf.

Hertog, S. and G. Luciani, 'Energy and Sustainability Policies in the Gulf States', *The Transformation of the Gulf. Politics, Economics and the Global Order*, eds. D. Held and K. Ulrichsen, New York 2012, pp. 236–57.

Heydemann, S. and R. Leenders, eds. *Middle East Authoritarianisms. Governance, Contestation, and Regime Resilience in Syria and Iran*, Stanford 2013.

Husaini, M. and L. El-Katiri, 'Prospects for Renewable Energy in GCC States: Opportunities and the Need for Reform', *The Oxford Institute for Energy Studies (OIES)* 10, 2014, https://www.oxfordenergy.org/wpcms/wp-content/uploads/2014/09/MEP-10.pdf.

Hvidt, M., 'Economic and Institutional Reforms in the Arab Gulf Countries', *The Middle East Journal* 65.1, 2011, pp. 85–102.

Kamrava, M., 'Royal Factionalism and Political Liberalization in Qatar', *The Middle East Journal* 63.3, 2009, pp. 401–20, doi: https://doi.org/10.3751/63.3.13.

Khatib, L., 'Qatar and the Recalibration of Power in the Gulf', *Carnegie Middle East Center*, 2014, http://carnegie-mec.org/2014/09/11/qatar-and-recalibration-of-power-in-gulf-pub-56582.

Kneuer, M. and T. Demmelhuber, 'Gravity Centres of Authoritarian Rule: A Conceptual Framework', *Democratization* 23.5, 2016, pp. 775–96, doi: http://dx.doi.org/10.1080/13510347.2015.1018898.

Luomi, M., *The Gulf Monarchies and Climate Change. Abu Dhabi and Qatar in an Era of Natural Unsustainability*, London 2012.

Luomi, M., 'The International Relations of the Green Economy in the Gulf: Lessons from the UAE's State-led Energy Transition', *Oxford Institute for Energy Studies (OIES)* 12, 2015, https://www.oxfordenergy.org/publications/the-international-relations-of-the-green-economy-in-the-gulf-lessons-from-the-uaes-state-led-energy-transition/.

Luomi, M., 'Mainstreaming Climate Policy in the Gulf Cooperation Council States', *Oxford Institute for Energy Studies (OIES)* 7, 2014, https://www.oxfordenergy.org/publications/mainstreaming-climate-policy-in-the-gulf-cooperation-council-states/.

Meltzer, J., N. Hultman and C. Langley, 'Low-Carbon Energy Transitions in Qatar and the Gulf Cooperation Council Region', *Global Economy and Development program at the Brookings Institution*, 2014, https://www.brookings.edu/research/low-carbon-energy-transitions-in-qatar-and-the-gulf-cooperation-council-region/.

Never, B., 'Regional Power Shifts and Climate Knowledge Systems: South Africa As a Climate Power?', *GIGA German Institute for Global and Area Studies* 125, 2010, https://www.giga-hamburg.de/de/system/files/publications/wp125_never.pdf.

'New milestones make Qatar a hub for renewable energy and sustainability', *Arab Sustainability Association* 3 April 2013, http://www.ifpinfo.com/asa/asa-news.php?news_id=2451.

Al Othman, W. and S. F. Clarke, 'Charting the Emergence of Environmental Legislation in Qatar. A Step in the Right Direction or Too Little Too Late?', *Sustainable Development: An Appraisal of the Gulf Region*, ed. P. Sillitoe, New York 2014, pp. 116–32.

Olayiwola, N., 'Emir calls for "farsighted" action on climate change', *Gulf Times* 5 December 2012, http://www.gulf-times.com/story/334545/Emir-calls-for-farsighted-action-on-climate-change.

Peterson, J. E., 'Qatar and the World: Branding for a Micro-State', *Middle East Journal* 60.4, 2006, pp. 733–48.

Qatar Foundation, 'Foundations for a Green Future', 2015, http://www.qf.org.
    qa/content/the-foundation/issue-73/foundations-for-a-green-future.
'Qatar Hosts Climate Summit Amid Criticism', *Al-Jazeera* 25 November 2012,
    http://www.aljazeera.com/news/middleeast/2012/11/201211256573379361.
    html.
'Qatar Sustainability Network successfully launched to enhance
    research and sustainability', *Qatar Construction Guide* 2012, http://
    qatarconstructionguide.com/index/index.php?id=3&art=221&lang=en.
Quaile, I., 'Green energy revolution in the Gulf?', *Deutsche
    Welle* 21 February 2013, http://www.dw.com/en/
    green-energy-revolution-in-the-gulf/a-16608352.
Raouf, M. and M. Luomi, eds., *The Green Economy in the Gulf*, London 2016.
Reiche, D., 'Energy Policies of Gulf Cooperation Council (GCC) Countries –
    Possibilities and Limitations of Ecological Modernization in Rentier states',
    Energy Policy 38.5, 2010, pp. 2395–403.
Scharfenort, N., 'Urban Development and Social Change in Qatar. The Qatar
    National Vision 2030 and the 2022 FIFA World Cup', *Journal of Arabian
    Studies* 2.2, 2012, pp. 209–30, doi: http://dx.doi.org/10.1080/21534764.2012
    .736204.
Scharpf, F. W., 'Legitimacy in the Multilevel European Polity', *Max Planck
    Institute for the Study of Societies* 9.1, 2009, http://www.mpifg.de/pu/
    workpap/wp09-1.pdf.
Schlumberger, O., 'Opening Old Bottles in Search of New Wine: On
    Nondemocratic Legitimacy in the Middle East', *Middle East Critique* 19.3,
    2010, pp. 233–50, doi: http://dx.doi.org/10.1080/19436149.2010.514473.
Todaro, M. P. and S. C. Smith, *Economic Development*, Boston 2011.
United Nations Framework Convention for Climate Change (UNFCCC),
    'Conference of the Parties Eighteenth session doc. FCCC/CP/2012/MISC.2:
    Submission from Bahrain, Saudi Arabia, Qatar and United Arab Emirates',
    2013, http://unfccc.int/documentation/submissions_from_parties/items/5916.
    php.
Vidal, J., 'Doha climate conference diary', *The Guardian* 2 December
    2012, https://www.theguardian.com/environment/blog/2012/dec/03/
    doha-climate-conference-diary.
Wang, A., 'The Search for Sustainable Legitimacy: Environmental Law and
    Bureaucracy in China', *Harvard Environmental Law Review* 37, 2013, pp.
    367–440.

World Wide Fund (WWF), 'Living Planet Report: Species and Spaces, People and Places', 2014, http://www.wwf.de/fileadmin/fm-wwf/Publikationen-PDF/WWF-LPR2014-EN-LowRes.pdf.

Yom, S., 'Collaboration and Community amongst the Arab Monarchies', *Project on Middle East Politics (POMEPS)*, 2016, memo prepared for the workshop International Diffusion and Cooperation of Authoritarian Regimes, Hamburg, 8–9 June 2016, http://pomeps.org/2016/07/15/collaboration-and-community-amongst-the-arab-monarchies/#_ftn1.

Zumbrägel, T., 'Is Qatar really going green?', *Newsletter of the European Centre for Energy and Resource Security (EUCERS)* 55, 2016, pp. 5–7, https://www.kcl.ac.uk/sspp/departments/warstudies/research/groups/eucers/newsletter/newsletter55.pdf.

Zumbrägel, T., 'The Quest for Green Legitimation: Reconsidering the environmental enthusiasm of the Arab Gulf monarchies', *Orient* 85.1, 2017, pp. 54–9.

5

Oil, Heat and Climate Jobs in the MENA Region

Nancy Lindisfarne and Jonathan Neale

Introduction

The impact of global climate change on the Middle East and North Africa region is already marked and complex. In this chapter we look at three examples of this impact: Darfur since 1969, Afghanistan since 1970, and Syria since 2010. Then we discuss the politics of oil in the region and consider the possibility of campaigns for 'climate jobs'.

We start with the long tragedy of Darfur. The rains failed in Darfur in 1969 and have never fully recovered. Some years have been worse and some better, and in the worst years there has been drought and famine. Over the last forty years a rise of 1 degree in average temperatures has contributed to reduced crop yields. Struggles over land, water and pasture have exploded into bitter conflict, and famine and war have produced a large number of refugees.[1]

---

1 For early work on climate change in Darfur, see N. Zeng, 'Drought in the Sahel', *Science* 303, 2003, pp. 1124–7; and United Nations Environment Programme, *Sudan: Post-conflict Environmental Assessment*, Nairobi 2007. More recently, there is some evidence of at least partial recovery in rainfall in the Eastern Sahel, but not in East Africa, the Horn of Africa, Western Sudan or Darfur. For an overview see I. Niang, O. C. Ruppel, M. A. Abdrabo, A. Essel, C. Lennard, J. Padgham and P. Urquhart, 'Africa', *Climate Change 2014: Impacts, Adaptation, and Vulnerability*, Cambridge 2014, pp. 1196–265. For more detail see A. Park Williams *et al*, 'Recent summer precipitation trends in the Greater Horn of Africa and the emerging role of Indian Ocean sea surface temperature', *Climate Dynamics* 39.9, 2012, pp. 2307–28. And for a study on Darfur see C. Funk, G. Eilerts, J. Verdin, J. Roland and M. Marshall, *A Climate Trend Analysis of Sudan*, United States Geological Survey, 2011.

As Amartya Sen reminds us, famines are created by the neglectful actions of governments. A kaleidoscope of factors have fed the chaos in Darfur: a proxy oil war between the US and China; the wars between North and South in Sudan; splits in the Islamist military government; military interventions and destructive meddling from Chad, America, France, Libya, South Sudan, the African Union, China, and on a smaller scale from Britain, Israel, and even Eritrea; the behaviour of Chevron and Total; the NGOs and campaigns who lobbied so hard for armed American intervention; the machinations of many aspirant local warlord/business-man; and the cruelty of the Nimieri and Bashir dictatorships in Khartoum.[2]

This was no simple tale of famine, refugees and climate war. The suffering of Darfuris was exacerbated by outside forces precisely because they lived in an isolated and vulnerable place, where powerful forces could safely play with other people's lives. But underlying the vulnerability was the change in climate. In Darfur, settled farmers and migrant pastoralists had long shared water and grazing in traditional arrangements. The long years of low rainfall, and the fierce drought of 1984–1985 finally broke those arrangements, and famine was followed by war. There is not space here to follow the twists and turns of what followed. We can say, however, that at the centre of the long ordeal was a fight between small nomads and small farmers, killing each other for disappearing grass.

Darfur is just one case. There is, however, a tendency in recent literature to assume that climate change is the central driving force in most conflicts in the region and beyond Africa.[3] But we have to be careful; the situation in Chad seems

---

2 For more on climate change, war and politics in Darfur see A. de Waal, *Famine that Kills: Darfur, Sudan*, Oxford 2005; D. Keen, *The Benefits of Famine: A Political Economy of Famine and Relief in Southwestern Sudan, 1983–1989*, Princeton 1994; J. Flint and A. de Waal, *Darfur: A Short History of a Long War*, London 2005; G. Prunier, *Darfur: the Ambiguous Genocide*, Ithaca NY 2005; J. Neale, *Stop Global Warming: Change the World*, London 2008; J. Tubiana, 'Darfur: A War for Land', *War in Darfur and the Search for Peace*, ed. A. de Waal, Cambridge, MA 2007, pp. 68–91; M. O. Akasha, *Darfur: A Tragedy of Climate Change*, New York 2013; M. Mamdani, *Saviors and Survivors: Darfur, Politics and the War on Terror*, New York 2009; A. De Juan, 'Long-term environmental change and geographical patterns of violence in Darfur 2003–2005', *Political Geography* 45, 2015, pp. 22–33; A. de Waal, *The Real Politics of the Horn of Africa: Money, War and the Business of Power*, Cambridge 2015.

3 Many of the best of these books, such as C. Parenti, *Tropic of Chaos: Climate Change and the New Geography of Violence*, New York 2011, are uneven in their analysis but consistently interesting. The great strength of Parenti's work is that it is not Malthusian, and that he deals with mediated complexity. For an astringent view of what is wrong with the growing, and frankly silly, literature that tries to make statistical associations between climate and conflict, see T. Forsyth and M. Schomerus, *Climate Change and Conflict: A Systematic Evidence Review*, London School of Economics, 2013. For a good survey

to have much in common with Darfur. Southern Sudan and Somalia have also suffered from serious, long running climate change, although explanations for the tragedies occurring in those countries are more complex.

Our second example, Afghanistan, is different. The drought and famine of 1970–1972 and the long drought of 1998–2004 were very probably the result of climate change. The drought of 2013–2014 certainly was, and the long-term outlook for both pastoralists and farmers is not a pleasant one.[4] The royal government's policies turned the first of those droughts into a famine, and the resulting anger and disgust were partly responsible for the fall of the monarchy soon afterwards.

Bayakhan, a young Pashtun from north-central Afghanistan, wept as he spoke of the drought and famine and the terrible winter of 1971–1972:

In the autumn, it became clear that it was going to be a bad winter. There was no grass left in the steppe where the sheep were grazing, it was all dust, just like the tracks. Then for two nights there was a foul dust storm. The first night, a whirlwind came from downriver. You couldn't see your hand in front of your face. In the morning when we went out to the steppe to look for the animals, they were all over the place – and so were the wolves.

The carcasses stacked up. That was the sort of year it was. None of our animals died at first, but later they went hungry. Once a sheep 'falls from its stomach', it'll drop dead.

In other years, new grass was up by late February and the sheep and camels grazed their fill. This year the grass didn't grow until late March. At first you could find fodder here, at a price. But by late February it had ran out completely. My job was to find straw and take it to the sheep.

---

and bibliography of that literature, and of some qualitative studies in Africa, see T. Ide, 'Research methods for exploring the link between climate change and conflict', *Wiley Interdisciplinary Reviews: Climate Change*, January 2017.
4 The evidence is patchy. But see M. Savage, B. Dougherty, M. Hamza, R. Butterfield and S. Bharwani, *Socio-Economic Impacts of Climate Change in Afghanistan*, Stockholm 2013; V. Thomas, *Climate Change in Afghanistan: Perspectives and Opportunities*, Kabul 2016; A. K. Alim and S. S. Shobair, 'Drought and Human Suffering in Afghanistan', *SAARC Workshop in Drought Risk Management in South Asia*, Kabul 2010; United Nations Environmental Program, *Climate Change in Afghanistan: What Does It Mean for Rural Livelihoods and Food Security*, 2016; Parenti, *Tropic of Chaos*, pp. 97–112; J. Shroder, 'Characteristics and Implications of Climate Change in Afghanistan and Surrounding Regions', *Transboundary Water Resources in Afghanistan: Climate Change and Land-Use Implications*, eds. J. Shroder and S. J. Ahmad, Oxford 2016, pp. 145–60; and M. Barlow and A. Hoell, 'Drought in the Middle East and Central-Southwest Asia During Winter 2013/14', *Special Supplement to the Bulletin of the American Meteorological Society* 96, 2015, pp. 76–83.

My trousers were frozen stiff. It was so cold you couldn't raise your arms from your sides. When we went by night to places like the main valley, we could hear wolves howling out in the snow. Once, on our way back, we were with some Omarzai, and one of them fell behind; we saw some wolves on top of a ridge and we said, 'Watch out that fellow doesn't get eaten!' We watched, but he didn't make it.[5]

In the last forty years increased heat and droughts have added considerably to people's stresses. It may well be the case that farmers would have suffered far more if it had not been for foreign tolerance of a large and lucrative market for opium as a cash crop ever since the 1980s. For the time being, the impact of heat and drought has not been on the same scale as the effects of Soviet and American invasions. Bombing covers the land in unexploded ordnance, well over a million Afghans have died, another million have been maimed, and across two generations over fifteen million Afghans have been forced into exile or internal displacement.[6]

Our third example is Syria. In 2015, Colin Kelley and several other American scientists published a careful and measured paper, showing that from 2008 onwards climate-change induced drought has pushed at least a million and a half rural Syrians into migration to the cities. Western media has suggested that drought was the cause of the 2011 uprising, and in some quarters there is an argument that the wave of Syrian refugees into Europe were fleeing climate change.[7]

---

5 R. Tapper and N. Lindisfarne Tapper, *Afghan Village Voices: Stories from a Tribal Community in Time of Peace*, London (forthcoming).

6 There are now a great many books on the Afghan tragedy. Particularly useful are G. Dorronsoro, *Revolution Unending: Afghanistan – 1979 to the Present*, London 2000; A. Klaits and G. Gulmamadova-Klaits, *Love and War in Afghanistan*, New York 2005; J. Rico, *Blood Makes the Grass Grow Green: A Year in the Desert with Team America*, New York 2007; S. Cowper-Coles, *Cables from Kabul: The Inside Stories of the West's Campaign*, London 2011; and B. D. Hopkins and M. Marsden, eds., *Beyond Swat: History, Society and Economy along the Afghanistan-Pakistan Frontier*, London 2012. For regular, careful reports, see *Afghanistan Info*, published by the Swiss Committee for the Support of the Afghan People until 2017.

7 For the original, reasonable article that started the controversy, see C. P. Kelley, S. Mohtadi, M. A. Cane, R. Seager and Y. Kushnir, 'Climate change in the Fertile Crescent and implications of the recent Syrian drought', *PNAS* 112 .11, 2015, pp. 3241–6; and for a balanced judgement, see A. Randall, 'The role of climate change in the Syria crisis: how the media got it wrong', *New Internationalist blog* 10 June 2016. See also A. Voski, 'The Role of Climate Change in Armed Conflict across the Developing World and in the Ongoing Syrian War', *Carleton Review of International Affairs* 3, 2016, pp. 1201–40; S. Saleeby, 'Sowing the Seeds of Dissent: Economic Privation and the Syrian Social Contract Unravelling',

This is not what Kelley *et al* maintain. More importantly, this argument glosses over the forty-six-year rule of the Assads, and the deep hatred of most Syrians for that regime. This one-party, one-family rule has been extraordinarily repressive, during the course of which many people have disappeared, or have been killed in secret prisons.[8] The public measure of the brutality took place in 1982, when there was a popular uprising against the regime lead by the Muslim Brotherhood in the major city of Hama. This was quelled by Assad (the father) through bombing and killing some 20,000, perhaps even 40,000 citizens. The violence was so comprehensive, and effective, that it has never been possible to establish exactly how many Syrians perished. This onslaught was known internationally, but more or less ignored. Inside Syria, the massacre in Hama served to terrify the population, who remained relatively quiescent until 2011.

In 2011 hope was contagious during the Arab Springs, and Syrians, like others across the region, rose up to rid themselves of a tyrannical regime. In the five years of civil war since close to half a million people have died – the majority of whom were killed by Assad's forces, local and foreign sectarian militias, and Russian and American bombers. Syrians have been killing each other, but not because of climate change.[9] As Karim Bergaoui and colleagues wrote in the *Bulletin of the American Meteorological Society*, 'While the extent to which the 2007/08 drought in the Levant region destabilized the Syrian government continues to be debated, there is no questioning the enormous toll this extreme event took on the region's population.'[10] It was one more factor, and not a small one, which was followed by a further drought in 2014.

In Darfur, then, climate change was arguably the main driver in a long tragedy. In Afghanistan and Syria it was a cause for additional suffering. Looking forward, however, we can see similar climate disasters playing out again in those countries,

Jadaliyya 16 February 2012; and D. Verner and C. Breisinger, eds., *Economics of Climate Change in the Arab World: Case Studies from the Syrian Arab Republic, Tunisia and the Republic of Yemen*, Washington 2013, pp. 34–48 and 80–90.
8 The photographic evidence of the extent and horror of torture and murder in Assad's prisons is overwhelming. See G. le Caisne, '"They Were Torturing to Kill": Inside Syria's Death Machine', *The Guardian* 1 October 2015.
9 See R. Yassin-Kassab and L. Al-Shami, *Burning Country: Syrians in Revolution and War*, London 2016; J. Alford and A. Wilson, eds., *Khiyana: Daesh, The Left and the Unmaking of the Syrian Revolution*, London 2016; S. Yazbek, *A Woman in the Crossfires: Diaries of the Syrian Revolution*, London 2011; and S. Yazbek, *The Crossing: My Journey to the Shattered Heart of Syria*, London 2015.
10 K. Bergaoui, D. Mitchell, R. Zaaboul, R. McDonnell, F. Otto and M. Allen, 'The contribution of human induced climate change to the drought of 2014 in the Southern Levant Region', *Special Supplement*, 2015.

but elsewhere too, and in a much hotter world. It is useful to discriminate between three possible future effects of climate change. One is conflict and war. The second is famine. The third is long-term economic suffering. Betsy Hartmann has argued for some time that the discourse of climate refugees and climate wars serves to conceal the reality of invasions and normal capitalist economic suffering. More recently, in a brilliant essay in the *London Review of Books*, Alex de Waal has reminded us that for more than a century the truly terrible famines have occurred when a military force decides to starve a population as a weapon of war. He calls attention to the famines unfolding in Yemen and Somalia in 2017 as examples of just such manufactured starvation. 'Starve', he writes, can be a transitive verb.[11]

And, of course, both Hartmann and De Waal are right. Even so, we need to keep in mind both their points *and* the reality of climate-driven economic degradation. As suggested so far for the cases of Darfur, Afghanistan and Syria, there is no pure climate disaster. But equally, there will be no pure military or political disasters in future. There is always a balance of causes, tipping more one way or another in different situations. And as global warming bites harder, the balance will shift more toward climate change as a cause for disaster. Moreover, even if we downplay the threat of climate as a cause of war or famine, we are still left with the reality that the livelihoods of many millions are being destroyed. This will, in the long term, bitterly increase inequality in any society. And even if people do not rebel or wars are started, these will be catastrophes in the lives of the population affected.

Future impacts

The region will see two other important climate-change impacts in future. One is already beginning to unfold: urban heat. We are now seeing a marked jump in global warming. By June 2016 we had seen fourteen straight months of record temperatures. The fifteen years from 2001 to 2015 saw fifteen of the hottest sixteen years since records began (the outlier was 1998). And the earth is warming faster than climate scientists expected. Temperatures have been particularly high in the Gulf region. Through June and July Iraq and Kuwait saw the highest temperatures ever, often over 50 degrees, and reaching 54 in Kuwait, 53 in Basra, and

---

11 A. de Waal, 'The Nazis Used It, We Use It: Famine as a Weapon of War', *London Review of Books* 15 June 2017; and B. Hartmann, 'Rethinking Climate Refugees and Climate Conflict: Rhetoric, Reality and the Politics of Climate Discourse', *Journal of International Development* 22, 2010, pp. 233–46.

52 in Gotvand, Iran. A 2016 article by Pal and Altahir of MIT predicts periods with temperatures of over 60 in much of Southwest Asia throughout the present century – recent measurements suggest this may happen earlier than anticipated.[12]

The key thing to understand here is that temperature rises are usually stated as an average. With current emissions, we can expect a rise of at least four degrees. But this will be higher on particular days, in summer, in particular places, and higher in large cities by two to four degrees. So an increase of four degrees may well be an increase of ten or twelve degrees from time to time in Baghdad or Basra. Moreover, these cities are no longer built of the old materials adapted to the local climate. People live in concrete buildings, and in great heat they will depend on electricity for air conditioning. In Iraq electricity is already intermittent. At very high temperatures, electricity supply systems in many cities will break down, partly because of the level of demand, and partly because of the effects of heat on generation plants. When electricity breaks down, the supply of water will break down as well. This is a recipe for summers from hell.[13]

The other major likely impact from climate change will be economic collapse in countries dependent on oil revenue. There is little doubt that at some point governments will want to take decisive action. A global move to electric vehicles may be the telling moment, because such a move will permanently destroy the oil economy and take the price of oil well below the cost of production. The question is when, and after how much suffering, the shift away from oil occurs. But the price of oil will collapse long before the full shift happens. That collapse only requires enough movement out of oil to create marked over-capacity in the oil industry. The effects will be abrupt, and in some countries devastating.

A whole spate of recent books, like Chris Goodall's *The Switch*, Steve Levine's *Powerhouse*, Tony Serba's *Clean Disruption of Energy and Transportation*, and Ashlee Vance's *Elon Musk*, have recently argued that the moment of that collapse is not all that far away. Care is needed with all these books, and even more so with media reports on solar power and batteries, because there is a strong element of boosterism. But their general argument appears increasingly sound. They point to the very sharp falls in recent years in the price of solar power, and argue that similar falls will accelerate in the making of car batteries. The cost of developing a new car model for the global market is enormous. When the price of batteries

---

12 J. S. Pal and E. A. B. Eltahir, 'Future temperature in Southwest Asia projected to exceed a threshold for human adaptability', *Nature Climate Change* 6, 2015, pp. 197–200.
13 See E. Klinenberg, *Heatwave: A Social Autopsy of a Disaster in Chicago*, Chicago 2002, for an account of the devastating effects of a far less drastic heatwave on the urban population of Chicago in 1995.

falls below a certain point, and the number of miles they can power a car without recharging rises above a certain point, manufacturers are likely to decide that all new investment should go into electric cars.[14] In the summer of 2017 that moment seemed to be growing nearer. Volvo became the first major car manufacturer to announce that from 2019 all their new cars would be hybrid or wholly electric. In the same week, the new government in France announced plans to require all new cars in the country to be electric by 2040. Norway has already announced similar plans for 2015. Germany and India are also considering – but so far only considering – imposing similar rules by 2030. Political and economic competition has had a lot to do with this shift. The French initiative was explicitly framed as a riposte to Donald Trump's attempt to withdraw from the Paris climate agreement. And while Volvo is in most people's minds a Swedish car company, it is in fact owned by Geely, a Chinese holding company. Volvo announced that at first all the new electric and hybrid cars would be made in China. Although Volvo did not explicitly admit it, such a plan would serve to cement China's current lead in battery manufacture over the American corporations, and particularly over Elon Musk. This lead is the result of the kind of directed planning and continued support by the state that have made China the dominant force in global solar PV energy. Such political and economic pressures are not likely to abate. Rather, they are likely to push the technology on faster.[15]

Technological head starts, government support, and a number of years of very large investment will be crucial in adjusting the world to a disrupted and reconfigured auto manufacture and energy market. If the countries in the MENA region wait until the moment of disruption is upon them, the shock to state finances and migrant remittances will make it very difficult indeed to switch course. Taking action before that moment comes would save everyone a great deal of grief.

The centrality of oil

We have reviewed some of the climate related consequences of the global burning

---

14 C. Goodall, *The Switch*, London 2016; S. Levine, *Powerhouse: America, China and the Great Battery War*, New York 2015; T. Seba, *Clean Disruption of Energy and Transportation*, Beta 2014; and A. Vance, *Elon Musk: How the Billionaire CEO of SpaceX and Tesla is Shaping our Future*, London 2016.
15 A. Vaughan, 'All Volvo cares to be electric or hybrid from 2019', *The Guardian* 5 July 2017; A. Chrisafis and A. Vaughan, 'France to be ban sales of petrol and diesel cars by 2040', *The Guardian* 6 July 2017; H. Sanderson, T. Hancock and L. Lewis, 'Electric cars: China's battle for the battery market', *Financial Times* 5 March 2017.

of fossil fuels for the region. Now we turn our attention to the consequence of the global burning of fossil fuels for the politics of the region. There is a complex interaction between oil and inequality, foreign invasions, wars and dictatorships that have afflicted the region for the last century. Understanding the profound connection between oil politics and climate change is now imperative, but still a new field of research. We have written on this at greater length elsewhere. In this chapter we can only hope to provide some food for thought.

There are three useful ways of understanding the development of capitalism. One is to observe it as an international system of inequality between states backed by force – a perspective brilliantly developed in Sven Beckert's *Empire of Cotton: A New Global History of Capitalism*. A second approach is to look at the extraordinary dynamism and the class conflicts of an industrial revolution based on the accumulation of capital through competition and exploitation – the traditional Marxist method. The third, and more recent approach, is to understand capitalism as the story of fossil fuels, first coal and then oil. Three very good recent works of the last sort are Timothy Mitchell, *Carbon Democracy: Political Power in the Age of Oil*, Jason Moore, *Capitalism in the Web of Life*, and Andreas Malm, *Fossil Capital: The Rise of Steam Power and the Roots of Global Warming*.[16] All three approaches are necessary to understand both the world, and the region. We concentrate here, however, on the central importance of fossil fuels to the development of capitalism. There is, in particular, the importance of oil in war and to empires. This is partly a matter of controlling resources – as is often said, the decisive battle of the Second World War took place in Stalingrad because the Soviet Union had to stop the German army reaching the oil in Baku. There has been a somewhat similar scenario in the history of the American Sixth Fleet in the Gulf and the Mediterranean. But also, modern warfare – tanks, shock and awe, drones and all – would not be possible in a world of solar power and wind turbines. In that sense, all wars are now oil wars.

The centrality of oil to the growth of global capitalism also has had another effect. A focal part of the political conquest of the world by the shifting array of great powers has been the domination of the largest oil reserves. This, and not simply the interests of the oil companies, explains much of colonialism, but also of the unfolding tragedy since 2001. It is often said that recent US interventions

16 S. Beckert, *Empire of Cotton: A New Global History of Capitalism*, London 2014; T. Mitchell, *Carbon Democracy: Political Power in the Age of Oil*, London 2011; A. Malm, *Fossil Capital: The Rise of Steam Power and the Roots of Global Warming*, London 2016; and J. Moore, *Capitalism in the Web of Life: Ecology and the Accumulation of Capital*, London 2015.

happened because America did not enjoy 'energy independence'. This is to put the car before the horse. The United States has always consumed only small amounts of Middle Eastern oil, and uses even less now. 'Energy dependence' is a fiction used to justify wars to an American public who would rather not be involved. But it is true that domination of the world's oil reserves has long been a key part of global authority. Indeed, the exposure of American weakness in the region since 2001 has been a key part of the decline of US power. A similar trajectory has been true of Soviet, and then Russian, policy in the region. The Russian state has always needed Central Asian oil, but the prize further south is global influence.

Oil also increases social inequality within countries. There are several reasons for this. The point we are making is related to, but not the same as, Timothy Mitchell's convincing argument that, for a variety of reasons, workers in the oil industry find it much harder to exert trade union power than workers in coal or manufacturing. And where the unions in the central national industry are weak, this will affect all the unions. This in turn increases inequality, because workers find it harder to defend their incomes. We would add to this by maintaining that the oil industry requires a smaller number of workers. One result is that a small elite can monopolise a significant amount of wealth. This again reinforces inequality. Class inequality, and the transparent injustice of it, can only be held in place with a strong apparatus of repression. And, as Richard Wilkinson and Kate Pickett have discussed, the greater the inequality the unhappier the population, and the more social problems of all kinds. Unhappiness, in turn, increases tension in society.[17]

There is another turn of the screw. Linda MacQuaig has persuasively argued that the goal of imperial power has *not* been to keep the price of oil high but to keep profits high.[18] In 1928, the three largest global oil companies reached a secret agreement at Achnacarry Castle in Scotland, and the four other oil majors soon joined. The agreement shared the market between them and lasted for decades. As McQuaig puts it, 'Too much oil would drive the price down, which they obviously didn't want; on the other hand, too little oil would drive the price up, potentially creating a serious downturn in the world economy, which they also didn't want.'[19] It was this cartel structure that OPEC took over in the 1960s. Except for one brief period, the American government has been able until very recently to persuade

---

17 R. Wilkinson and K. Pickett, *The Spirit Level: Why Equality is Better for Everyone*, London 2009.
18 L. McQuaig, *It's the Crude, Dude: War, Big Oil and the Fight for the Planet*, Toronto 2004. See also J. Blair, *The Control of Oil*, New York 1978; and the discussion of 'cheap nature' in Moore, *Capitalism*.
19 McQuaig, *It's the Crude*, p. 211.

OPEC to continue keeping the price down, relying on their Saudi allies to open the taps when necessary to reduce the price of oil. More recently, the Saudi government has opened the taps to keep the price of oil low and drive fracked American oil off the market.

At first sight, these policies make no economic sense for oil producers. But there is a logic here. Not just oil, but cheap oil, is essential to capitalist development. American, British, Dutch and Saudi oil executives have always behaved as if they were obliged to respect a deeper need to keep the world economy expanding. The logic behind this is not just to secure the profit of one corporation or one industry, but to ensure the survival of the system. Nevertheless, the need to keep the price down pits the needs of the majority of the population in these countries against the policies of both local rulers and global powers. The commonality between national and global elites eats away at the legitimacy of the local rulers. That and the gross inequalities made possible from the great oil profits combine to increase repression in oil-rich countries. Reading Robert Fisk's magisterial and heart-breaking history, *The Great War for Civilisation*, there comes a moment when the reader stops, overwhelmed by the endless repetition of the same repressive relationships under so many different regimes.[20] It seems as if there are many ways of being the head of a state, but only one way to be an interrogator. And indeed, the similarity exists because everywhere the state stands between the majority of people and the oil wealth.

Our analysis falls into three parts. The first part focuses on small and great wars for the competition to control oil, producing invasions and civil wars that fuel each other, and how people are broken and degraded by the experience of war, repression, corruption and inequality. It is not only the oil and gas countries that pay a price. The countries that are geographically situated in-between are always 'strategically important', and are therefore often occupied or repressed. In all of this, the immediate causes of such tragedy and great grief are obvious, and so glaring that they become even harder to bear.

Our second focus is on resistance. Wars and violence may have been more bearable if Arabs, Turks, Iranians or Afghans conformed to the Orientalist trope of welcoming hierarchy and firm leadership. But conflicts tend to be fierce since the region's people, like people everywhere else, value liberty and equality. The latter fact fuels resistance, as we have seen for instance in the Arab Spring, but also many times before, throughout the whole of the 20th century, in national independent movements, Arab socialism, the revolution in Iran, and Islamism across the

---

20 R. Fisk, *The Great War for Civilisation: The Conquest of the Middle East*, London 2006.

region. In response to these internal conflicts, imperial and local powers invade, divide and rule, sell arms, and fight proxy wars. Sometimes various powers come together, as they have in Syria today, to stamp out any memory of the Arab Spring.

Finally, we must not forget oil corporations.[21] These corporations, through Cheney and Bush, were key instigators of the invasions of 2001 and 2003, but they had done so much else before. We need not rehearse the details here. Moreover, the oil and other carbon corporations are global powers in their own right. The top ten companies in the Fortune Global 500 list in 2016, measured by revenue, included five oil corporations (China National Petroleum, Sinopec, Shell, Exxon Mobil, and BP), two car producers (Volkswagen and Toyota), one electricity producer (State Grid of China), one vast parking lot (Walmart) – and Apple.[22] This formidable array of corporate power has, as we know from the work of Naomi Oreskes and Erik Conway, been mobilised to spread climate denial in the United States. More importantly, Oreskes and Conway point out, the corporations have been aiming not for outright denial but for muddying the waters for the majority of the audience.[23] Even more significant, however, has been the influence of oil corporations on American climate diplomacy in its various disastrous forms throughout the 20th century, and most recently under Bush the father, Clinton, Bush Jr. and then under Obama .

In sum, the burning of fossil fuels has had a plethora of impacts on the region. And there is worse to come, unless an alternative can be found. In the rest of this chapter we will sketch out that alternative and suggest which social forces might be able to put it into practice.

Climate jobs

We begin this section by explaining the concept of climate jobs, and then proceed to explore how it might apply in the region.[24]

There are now climate jobs campaigns in Canada, South Africa, Portugal, Norway, Britain, and the state of New York. Most of these campaigns began with climate organisations, but most also have strong support from national trade

---

21 See particularly N. Klein, *This Changes Everything: Capitalism vs. the Climate*, London 2014.
22 At beta.fortune.com/global500.
23 N. Oreskes and E. Conway, *Merchants of Doubt*, London 2010.
24 Information on the various national campaigns is posted regularly on the Global Climate Jobs website: www.globalclimatejobs.wordpress.com.

unions. The idea is quite simple.[25] To halt climate change, we need to turn to a very low carbon economy. Globally, this requires thousands of strategies. But four steps will make the difference: first, we have to cover the world with renewable energy, mostly solar and wind power, so that we can replace all fossil fuels in the manufacture of electricity; second, we need a massive switch from cars to public transport, and we need to run almost all transport on renewably generated electricity; third, we need to convert all housing and commercial buildings in the cooler and the hottest countries in such a way that much less energy – in the form of renewable electricity – is required for heating and cooling; and finally, in many countries we need to conserve and extend dense tropical rainforests.

These measures would, it is often said, be enormously expensive. But stop and think for a moment. Enormously expensive ventures entail the creation of a very large number of jobs – that is the expense. Instead of thinking of a low-carbon world as a cost for business and governments, we should think of it as a gain for working people – and the climate. Climate jobs campaigns have conducted detailed studies in several countries so far. On a global level, they estimate that about 140 million workers could cut greenhouse gas emissions by more than 80% in twenty years, using the technology we have now. These would have to be public projects. Only governments have the necessary resources, or the necessary motivation. This will not work on the scale required simply through market forces. Government regulation will be necessary.

This would be an expensive measure, but the money can be found. Some of it could be repaid in electricity bills and bus and train tickets. In richer countries, much of the cost of increased public employment would be recouped in lower benefits and higher tax payments. The remainder of the money could be raised by taxing the income or the wealth of the very rich. This is an ambitious plan,

25 For more details on how the idea of climate jobs could work in practice, see J. Neale, ed., *One Million Climate Jobs: Tackling the Environmental and Economic Crises*, London 2014; *One Million Climate Jobs: A Just Transition to a Low Carbon Economy to Combat Unemployment and Climate Change*, Cape Town 2012; A. Ytterstad, *100,000 Climate Jobs and Green Workplaces Now: For a Climate Solution from Below* (in Norwegian), Oslo 2013; H. Ryggvik, *Norwegian Oil and the Climate: An Outline of Cooling Down* (in Norwegian), Oslo 2103; A. Ytterstad, ed., *Broen til Framtiden*, Oslo 2015; Bizi!, *Demain, 10 000 emplois climatique in Pay Basque nord*, Bayonne 2015; H. Min Cha and L. Skinner, *A Climate Jobs Programme for New York State: Reversing Inequality, Combatting Climate Change: Preliminary Recommendations*, New York 2016; M. Mineo-Paluello, *Jobs in Scotland's New Economy*, a report commissioned by the Scottish Green MSPs, 2015; Attac, *Un million d'emplois pour le climat*, Paris 2017; and J. Neale, *Our Jobs, Our Planet: Transport Workers and Climate Change*, Climate and Capitalism 2012.

but expenditure on this scale is what governments do when something matters to them. It is exactly what happened when belligerents on all sides transformed their economies during the Second World War. And during the 2008 financial crash we learned that the Federal Reserve Bank could come up with 400 billion dollars in one day if they had to. If the Earth was a bank, they would already have saved her. The climate jobs campaign's motto is 'Earth is too big to fail'.

One enormous advantage of the climate jobs campaign is political. The mainstream environmental approach to climate change has been to demand generalised sacrifice – often called 'degrowth' – to solve the problem. There is an intellectual problem with this solution. We have to decrease global emissions by at least 80% to 90%, and cuts on this level cannot be achieved by reducing consumption. The great majority of the cuts have to be done through using energy differently. Indeed, a reduction of 98% could be achieved by simply using energy differently. But there is an even bigger political difficulty with the 'degrowth' approach. Demands for cuts for sacrifice and degrowth are coming from a largely white, affluent movement, overwhelmingly from the richer countries. Calls are for small falls in the standard of living in the Global North, and an absolute block to poorer countries catching up. These calls, moreover, ring out in a context of austerity, while the majority of ordinary people in many countries are already sacrificing a great deal.

Things are changing. There are carrots and sticks. Investment in renewables is happening all over the world. Portugal kept its lights on with renewable energy alone for four consecutive days in April 2016. In Britain, the Crown Estate has joined the debate about the Hinkley Point by 'pointing out that offshore windfarms are already being built at cheaper prices than the proposed atomic reactors for Somerset'. In Saudi Arabia, the cabinet is backing a far-reaching plan to unshackle the economy from reliance on oil. Many more examples can be given. On the other hand, because of huge public opposition, France, Bulgaria, Germany and Scotland have made fracking illegal, Obama vetoed the Keystone pipeline from the Canadian tar sands to Texas, the Ogoni resistance has paralysed Shell, and the US coal giant Peabody has filed for bankruptcy, which experts have seen as 'a sign that the most carbon-intensive fossil fuel was threatened by tightening environmental regulation'.[26]

26 A. Neslen, 'Portugal reaches clean energy milestone', *The Guardian* 19 May 2016; T. Macalister, 'US coal giant Peabody files for bankruptcy as prices fall', *The Guardian* 14 April 2016; T. Macalister, 'Crown estate says future is in wind, not Hinkley', *The Guardian* 15 August 2016; I. Black, 'Saudi cabinet backs far-reaching plan to unshackle economy from reliance on oil', *The Guardian* 26 April 2016.

Although things are changing, they are not changing fast enough. For example, in Morocco, some 20% of electricity will soon be produced by renewable energy, but this is only 2% of the energy used in the economy as a whole. And a second example is perhaps even more disturbing. A considerable proportion of oil produced in the Middle East is used for domestic consumption. To cover these energy requirements and leave more oil for export, a number of Middle Eastern countries, including Saudi Arabia, Iran and Algeria, are now investing in nuclear rather than sustainable wind or solar power.[27] We will not find it easy to decarbonise the world. The leaders of the world and the corporate powers are not taking the necessary actions. We need to build a mass movement to force them to act. This may not be impossible, but will certainly be difficult. More than half of global emissions now come from the poorer countries. These emissions cannot be reduced without the enthusiastic support of majorities in those countries. We will never get that support for degrowth. And – crucially – we do not need to.

A place where the argument for sacrifice will go absolutely nowhere is the Middle East and North Africa. This is obvious in the poorer countries like Sudan and Afghanistan. But it is equally true in Iraq, Saudi Arabia, the Gulf and Algeria, the oil and gas producers, which face the prospect of economic collapse. We need an alternative that allows growth in a different economy with different fuels, that provides jobs and hope for ordinary people. There are obvious difficulties in applying a climate jobs perspective in the MENA region, and we will return to these challenges. First, though, let us look at some of the ways a strategy for nearly total decarbonisation makes particular technical sense in this region.

---

27 *Middle East Solar Outlook for 2016*, Middle East Solar Industry Association 2016; *Evaluating Renewable Energy Manufacturing Potential in the Mediterranean Partner Countries*, International Renewable Energy Association 2015; C. Roselund, 'Solar in the Middle East and North Africa: Potential and Development', *Solar Server* 2016; A. Neslen, 'Morocco to switch on first phase of world's largest solar plant', *The Guardian* 4 February 2016; D. Cusick, 'Solar Power Invades Oil-Rich Middle East', *Scientific American* 28 September 2015; and E. Brutto and F. Abdul Magid, *Solar Energy Market in Middle East and North Africa 2016: Overview of the Solar Heat Market Trends*, DNV GL – Energy 2016. But see also the words of warning in O. Reyes, *Maps and Legends: A Critical Look at Desertec*, Devon 2012. For nuclear expansion, see B. Parkin and J. Jones, 'Petrocide: Oil in the Context of Imperialism, Resource Conflicts and Environmental Crisis', paper presented at the Historical Materialism Conference, School of Oriental and African Studies, London, 5–8 November 2015. For more recent developments in solar power, see I. Tsarpas, 'Building Big in MENA', *PV Magazine* 21 February 2017; and for Turkish plans for large scale domestic manufacture of PV cells behind a tariff wall, see I. Clover and I. Tsagas, 'Analysis: UGW Konya deal in Turkey could mark beginning of new manufacturing capacity', *PV Magazine* 21 March 2017.

On one level this is obvious – there is an enormous amount of sun in the region, and large amounts of empty space. Vast expanses of desert lands are not enough, however. Both main methods in use for generating solar power – i.e. photovoltaic cell arrays and concentrated solar power – require considerable amounts of water. However, there is still plenty of space. Moreover, the region is particularly fitted to Concentrated Solar Power (CSP). CSP is now a great deal more expensive than PV arrays, but it has the great advantage of being able to store heat throughout the night and then produce large amounts of electricity at night – PV arrays cannot do this. CSP also needs much less land. This is important because an energy system that uses some renewable energy cannot rely on solar power alone. An energy system run completely, or almost completely, on renewable energy confronts the problem of irregular supply. The sun shines only during the day, and the wind blows strong and weak in any one area. But the wind blows when the sun is not out, and when the wind falls in the Nile Delta, it is likely to be picking up in northern Sudan and Turkey. A mixture of various kinds of supply, and a mixture of supplies over long distances, is essential. That is entirely possible with modern long-distance cables. In this context, the wind resources of the region matter. There are substantial possibilities offshore everywhere. There are also enormous wind resources in Turkey and in Kazakhstan.

One consequence of this necessity to mix energy is that, contrary to common wisdom, no 'solar revolution' can be decentralised. This is partly because renewable energy cannot be entirely solar. But it is also because models of decentralised solar energy always focus on the provision of domestic energy, while more than half the electricity we need services transport and industry. However, there are two ways in which decentralised solar suits the region particularly well. First, it can be of use in poorer countries where the grid does not reach many villages. The portable tent top solar units utilised by yak herders in Tibet can be used as an example of a system that could work. But perhaps more importantly, local roof-top solar systems are a very good fit for urban air conditioning – you need air conditioning when the sun is shining, and in proportion to the heat. Second, renewable energy carries the possibility of transforming the economies of countries without oil or gas. To understand this, we need to think of local, national industrial capacity. The enormous renewable energy reserves of the Sahara are usually discussed in terms of potential for exports to Europe. However, for countries like Morocco, Tunisia, and Syria very large amounts of renewable electricity would make it possible for the countries to reduce the enormous cost of imported oil to almost nothing – and to power considerable industrial growth.

Transport and industry matter a great deal. On a global level, and in the Middle

East, domestic electricity is a less important end user. After all, in a post-carbon world, the oil rich and oil poor countries of the region will each still need to have an economy. These are mostly highly urbanised countries. They will need industry. That must be partly a matter of diversified manufacturing. But renewable energy manufacture, operations and export will also have to be part of that picture.

Finally, there is the matter of state action and financial reserves. Projects on the scale we are talking about can only possibly work in the necessary time scale with massive government intervention and expenditure. In this respect, many countries in the region are relatively well-placed. The oil and gas states have traditions of massive government intervention. These states have developed urban systems, secondary and higher education, health provision, and much more, sometimes from almost nothing to world-class standards. And there are very large sovereign wealth funds in some of the region's countries, as well as untapped tax bases in others. In several countries, it would make far more sense to use those funds to decarbonise the economy and build a new industrial base.

The problem of agency

That all sounds very nice. But the barriers to any such transformation of the region are numerous. These are political, and not technical, barriers. The great powers who dominate the region are committed to fossil fuels. As are the more powerful national governments, the global and national oil corporations and most of the elites. We should not underestimate the importance of the fact that all the foreign and local military forces are utterly dependent on machinery driven by fossil fuels, to which there is no real alternative.

This situation may be extreme, but it mirrors a much broader problem around the world. The Paris climate talks in 2015 made it quite clear that national governments and global elites in general are not prepared to act. The Paris agreement, in fact, provides for rising emissions every year from now to 2030. Difficult as it may be, only mass movements will be able to force governments to reduce emissions, country by country. Such conclusion makes things look particularly bleak in the MENA region. Trade union movements are relatively weak and sometimes illegal, and NGOs are often hemmed in. Mass popular movements face enormous obstacles and dangers. They have quite different, pressing, immediate concerns, and they look to ideologies quite different from northern environmentalism. Almost all movements of resistance would say they have more important things than climate change to cope with at the moment.

There are reasons enough to despair. We all know that. And yet, the popular movements of the region keep coming back, again and again, in ever changing forms, after defeat, after betrayals, after all the blood, because the region's people insist upon fairness and freedom. It is not time, quite yet, to write-off the possibility of democracy and equality in the MENA region. And if there is a resurgence in the power of ordinary people in the region, then it would be possible to make the argument for climate action. That could work – if the matter is framed as an argument for hundreds of thousands, and millions, of jobs now, and for an alternative to economic collapse later. And if the transformation is framed as an alternative to a world run by global oil companies, global military powers and their local allies. That could, just possibly, seize the imaginations of many people.

Summary and conclusion

We can now summarise the argument proposed in this chapter. Oil is the main problem in the MENA region, because of climate change, and because the regional economy is based on it. Heat is the consequence which will make life in much of the region very difficult, and in some places impossible. Creating climate jobs is a solution which offers the region an economic and environmental alternative. And oddly enough, oil can also be the solution, because the wealth accumulated from oil makes a swift transition to wind and solar power possible.

We are, however, still stuck in a hard place, between a menacing future and a hope which may well not come into fruition. What we need is a middle ground, a more realistic and likely scenario for the future. The difficulty is that there is no middle ground. In much of life and politics, there can always be compromises. No matter how flawed, grudging or temporary, those compromises and peace deals often allow people to muddle through. But this works only when negotiation is between people. In the current case, one negotiator is the atmosphere of the Earth. And the physics of the atmosphere do not compromise, do not listen and do not forgive. This closes the middle ground, which does not mean we should throw up our hands and insist on our revolution or nothing. The argument for climate action has been a long one, and it will stretch some time into the future. Along that journey every debate, every plan, every wind farm and solar array matters.

Bibliography

Akasha, M. O., *Darfur: A Tragedy of Climate Change*, New York 2013.
Alford, J. and A. Wilson, eds., *Khiyana: Daesh, The Left and the Unmaking of the Syrian Revolution*, London 2016.

Alim, A. K. and S. S. Shobair, 'Drought and Human Suffering in Afghanistan', *SAARC Workshop in Drought Risk Management in South Asia*, Kabul 2010.

Attac, *Un million d'emplois pour le climat*, Paris 2017.

Barlow, M. and A. Hoell, 'Drought in the Middle East and Central-Southwest Asia During Winter 2013/14', *Special Supplement to the Bulletin of the American Meteorological Society* 96, 2015, pp. 76–83.

Beckert, S., *Empire of Cotton: A New Global History of Capitalism*, London 2014.

Bergaoui, K., D. Mitchell, R. Zaaboul, R. McDonnell, F. Otto and M. Allen, 'The contribution of human induced climate change to the drought of 2014 in the Southern Levant Region', *Special Supplement*, 2015.

Bizi!, *Demain, 10 000 emplois climatique in Pay Basque nord*, Bayonne 2015.

Black, I., 'Saudi cabinet backs far-reaching plan to unshackle economy from reliance on oil', *The Guardian* 26 April 2016.

Blair, J., *The Control of Oil*, New York 1978.

Brutto, E. and F. Abdul Magid, *Solar Energy Market in Middle East and North Africa 2016: Overview of the Solar Heat Market Trends*, DNV GL – Energy 2016.

Chrisafis, A. and A. Vaughan, 'France to be ban sales of petrol and diesel cars by 2040', *The Guardian* 6 July 2017.

Clover, I. and I. Tsagas, 'Analysis: UGW Konya deal in Turkey could mark beginning of new manufacturing capacity', *PV Magazine* 21 March 2017.

Cowper-Coles, S., *Cables from Kabul: The Inside Stories of the West's Campaign*, London 2011.

le Caisne, G., '"They Were Torturing to Kill": Inside Syria's Death Machine', *The Guardian* 1 October 2015.

Cusick, D., 'Solar Power Invades Oil-Rich Middle East', *Scientific American* 28 September 2015.

Dorronsoro, G., *Revolution Unending: Afghanistan – 1979 to the Present*, London 2000.

Evaluating Renewable Energy Manufacturing Potential in the Mediterranean Partner Countries, International Renewable Energy Association 2015.

Fisk, R., *The Great War for Civilisation: The Conquest of the Middle East*, London 2006.

Flint, J. and A. de Waal, *Darfur: A Short History of a Long War*, London 2005.

Forsyth, T. and M. Schomerus, *Climate Change and Conflict: A Systematic Evidence Review*, London School of Economics 2013.

Funk, C., G. Eilerts, J. Verdin, J. Roland and M. Marshall, *A Climate Trend Analysis of Sudan*, United States Geological Survey 2011.

Goodall, C., *The Switch*, London 2016.

Hartmann, B., 'Rethinking Climate Refugees and Climate Conflict: Rhetoric, Reality and the Politics of Climate Discourse', *Journal of International Development* 22, 2010, pp. 233–46.

Hopkins, B. D. and M. Marsden, eds., *Beyond Swat: History, Society and Economy along the Afghanistan-Pakistan Frontier*, London 2012.

Ide, T., 'Research methods for exploring the link between climate change and conflict', *Wiley Interdisciplinary Reviews: Climate Change*, January 2017.

De Juan, A., 'Long-term environmental change and geographical patterns of violence in Darfur 2003–2005', *Political Geography* 45, 2015, pp. 22–33.

Keen, D., *The Benefits of Famine: A Political Economy of Famine and Relief in Southwestern Sudan, 1983–1989*, Princeton 1994.

Kelley, C. P., S. Mohtadi, M. A. Cane, R. Seager and Y. Kushnir, 'Climate change in the Fertile Crescent and implications of the recent Syrian drought', *PNAS* 112.11, 2015, pp. 3241–6.

Klaits, A. and G. Gulmamadova-Klaits, *Love and War in Afghanistan*, New York 2005.

Klein, N., *This Changes Everything: Capitalism vs. the Climate*, London 2014.

Klinenberg, E., *Heatwave: A Social Autopsy of a Disaster in Chicago*, Chicago 2002.

Levine, S., *Powerhouse: America, China and the Great Battery War*, New York 2015.

Macalister, T., 'Crown estate says future is in wind, not Hinkley', *The Guardian* 15 August 2016.

Macalister, T., 'US coal giant Peabody files for bankruptcy as prices fall', *The Guardian* 14 April 2016.

Malm, A., *Fossil Capital: The Rise of Steam Power and the Roots of Global Warming*, London 2016.

Mamdani, M., *Saviors and Survivors: Darfur, Politics and the War on Terror*, New York 2009.

McQuaig, L., *It's the Crude, Dude: War, Big Oil and the Fight for the Planet*, Toronto 2004.

Middle East Solar Outlook for 2016, Middle East Solar Industry Association 2016.

Min Cha, H. and L. Skinner, *A Climate Jobs Programme for New York State: Reversing Inequality, Combatting Climate Change: Preliminary Recommendations*, New York 2016.

Mineo-Paluello, M., *Jobs in Scotland's New Economy*, a report commissioned by the Scottish Green MSPs, 2015.

Mitchell, T., *Carbon Democracy: Political Power in the Age of Oil*, London 2011.

Moore, T., *Capitalism in the Web of Life: Ecology and the Accumulation of Capital*, London 2015.

Neale, J., ed., *One Million Climate Jobs: A Just Transition to a Low Carbon Economy to Combat Unemployment and Climate Change*, Cape Town 2012.

Neale, J., ed., *One Million Climate Jobs: Tackling the Environmental and Economic Crises*, London 2014.

Neale, J., *Our Jobs, Our Planet: Transport Workers and Climate Change*, Climate and Capitalism, 2012.

Neale, J., *Stop Global Warming: Change the World*, London 2008.

Neslen, A., 'Morocco to switch on first phase of world's largest solar plant', *The Guardian* 4 February 2016.

Neslen, A., 'Portugal reaches clean energy milestone', *The Guardian* 19 May 2016.

Niang, I., O. C. Ruppel, M. A. Abdrabo, A. Essel, C. Lennard, J. Padgham and P. Urquhart, 'Africa', *Climate Change 2014: Impacts, Adaptation, and Vulnerability*, Cambridge 2014, pp. 1196–265.

Oreskes, N. and E. Conway, *Merchants of Doubt*, London 2010.

Pal, J. S. and E. A. B. Eltahir, 'Future temperature in Southwest Asia projected to exceed a threshold for human adaptability', *Nature Climate Change* 6, 2015, pp. 197–200.

Parenti, C., *Tropic of Chaos: Climate Change and the New Geography of Violence*, New York 2011.

Park Williams, A. *et al*, 'Recent summer precipitation trends in the Greater Horn of Africa and the emerging role of Indian Ocean sea surface temperature', *Climate Dynamics* 39.9, 2012, pp. 2307–28.

Parkin, B. and J. Jones, 'Petrocide: Oil in the Context of Imperialism, Resource Conflicts and Environmental Crisis', paper presented at the Historical Materialism Conference, School of Oriental and African Studies, London, 5–8 November 2015.

Prunier, G., *Darfur: the Ambiguous Genocide*, Ithaca, NY 2005.

Randall, A., 'The role of climate change in the Syria crisis: how the media got it wrong', *New Internationalist blog* 10 June 2016.

Reyes, O., *Maps and Legends: A Critical Look at Desertec*, Devon 2012.

Rico, J., *Blood Makes the Grass Grow Green: A Year in the Desert with Team America*, New York 2007.

Roselund, C., 'Solar in the Middle East and North Africa: Potential and Development', *Solar Server* 2106.

Ryggvik, H., *Norwegian Oil and the Climate: An Outline of Cooling Down* (in Norwegian), Oslo 2103.

Saleeby, S., 'Sowing the Seeds of Dissent: Economic Privation and the Syrian Social Contract Unravelling', *Jadaliyya* 16 February 2012.

Sanderson, H., T. Hancock and L. Lewis, 'Electric cars: China's battle for the battery market', *Financial Times* 5 March 2017.

Savage, M., B. Dougherty, M. Hamza, R. Butterfield and S. Bharwani, *Socio-Economic Impacts of Climate Change in Afghanistan*, Stockholm 2013.

Seba, T., *Clean Disruption of Energy and Transportation*, Beta 2014.

Shroder, J., 'Characteristics and Implications of Climate Change in Afghanistan and Surrounding Regions', *Transboundary Water Resources in Afghanistan: Climate Change and Land-Use Implications*, eds. J. Shroder and S. J. Ahmad, Oxford 2016, pp. 145–60.

Tapper, R. and N. Lindisfarne Tapper, *Afghan Village Voices: Stories from a Tribal Community in Time of Peace*, London (forthcoming).

Thomas, V., *Climate Change in Afghanistan: Perspectives and Opportunities*, Kabul 2016.

Tsarpas, I., 'Building Big in MENA', *PV Magazine* 21 February 2017.

Tubiana, J., 'Darfur: A War for Land', *War in Darfur and the Search for Peace*, ed. A. de Waal, Cambridge, MA 2007, pp. 68–91.

United Nations Environment Programme, *Sudan: Post-conflict Environmental Assessment*, Nairobi 2007.

United Nations Environmental Program, *Climate Change in Afghanistan: What Does It Mean for Rural Livelihoods and Food Security*, 2016.

Vance, A., *Elon Musk: How the Billionaire CEO of SpaceX and Tesla is Shaping our Future*, London 2016.

Vaughan, A., 'All Volvo cares to be electric or hybrid from 2019', *The Guardian* 5 July 2017.

Verner, D. and C. Breisinger, eds., *Economics of Climate Change in the Arab World: Case Studies from the Syrian Arab Republic, Tunisia and the Republic of Yemen*, Washington 2013, pp. 34–48 and 80–90.

Voski, A., 'The Role of Climate Change in Armed Conflict across the
    Developing World and in the Ongoing Syrian War', *Carleton Review of
    International Affairs* 3, 2016, pp. 1201–40.
de Waal, A., *Famine that Kills: Darfur, Sudan*, Oxford 2005.
de Waal, A., 'The Nazis Used It, We Use It: Famine as a Weapon of War',
    London Review of Books 15 June 2017.
de Waal, A., *The Real Politics of the Horn of Africa: Money, War and the
    Business of Power*, Cambridge 2015.
Wilkinson, R. and K. Pickett, *The Spirit Level: Why Equality is Better for
    Everyone*, London 2009.
Yassin-Kassab, R. and L. Al-Shami, *Burning Country: Syrians in Revolution
    and War*, London 2016.
Yazbek, S., *A Woman in the Crossfires: Diaries of the Syrian Revolution*,
    London 2011.
Yazbek, S., *The Crossing: My Journey to the Shattered Heart of Syria*, London
    2015.
Ytterstad, A., *100,000 Climate Jobs and Green Workplaces Now: For a Climate
    Solution from Below* (in Norwegian), Oslo 2013.
Ytterstad, A., ed., *Broen til Framtiden*, Oslo 2015.
Zeng, N., 'Drought in the Sahel', *Science* 303, 2003, pp. 1124–7.

6

MENA Water and Food Security Since 1950: Adaptation and Economic Diversification

Marta Antonelli and J. A. (Tony) Allan

Food security – a very emotional and an extremely politicised issue

The purpose of this chapter is to highlight the importance of the link between water and food and the significant role of *food-water* in ensuring the sustainable stability of Middle Eastern and North African (MENA) economies. *Food-water* is the water consumed in producing food. In general, it accounts for about 92% of the water needed by an economy. *Non-food* water, i.e. water that is consumed by domestic and industrial users, comprises the other 8%.[1]

There are two contradictory water and food security narratives surrounding food-water. The first is the popular discourse generated by politicians, the media and the general public based on the evidence that householders and industry have access to water services and to food that is affordable. The second narrative is based on the underlying fundamentals of water endowments, the capacity of the global system to provide affordable food imports and the diversification and

---

1 M. M. Mekonnen and A. Y. Hoekstra, 'The green, blue and grey water footprint of crops and derived crop products', *The Value of Water Research Report Series* 47, 2010, Delft: UNESCO-IHE; M. M. Mekonnen and A. Y. Hoekstra, 'The green, blue and grey water footprint of crops and derived crop products', *The Value of Water Research Report Series* 48, 2010, Delft: UNESCO-IHE; M. M. Mekonnen and A. Y. Hoekstra, 'The green, blue and grey water footprint of crops and derived crop products', *Hydrological Earth Systems Science* 15, 2011, pp. 1577–600.

capacity of individual economies. This second narrative explains why the MENA region enjoys a measure of food and water security. But this latter narrative is backgrounded because it reveals strategic dependencies.

The first water and food security narrative – truisms that are not truisms

The first narrative that has been widely accepted since the 1950s by national leaders, as well by people in the street, has evolved over many centuries from a time when the region was water and food self-sufficient. This *sanctioned discourse* that water scarcity is a future problem and not an immediate one is deeply embedded in the minds of food consumers and legislators. Until the 1990s, it was even accepted by water scientists. Sanctioned discourse can be described as 'the prevailing dominant opinion and views which have been legitimised by the discursive elite'.[2] The accepted narrative or sanctioned discourse has been established in circumstances of asymmetric power.[3] In other words, those enjoying power engage with other players to establish a narrative that is socially and politically stabilising. At the same time, it projects the idea, with respect to elemental issues such as water and food security, that everything is under control. The evidence is the availability of affordable food in the shops.

The prevailing narrative on food and water security in the MENA region runs roughly as follows:

There is food on the shelves of our shops and supermarkets and it is essential that this food be affordable for low-income families. Food insecurity has been kept at bay so there must be enough water to raise the nation's food. National water resources that currently underpin essential domestic, industrial and irrigation water services are secure but limited. No water can possibly be shared with neighbouring economies. Nor can existing water resources be decreased by the actions of neighbours as a consequence of increases in their water consumption. Serious water conflict is a risk, but it is a future problem, not an immediate problem.

2 A. Jägerskog, 'The sanctioned discourse – a crucial factor for understanding water policy in the Jordan River Basin', *Occasional Paper*, Department for Water and Environmental Studies, Linköping University, No. 41, 2002.
3 M. Zeitoun, 'The conflict vs. cooperation paradox: fighting over or sharing of Palestinian – Israeli groundwater?', *Water Policy* 8, 2007, pp. 105–20.

Notes:
1 The fact that water and food security is dependent on food imports has been *known* by water scientists and professionals in the region since the 1990s. Yet it has been made *unknown*. Awareness that the MENA economies have achieved the current version of food and water security through economic diversification which enables food imports has also been made *unknown*.
2. The situations in Palestine and Yemen are not captured by the above narrative.

There are a number of essential but dangerous assumptions underpinning this deluded popular narrative. The adoption of these assumptions and the need for their existence are, however, entirely explicable politically. The main blind spot is the relative proportions of water needed by domestic, industrial and agricultural water users. Citizens and legislators in the MENA region do not realise that domestic water consumption accounts for only about 4% of the total water consumption of an individual or an economy. Industrial consumption is also about 4%. These two non-food water uses have to be met with local water resources. Unlike non-food water, food-water does not have to be locally sourced; it can be 'imported'. Water embedded in MENA food imports enables the region's economies to escape the limits of their own water endowments. MENA economies are amongst the highest net food importers in the world. Local water resource endowments are not sufficient to meet their food demands (see Figures 11 and 12).

The assumption that water for domestic and industrial consumption is a current critical problem is true for Yemen, Jordan and Palestine. For the other MENA economies it is not. All MENA economies can meet their domestic and industrial water needs. If they are beginning to find it difficult, they can recycle domestic and industrial water after first use. They can also desalinate brackish water and seawater.

The major delusion is that affordable food in the shops is a sign of a secure system. The MENA region is in practice highly dependent on international food commodity markets for its food security. It achieves a version of food and water security by consuming food grown with food-water in other economies that currently have surplus water resources after they have produced their own food needs.

The security and long-term stability of the MENA food-water system has been tested twice since 1950. There have been two serious international food commodity price spikes in the past half century – in 1974–1980 and in 2008–2016. In both cases public officials and private sector organisations along with international private sector traders brought global food prices back down. The FAO international food price index was 161.4 in 2007 and 161.9 in 2016.[4] In practice the MENA region has been strategically adapting to significant food deficits since the 1950s. Some of the region's economies ceased to be food self-sufficient in the 1950s, for example the economies in the Gulf and in Libya in North Africa. By 1970, all the economies of the region, except Syria and Turkey, no longer enjoyed food self-sufficiency. Even Syria and Turkey need to import food when seasonal winter rains are low.

The downward trend in international food prices has been analysed recently by Baldos and Hertel (2013).[5] They have employed the widely used SIMPLE model (Simplified International Model of Agricultural Prices, Land Use and the Environment[6]) to estimate international food prices up to 2050. They conclude that food prices will continue to fall. This conclusion is favourable for the MENA region in that it will still be a major food importing region for the rest of the century. Perhaps the narrative that water scarcity is a future problem and not an immediate one will still be in place.

The second narrative – the known that must become unknown

The second narrative identifies the underlying hydrological and economic systems and processes that enable a degree of water and food security to be enjoyed in individual MENA economies. This narrative, which cannot be recognised by political elites, legislators and the man and woman on the street, runs as follows:

> Overall, Middle Eastern economies are about 50% dependent on imported food. Some Gulf economies are over 90% dependent on imported food. Their food and water security depend on the availability of international food commodity imports, raised in water surplus economies. The MENA economies benefit in two ways from the availability of food in the global food system. First, they avoid the environmental costs and the political stress associated with the overuse of their own scarce water resources. These

4 FAOSTAT, 'Food price index', Fao.org, http://www.fao.org/worldfoodsituation/foodpricesindex/en/.

5 U. L. C. Baldos and T. W. Hertel, 'Debunking the "new normal". Why world food prices are expected to resume their long run downward trend', *Global Food Security* 8, 2016, pp. 27–38, https://doi.org/10.1016/j.gfs.2016.03.002.

6 U. L. C. Baldos and T. W. Hertel, 'Looking back to move forward on model validation: insights from a global model of agricultural land use', *Environmental Research Letters* 8.3, 2013, 034024, doi:10. 1088/1748-9326/8/3/034024.

costs are borne by the food exporting economies that provide the imported food. Second, they have benefitted from the long-term downward trend in global food commodity prices. There is no prospect of access to significant volumes of *new low-cost water* locally for crop production to meet the needs of a doubled population. The demand for food commodity imports can only increase. The MENA economies have diversified sufficiently to meet the costs of rising levels of food imports that have been, fortunately for them, under-priced for decades. Future water and food security will depend mainly on further economic diversification and expert engagement in the political economy of global food commodity trade.

This second narrative explains why the MENA region has achieved a remarkably effective model of water and food security. But it is not an explanation that works for those running an economy as it is intuitively destabilising. The apparent water security and food security are very welcome; the message of dependency is not. Hence, the knowns identified by water scientists and those involved in trading food have to be made unknown.

This chapter provides an overview of the scale of MENA food production in relation to food demand. It also identifies the rising trend in past and future food consumption that has been met by the global food system. It will conclude that the MENA region can only be food and water secure if it accelerates the diversification of its economies. It will also answer the following questions:

- What are the existing trends in demand for food-water in the MENA region?
- How has the MENA water resource deficit been addressed?
- What version of food and water security can the MENA economies enjoy in future?
- Is food-water security too difficult to understand? And why will truisms that are not truisms prevail and the critical known continue to be constructed as an unknown?

Trends in the MENA demand for food-water and the types of water that meets this demand

Levels of water consumption are closely related to population. An individual consumes between 2.5 and 5.0 cubic metres of water per day for their food, their household needs and for their jobs. The difference between the high figure of 5.0

and the low figure of 2.5 is accounted for mainly by their food choices and the different volumes of water associated with their food choices. About 5.0 cubic metres of water per day are consumed by someone who eats a lot of meat. A vegetarian only consumes about 2.5 cubic metres per day. Water consumption at home is relatively very small and only amounts to about 0.1 cubic metres (100 litres) per day per person. A similar volume is consumed on average by an individual in their employment.[7]

Per capita domestic water consumption increases as standards of living and family incomes rise. International experience shows that current household per capita water consumption in advanced economies worldwide is only about 0.15 cubic metres (150 litres) per day and is tending to fall. Where more household and industrial water is needed in future in MENA economies, it will be diverted from low value uses in irrigated agriculture. This transition can be politically stressful, but it will be manageable.

Figure 9 shows the proportions of domestic, industrial and agricultural water consumption of fifteen MENA economies. The diagram has been constructed to make it possible to illustrate the small proportions of water devoted to domestic and industrial consumption. The message is that over 90% of water consumption is in irrigated agriculture and accounts for 1,772 m³/cap/year on average. In UAE, Israel, Tunisia, Syria and Lebanon it reaches up to 2,000 m³/cap/year. In this diagram the water consumed in agriculture is both effective rainfall – sometimes known as green water, and surface and ground water – sometimes referred to as blue water.

Notes on Figure 9:

1. The agricultural footprint includes both green and blue water. Green water is water in the soil profile after rainfall. It is sometimes referred to as effective rainfall. Blue water is water that has been diverted from surface sources such as rivers and pumped from groundwater.

2. In order to present the proportions of domestic and industrial water at a scale that is readable, the diagram only shows data for the 75%–100% part of the scale.

3. The proportions of water consumption in MENA oil economies are different from non-oil economies.

4. The data for Israel are typically those of a diversified OECD economy.

---

7 M. M. Mekonnen and A. Y. Hoekstra, 'The green, blue and grey water footprint of crops and derived crop products', *Hydrological Earth Systems Science* 15, 2011, pp. 1577–600.

The data for the other MENA economies will converge on the Israeli pattern of consumption during the rest of the 21st century as they diversify and strengthen.

Notes on Figure 10:

1. The degree of food-water scarcity is here defined as the percentage ratio between a country's individual total availability of food-water and their total water requirements for producing a diet of 3,000 kcal per capita per day. Countries with food-water scarcity metrics of over 100% have sufficient water resources to provide 3,000 kcal per capita per day.
2. The availability of food-water is hereby defined by considering both green and blue water resources.
3. It is noteworthy that the data deployed refer to water scarcity considered at the national scale and that, if the analysis were pursued at the subnational (grid) level, the picture would change as some of the countries considered here endure different climatic conditions within their territory.

How has the MENA water resource deficit been addressed?

Water consumption has been increasing in the MENA region because of the rising demand for food from the rising populations of all countries in the region. The population of the region has increased almost fourfold since 1960 from 116 million to 424 million in 2015.[8] The current population of over 400 million requires about twice the water resources available in the region to meet its food needs. Figure 11 confirms this situation by showing that the MENA region imports about 500 m3/person/year of water, which is about half the approximately 1000 m3/person/year needed by an individual each year.

Figure 11 is useful in allowing comparison between the MENA region and other world regions in terms of virtual water 'imports', which are on the increase. But so are those of economies in other regions. The EU economies, for example, engage in the importation of food commodities at a much higher level than the MENA economies.

It is normal for economies to import their food requirements and over 160

8 World Bank, 'Demographic database', Worldbank.org, 2016, http://data.worldbank.org/indicator/SP.POP.TOTL?view=map.

economies out of the world's 210 economies are net food importers.[9] As a consequence of the rising global demand for food for a future population of 11 billion by
the end of the century there will be a tightening of future global food commodity
markets. Those managing Middle Eastern economies should note that UN-DESA
has estimated that Africa's population will be 4.3 billion by 2100, exceeding that
of Asia at 4.1 billions.[10] The idea that the MENA governments and private sector
entrepreneurs could invest effectively to secure future food supplies from Africa
as envisaged during the recent period of food price volatility is unrealistic.[11] Africa
is currently a food importing continent and it will still be a food importing continent in 2100. It will not be a secure source of food.

The strategic significance and scale of the current and future dependence on
food commodity imports is illustrated in Figure 12. The diagrams show three
things: First, that food imports are very sensitive to food price volatility. The
price spikes of 2008 and 2011 reduced the volume of food imports. Second, the
MENA region is fortunate that by volume the region is mainly dependent on high
volumes of low-value food commodities such as cereals. These crops are raised
with green water used to produce staple food commodities on rainfed tracts in the
food basket economies of North and South America. Third, the bottom left figure
shows that the MENA region is using its scarce blue water to generate income in
raising high-value crops that can be used to pay for the substantial volumes of low
cost imported food commodities.

Woertz[12] has shown that food imports play a very significant role in the relations of the MENA region with the world's major powers. The 1973–1980 period
was a period of political instability. There were brief periods of armed conflict in
the region with associated global economic impacts. The OPEC economies constrained oil exports to economies that were seen to be closely aligned with Israel.
The United States responded by restricting food commodity exports to the region.
By the early 1970s the Soviet Union and its allies proved that they did not have the
capacity to export cereals to the Middle East. Egypt was the main customer. Evidence of the vital significance of access to secure food, preferably under-priced,
occurred in the early 1970s.

---

9 M. Kivela, *Virtual water 'flows' in international food trade*, Unpublished thesis in the
Geography Department, King's College, London 2013.
10 UN-DESA, *Population data for the world's countries and regions*, New York 2016.
11 M. Keulertz and S. Sojamo, 'Inverse globalisation? The global agricultural trade system
and Asian investments in African land and water resources', *Handbook of land and water
grabs in Africa*, London 2013.
12 E. Woertz, *Oil for food: the global food crisis in the Middle East*, Oxford 2015.

The period 1970 to 1973 was a pivotal moment in the history of food and water security in Egypt. The High Dam had just been commissioned in July 1970. This infrastructure immensely enhanced the agricultural potential of Egypt. But improved national production and productivity were not sufficient to meet Egypt's rising demand for cereals. Egypt had to import more food. The Soviet Union, which had been Egypt's main ally, was faced with the challenge of purchasing US grain to secure the Egyptian economy. The Soviet Union did not have the hard currency to sustain the assistance. Under Sadat, Egypt chose to change its sponsor from one that could not address its food and water insecurity to the other superpower that could.

The global market for cereals has been transformed since the end of communism in Russia and Ukraine in 1992. By 2010, Russia became one of the top four sources of food for Egypt and other regional economies as a consequence of the adoption of reforms in its agricultural sector and engagement with the four major global cereal traders. The increasing levels of cereal consumption in the cereal importing regions have been shown by Cargill (2012).[13] North America is still the pivotal producer of cereals, but South America has caught up and Eastern Europe and Russia have become major global players since 1990. Understanding these global dynamics is more strategic than the management of the internal water resources of the MENA region.

What version of food and water security can the MENA economies enjoy in future?

The population of the MENA region is set to double by the late twenty-first century. Its capacity to produce food will increase with improved water and agricultural technologies. But the probable further decline in rainfall will reduce the food production potential of the region.

The Middle East and North Africa has the advantage of favourable growing conditions where water is available and there will be an increasing trend towards the production of high-value food commodities on demand in world markets.

The other economies of the region have already emulated the example of Israel in ceasing to increase food production to match the trend in the demand for food consequent on rising populations. This change in policy is called decoupling.[14]

13 Cargill, 'How to feed a planet', *The Economist* May 2012, https://www.economist.com/blogs/feastandfamine/2012/05/food.
14 M. Gilmont, 'Decoupling dependence on natural water: reflexivity in the regulation and allocation of water in Israel', *Water Policy* 16.1, 2014, pp. 79–101.

The progressive increase in food production, and water consumption, after 1948 ceased to match rising national food demand in 1961. Policy changed to a one of dependence on the importation of very affordable water intensive food staples. This first step towards decoupling has already been adopted by the other economies in the region. The volumes of the food imports continue to rise as populations increase. In all cases this decoupling has proved to be a politically non-stressful process despite the expense of the very substantial and rising levels of food imports. According to Mekonnen and Hoekstra[15] between 1996 and 2005 Israel 'imported' on average 7.9 km3 of water per year embedded in food, while it 'exported' 1.4 km3 per year. Israel has access to only about 1.4 km3 per year of natural water.[16]

The first decoupling was enabled by a strong and diversified economy and international trade. The second decoupling has been enabled by two technologies; recycled urban and industrial water and desalinated seawater have been substituted for a relatively large volume of natural water that was being used unsustainably. Recycled water became available in 1988 and desalinated water in 2006.[17] These sources of water have by 2014 enabled a reduction of 0.8 km3 per year in natural water consumption. The volume of water involved in the second decoupling is about one tenth of that involved in the first trade related decoupling. The first decoupling went unnoticed and was politically stress free. The second decoupling has been predictably very stressful because it impacted irrigators.[18] The first decoupling required that the economy was sufficiently strong and diversified to import food from a world market that was oversupplied with subsidised and under-priced food. The second decoupling required that farmers be incentivised and encouraged to use recycled city water and desalinated water on occasions when desalinated water is in surplus. The second decoupling has clearly had a

---

15 M. M. Mekonnen and A. Y. Hoekstra, 'The water footprint of production and consumption', *Value of Water Research Report* 50.2, 2011, appendices, Delft: IHE.
16 M. Gilmont, 'Decoupling dependence on natural water: reflexivity in the regulation and allocation of water in Israel', *Water Policy* 16.1, 2014, pp. 79–101.
17 M. Gilmont, L. Nassar, H. S. Salem, N. Tal, E. Harper and S. Rayner, 'Achieving water and food security in the MENA: evidence and potential for decoupling economic and population growth from national water needs', paper presented at the LMEI/SOAS Centenary Conference, *Environmental Challenges in the MENA Region: the long road from conflict to cooperation*, October 2016.
18 M. Gilmont, L. Nassar, H. S. Salem, N. Tal, E. Harper and S. Rayner, 'Achieving water and food security in the MENA: evidence and potential for decoupling economic and population growth from national water needs', paper presented at the LMEI/SOAS Centenary Conference, *Environmental Challenges in the MENA Region: the long road from conflict to cooperation*, October 2016.

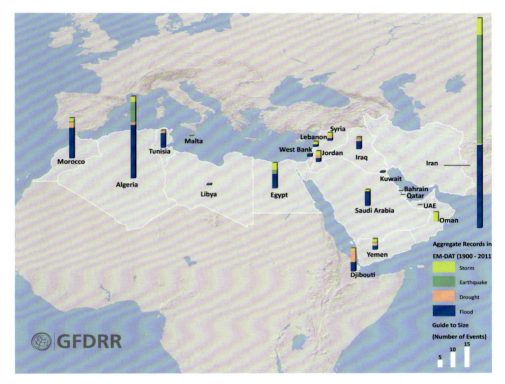

Figure 1: Number of disasters stacked by type of disaster, 1980–2006. Source: World Bank: Adapting to climate change in the Arab countries.

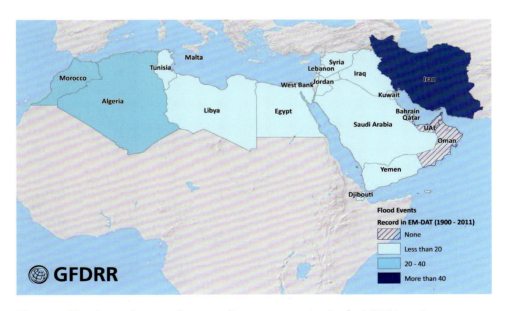

Figure 2: Floods are the most frequent disasters occurring in the MENA region, 1900–2011. Source: World Bank: Adapting to climate change in the Arab countries.

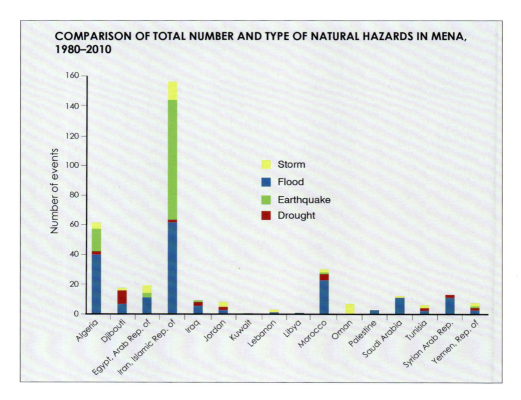

Figure 3: Comparison of the total, by country and type, of natural hazards in the MENA region, 1980–2010. Source: World Bank: Adapting to climate change in the Arab countries.

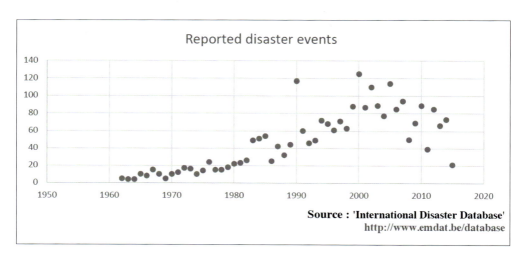

Figure 4: Reported disasters since 1960.

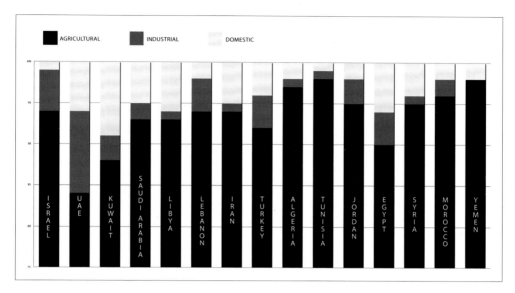

Figure 9: Water footprints of national consumption by sector (% per capita) in the MENA countries, ranked according to the Human Development Index (HDI). Data are averages for the 1996–2005 period. Source: Authors' elaboration based on Hoekstra and Mekonnen, 2012.

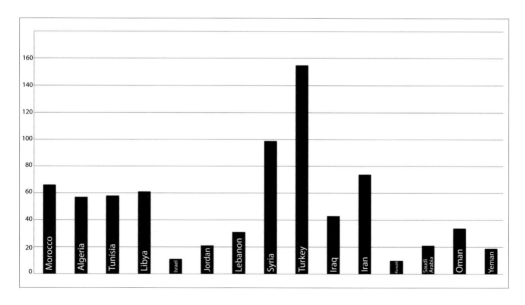

Figure 10: Food-water scarcity for 15 economies in the MENA region. Source: Authors' elaboration based on Gerten *et al.*, 2011.

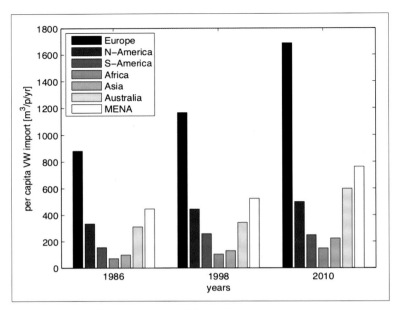

Figure 11: Virtual water 'imports' by region (m3/capita/year) in 1986, 1998, and 2010. Note that Europe is as dependent on food imports as the MENA economies. Source: Antonelli and Tamea, 2015, p. 331.

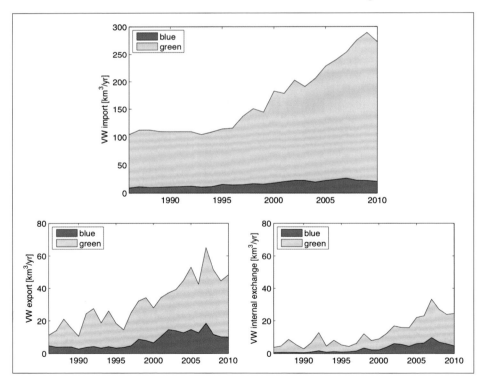

Figure 12: Trends in green water (effective rainfall), blue water (surface and ground water) and total virtual water volumes 'imported' (top), 'exported' (bottom left) and 'exchanged' internally (bottom right) by MENA, in km3 per year. Source: Antonelli and Tamea, 2015, p. 332.

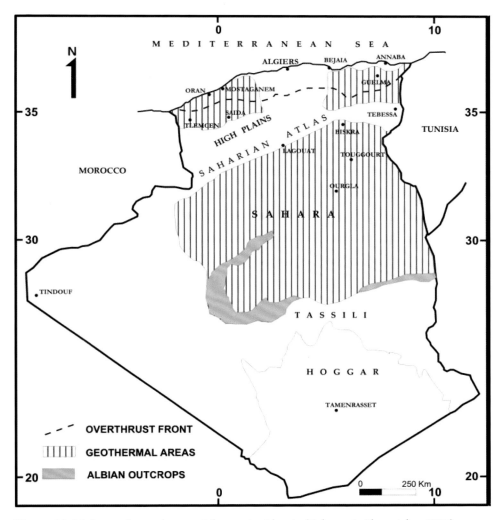

Figure 16: Main geothermal potential areas in Algeria (Fekraoui, Abouriche, 1995).

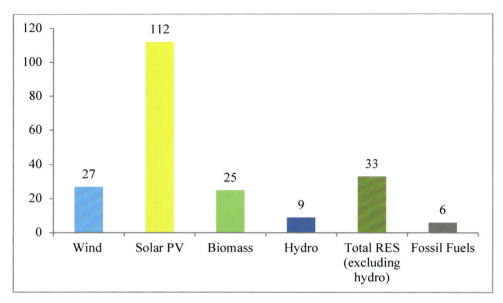

Figure 17: Percentage of annual average growth rate of electricity production within MENA, 2008–2011. Source: Bryden, Riahi, and Zissler, *MENA Renewables Status Report*, p. 9.

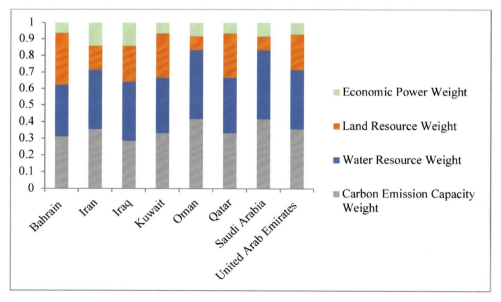

Figure 18: Calculated weights of the four indicators (cost and footprints) for the Persian Gulf countries.

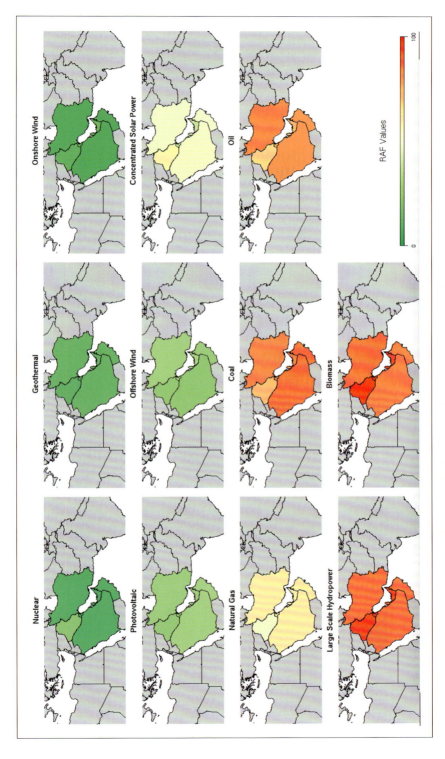

Figure 19: Desirability of energy technologies for the Persian Gulf region, according to their environmental and economic capacity.

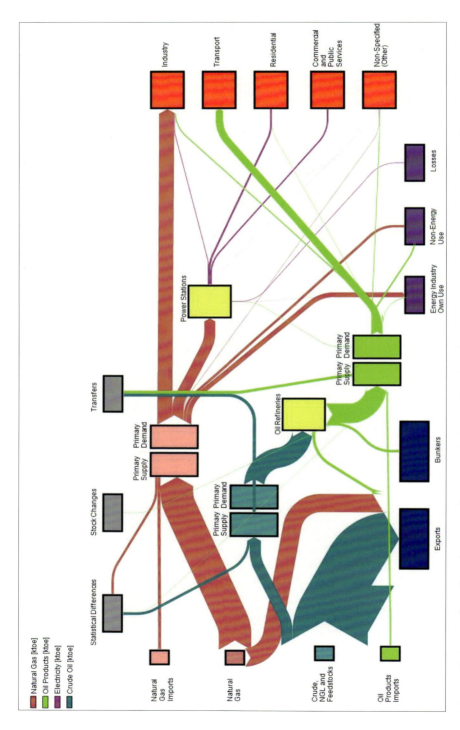

Figure 20: Energy flow chart for Oman for 2013–2014. Based on this chart, the energy sector in Oman is divided into three main sectors: the supply (primary) sector, the intermediary sector and the demand (end-use) sector.

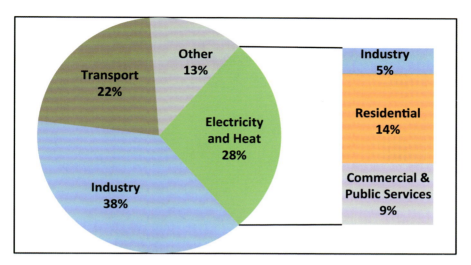

Figure 21: Breakdown of Oman's CO_2 emissions from fuel combustion by sector for the year 2013. From this chart it is clear that the industrial sector, followed by electricity and heat production, are the main contributors to CO_2 emissions in Oman.

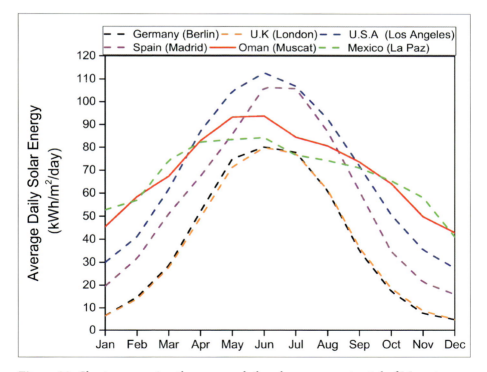

Figure 22: Charts comparing the average daily solar energy potential of Muscat, calculated as the product of average daily irradiance and daylight hours, with the rest of the world.

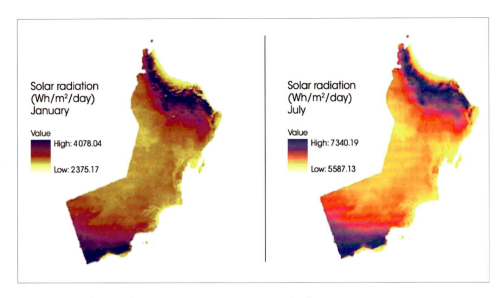

Figure 23: Solar irradiance in Oman in January and July.

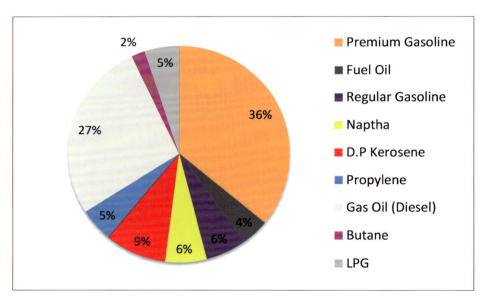

Figure 24: Oil products produced in Oman in 2013. The two main products produced by Oman's refineries are premium gasoline and gas oil (diesel). These are used in transport and electricity generation.

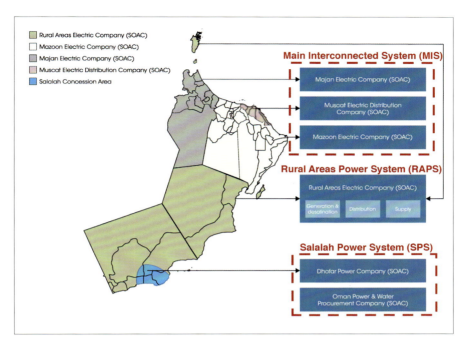

Figure 25: The regions in Oman in which the three electricity markets, MIS, SPS and RAPS operate. This chart shows that each system serves a different region in the country and hence there is no competition between these systems.

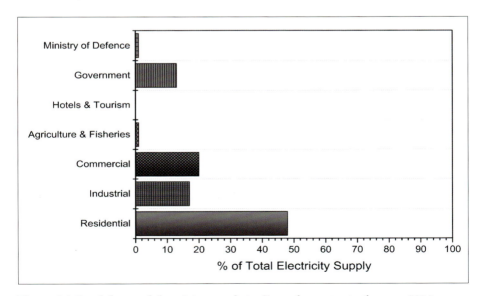

Figure 26: Breakdown of electricity supply in Oman by sector in the year 2014 when total electricity supply was 25 TWh. This chart shows that the residential sector is the largest electricity consuming sector in Oman.

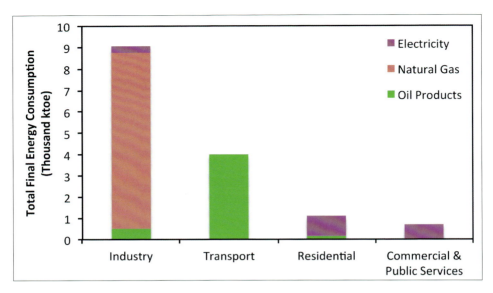

Figure 27: Total final energy consumption of Oman's end-users by fuel type in the year 2013. The industrial sector is the largest consumer of energy in Oman, with 91% of its energy consumption coming directly from natural gas. The transport sector is the second largest consumer of energy in Oman with all its energy consumption coming from oil products. Although the residential and commercial and public services sectors are the smallest energy consumers, they are the largest consumers of electricity in Oman.

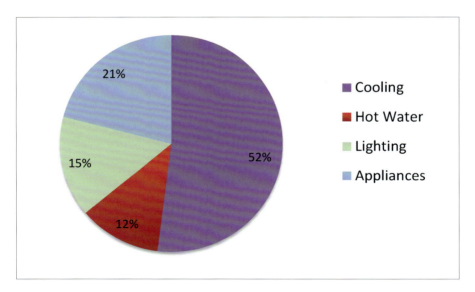

Figure 28: Breakdown of domestic energy consumption in Oman as modelled by Sweetnam *et al.* This chart shows that over 50% of energy demand in Oman is for cooling purposes, indicating the importance of reducing cooling demand in order to reduce overall residential electricity demand.

number of technological dimensions. A feature that should be noted by all those managing other MENA economies is that effectiveness of water governance is just as important as the capacity to afford the new technologies of recycling and desalination.

Is food-water security too difficult to understand?

It has been shown that there are two water security narratives in the MENA region. One is the popular narrative that misrepresents the position. This narrative is wrong but it is easily believed because it enables communities and politicians to feel comfortable with what is in fact a serious level of water and food insecurity. The other narrative is uncomfortable. It is the one identified and discussed by water scientists and economists. In practice political processes have easily backgrounded this narrative. This outcome is unhelpful as it prevents the adoption of knowledge that would accelerate the implementation of essential water consuming policies that would reduce water consumption in all sectors to more sustainable levels.

Those wanting to promote policies that will bring food and water security to the MENA region need to do four things. First, they need to understand the limited capacity of the region to meet the food-water needs of a doubled population. Second, they need to be thoroughly acquainted with the global population dynamics and future patterns of global demands for food. Third, they need to understand the global food system and where food production systems are already placing unsustainable demands on water resources. This system has an extraordinary capacity to trade food internationally, enabling water scarce regions such as the Middle East and North Africa to enjoy a form of food and water security – albeit a dependent version. Fourth, and most importantly, they need to recognise the extent to which the diversification of the region's economies have for the past forty years increasingly underpinned the current version of MENA food and water security. Future increased demand for food can only be met by an acceleration in the diversification of national economies.

Bibliography

Antonelli, M. and S. Tamea, 'Food-water security and virtual water trade in the Middle East and North African region', *International Journal of Water Resources Development* 31.3, 2015, pp. 326–42, doi:10.1080/07900627.2015 .1030496.

Baldos, U. L. C. and T. W. Hertel, 'Debunking the "new normal". Why world food prices are expected to resume their long run downward trend', *Global Food Security* 8, 2016, pp. 27–38, https://doi.org/10.1016/j.gfs.2016.03.002.

Baldos, U. L. C. and T. W. Hertel, 'Looking back to move forward on model validation: insights from a global model of agricultural land use', *Environmental Research Letters* 8.3, 2013, 034024, doi:10.1088/1748-9326/8/3/034024.

Cargill, 'How to feed a planet', *The Economist* May 2012, https://www.economist.com/blogs/feastandfamine/2012/05/food.

FAOSTAT, 'Food price index', Fao.org, http://www.fao.org/worldfoodsituation/foodpricesindex/en/.

Gerten, D., J. Heinke, H. Holger, H. Biemans, M. Fader and K. Waha, 'Global water availability and requirements for future food production', *J. Hydrometeorol* 12, 2011, pp. 885–99, doi:10.1175/2011JHM1328.1.

Gilmont, M., 'Decoupling dependence on natural water: reflexivity in the regulation and allocation of water in Israel', *Water Policy* 16.1, 2014, pp. 79–101.

Gilmont, M., L. Nassar, H. S. Salem, N. Tal, E. Harper and S. Rayner, 'Achieving water and food security in the MENA: evidence and potential for decoupling economic and population growth from national water needs', paper presented at the LMEI/SOAS Centenary Conference, *Environmental Challenges in the MENA Region: the long road from conflict to cooperation*, October 2016.

Jägerskog, A., 'The sanctioned discourse – a crucial factor for understanding water policy in the Jordan River Basin', *Occasional Paper*, Department for Water and Environmental Studies, Linköping University, No. 41, 2002.

Keulertz, M. and S. Sojamo, 'Inverse globalisation? The global agricultural trade system and Asian investments in African land and water resources', *Handbook of land and water grabs in Africa*, London 2013.

Kivela, M., *Virtual water 'flows' in international food trade*, Unpublished thesis in the Geography Department, King's College, London 2013.

Mekonnen, M. M. and A. Y. Hoekstra, 'The green, blue and grey water footprint of crops and derived crop products', *The Value of Water Research Report Series* 47, 2010, Delft: UNESCO-IHE.

Mekonnen, M. M. and A. Y. Hoekstra, 'The green, blue and grey water footprint of crops and derived crop products', *The Value of Water Research Report Series* 48, 2010, Delft: UNESCO-IHE.

Mekonnen, M. M. and A. Y. Hoekstra, 'The green, blue and grey water footprint of crops and derived crop products', *Hydrological Earth Systems Science* 15, 2011, pp. 1577–600.

Mekonnen, M. M. and A. Y. Hoekstra, 'The water footprint of humanity', *Proceedings of the National Academy of Sciences* 109.9, 2012, pp. 3232–7.

Mekonnen, M. M. and A. Y. Hoekstra, 'The water footprint of production and consumption', *Value of Water Research Report* 50.2, 2011, appendices, Delft: IHE.

UN-DESA, *Population data for the world's countries and regions*, New York 2016.

Woertz, E., *Oil for Food: The Global Food Crisis in the Middle East*, Oxford 2015.

World Bank, 'Demographic database', Worldbank.org, 2016, http://data.worldbank.org/indicator/SP.POP.TOTL?view=map.

Zeitoun, M., 'The conflict vs. cooperation paradox: fighting over or sharing of Palestinian – Israeli groundwater?', *Water Policy* 8, 2007, p. 105–20.

7

Extreme Environmental Challenges in the Context of Lasting Political Crisis: The Case of Yemen

Helen Lackner

Introduction

Yemen is currently in the midst of a war which shows little sign of ending, so it is not yet on the road out of conflict or heading for cooperation over environmental or any other issues. This chapter addresses the pre-war situation in Yemen and, except when explicitly stated, does not mention the worsening impact of the war. Although most discussions about Yemen focus on the military situation, foreign intervention, the failure of the country's transition from autocracy, its 'tribal' politics,[1] and its disastrous humanitarian situation, the role of climate change and environmental challenges in these crises should not be ignored as they are part of the overall problem and threaten Yemen's very existence as a habitable area[2] within a generation. What limited concern exists is rightly focused on water, and water

1 For my analysis of Yemen's social and political development in the past half century, see H. Lackner, *Yemen in Crisis: Autocracy, Neo-Liberalism and the Disintegration of a State*, London 2017. I also discuss the role of tribes and social change in H. Lackner, *Understanding the Yemeni Crisis: The Transformation of Tribal Roles in Recent Decades*, Middle East Papers, Luce fellowship paper no. 17, Durham 2016.
2 Alongside other relevant chapters, I address these issues in greater detail in chapter six, H. Lackner, 'Climate Change and Security: Major Challenges for Yemen's Future', *Climate Hazard Crises in Asian Societies and Environments*, ed., T. Sternberg, London 2017, pp. 103–19. Some basic information and data from that chapter are included here. The editors and the author thank Routledge for permission to use this material.

will take prime of place in this chapter too, but other aspects of the climate/social equation are equally deserving of close attention. Yemen presents an extreme example of the urgent necessity of addressing political, social, cultural and climatic aspects of these stresses through an integrated approach. While this study focuses on Yemen many of its lessons are relevant for other Middle Eastern states suffering from climate stress, water scarcity, political instability and authoritarian regimes.

Methodology

The chapter is based on examination of publicly available data on climate change in the region, Yemeni and international official and other documents on policies both stated and implemented, as well as on over 40 years of direct experience of working in rural development in Yemen. I am a social anthropologist, not a geographer or climatologist, so my focus will be on the social and political impacts of the interaction between humans and nature and how climate change is affecting future prospects for the survival of the population and the country's rich cultural heritage. Data and experience are focused on my own involvement in the country from the 1970s to date.

Yemen's environmental challenges

Yemen is particularly vulnerable to climate hazards of various types. In particular, their impact on agriculture and rural life is relevant as 70% of its population live in rural areas and over 55% are directly dependent on agriculture and livestock husbandry, while a further 5% depend on coastal fisheries. Urban environments are affected through inappropriate infrastructure planning which ignores the likelihood of rising sea levels, sudden floods and other disasters; the country's unique cultural heritage is also threatened by a combination of ill-constructed infrastructure and extreme climatic events.

While climate change is a recognised fact, its future impact cannot be predicted with certainty. The World Bank has foreseen three main climate scenarios for Yemen, the most likely ones being 'hot and dry' and 'warm and wet'. Regardless of which scenario actually materialises, 'Yemen will be getting warmer, most likely at a faster rate than the global average... there will be more variability of rainfall patterns within years [and] there will probably be an increased frequency of intense rainfall events and therefore possibly an increased risk of floods'.[3]

3 World Bank, *Assessing the Impacts of climate Change and variability on the Water and Agricultural Sectors and the Policy Implications*, 2010, report no. 54196-YE, p. 20.

Extreme water scarcity

Water is the fundamental constraint to Yemen's future.[4] I believe it is the most urgent and immediate problem Yemenis must address regardless of politics, if future generations are to continue living in the country.[5] The shortage of water in Yemen is absolute: currently annual use, at 3.5 billion m³, exceeds renewable resources by 1.4 billion m³. In plain English, one third of the water used is mined from a non-renewable fossil aquifer. With a population which has risen to 28 million people in 2018, per capita availability of renewable water has dropped to less than 85m³, which is significantly below 10% of the internationally recognised scarcity threshold [1000m³]. The World Bank estimates that ground water reserves are likely to be depleted in about three decades.[6]

With the exception of the rain-fed agricultural areas, Yemen depends on ground water.[7] Renewable aquifers depend on annual rainfall. Climate change is manifested in more violent and irregular rainfall episodes which rush down the mountains and reduce the water available to replenish shallow aquifers.

Rural water

Deterioration in water availability varies between regions. In the western highlands, which are the most densely populated areas, rainfall is highest, but water retention in the aquifers is limited and reducing as a result of increasingly violent downpours on areas where the topsoil has vanished, so less water is available to replenish the aquifers. The deterioration of terraces in the past half century has considerably worsened this problem. The replenishment to rainfall ratio is dropping just when need and demand are increasing for domestic use, thanks to rapid population increase and improved hygiene and while in agriculture powerful pumps are used for irrigation. Long-term water scarcity in these areas is highest and most affects the population, and per capita available water resources are diminishing.

In the coastal plains, limited flows come from seasonal rains in the highlands and much of it is controlled by spate irrigation systems, both traditional and modernised. These irrigate the main agricultural producing areas, complemented by well water. The latter is increasingly saline as one gets closer to the coast and its

4 M. Weiss, 'A perfect Storm: the causes and consequences of severe water scarcity, institutional breakdown and conflict in Yemen', *Water International*, 2015.
5 For more details see my analysis of state policies, 'Water Scarcity: Why doesn't it get the attention it deserves?', *Why Yemen Matters*, ed. H. Lackner, London 2014, pp. 161–82.
6 World Bank (2010) *op cit*, p. 21.
7 See C. Ward, *The Water Crisis in Yemen*, London 2015.

salinity worsens through increased sea water intrusion, as extraction is significantly beyond fresh water replenishment. Water supply in the aquifers also benefits from the rainfall in the highlands, which is restricted by the problem of the
reduced aquifer absorption resulting from more violent and irregular downpours.

Like the coastal areas, eastern slopes are also largely dependent on groundwater replenished by rainfall in the western highlands, and suffer the same problems, though here population density is lower and these areas may also have some
access to very deep fossil aquifers. These advantages are reduced by the additional
problem of increased transformation of agricultural and pasture land into desert,
resulting from water scarcity, erosion and climate change. Much of these areas
also share aquifers with Saudi Arabia (the Wasia-Biyadh-Aruma aquifer south and
the Wajid aquifer system).[8]

In Hadramaut the situation is less grave thanks to the presence of a large deep
aquifer, but the areas gradually sloping towards the Rub' al-Khali are entirely
dependent on wells and have much lower rainfall than the western highlands. The
deep aquifer is shared with Oman, the UAE and Saudi Arabia.

Urban water

Most urban households purchase, at high cost, tanker loads that are stored at
ground level, underground and in roof-top reservoirs. For the few households
who are connected to urban networks, the amount of water they need to buy
depends both on their storage capacity and their levels of consumption, which in
each instance is affected by income levels. Others have to buy all their water from
the private sector. By the beginning of the 21st century, hardly any urban residents
could rely entirely on the water supply from their municipal authorities.

Urban water comes from the same sources as agricultural water, and the basins
of Amran, Sana'a and Sa'dah are already extremely depleted, causing massive
shortages, particularly in the largest city, Sana'a, which is often described in
media as the first capital city which will run out of water. There the urban water
supply system only served 41 per cent of the population in 2007,[9] dropping from
61 per cent in 1984,[10] though the population increased during that period. Over
the first decade of this century, frequency of service has been reduced from three

8 World Bank, *Beyond Scarcity, Water Security in the Middle East and North Africa*,
Washington, DC 2017, pp. 101–2.
9 C. Ward, *The Water Crisis in Yemen*, London 2015, p. 189.
10 C. Ward, *The Water Crisis*, p. 184. Between 1984 and 1987, coverage dropped from 61 per
cent to 58 per cent.

times a week to once or twice at best. Even Aden now suffers water shortages and its water comes from further and further away, while the growth of the city as well as increasing shortages mean that most people, even those living in apartments, are now storing as much water as possible to compensate for the shortages, whereas even in the1980s everyone relied on water coming out of the tap, directly from the urban network. Yemen's other major city, Hodeida, mainly suffers from low water quality and saline intrusion into the aquifers which supply it.

Taiz, the country's fourth largest city, provides the most acute example of dramatic water shortages and also of the mechanisms used to mitigate the problem. Taiz has been suffering water shortages since the 1980s, and extreme ones since the 1990s. By 2010, less than 40% of homes in Taiz were connected to the urban network and these only received water about once every two months, making the connection largely irrelevant to the city's citizens. In previous decades, access to the network had ranged from about once every 40 days in the mid-1990s, rising to the high frequency of once every 20 days at the end of that decade, to drop back systematically thereafter. These problems not only stem from the city's geological circumstance, which precludes considerable storage in natural aquifers despite the city having among the highest rainfall rates in the country, but in addition both rapid population growth and serious leakages in the network add up to a major crisis situation.

Taiz also illustrates a major predicament which is likely to intensify and affect other cities in the future, namely competition between rural and urban areas over access to aquifers. Although this problem is obviously relevant to the other cities whose water increasingly comes from wells located well beyond the city – and this is particularly true of Aden whose water now comes from over 100 kilometres away in lower Yafa' and from agricultural areas in Lahej – Taiz is the only place where this competition over use has already, for over two decades, caused systematic conflict between the state authorities responsible for urban water supply and the rural communities whose own access is reduced as a result of water transfer from their aquifers to the city.

In Taiz, where wells were drilled in rural al Hayma to transfer water to the city in the 1980s, the initial 'compensation' provided to the rural community was given to a local shaykh who used it for his own benefit rather than to the benefit of the community; complete desertification of the rural district promptly followed, resulting in the rapid and widespread impoverishment of its population. When that source of water dried up and the authorities decided to drill for water in the next district [Habeer], the residents resisted despite the fact that the land was mostly owned by state. As armed confrontations ensued, an internationally-funded project was initiated to provide the rural community with investments and access to water, though the term 'compensation' was taboo in this context and was replaced by then fashionable terminology 'participatory approaches'. This measure failed to resolve the problem, both as a result of changes in project management and the simple fact that the community continued to perceive the loss of what they considered to be 'their' water as unacceptable. Eventually, some water was transferred to Taiz, but the quantities supplied were well below the projected amount; regardless, ongoing low-level conflict persisted. So although Taiz is the only case where the transfer of water from rural to urban use has led to open conflict between the authorities and the 'supplying' communities, there is clearly potential for similar outcomes in Sana'a, Aden and Hodeida, as well as many other smaller towns. This is an example of environmental challenges which lead to serious social and political problems.

A major issue with respect to domestic water supply in general is the fact that throughout Yemen there has been no systematic and imposed link between water supply and the provision of sanitation, despite World Health Organization recommendations and simple basic awareness of the health hazards of unhygienic disposal of used waters. Sanitation coverage systematically lags way behind water supply with only 53% of the country's population having access to improved sanitation facilities (92% urban, only 34% rural)[11] in 2012. The predictable health consequences of this neglect have been clear for decades with increasing rates of malaria and other mosquito-transmitted diseases, but it became all too evident in the 2017 cholera outbreak which escalated to becoming the worst and fastest spreading epidemic in the world by the middle of the year.

While the health implications of inadequate water and sanitation are well known and often mentioned, the impact of these issues on the country's cultural heritage are less frequently noted. The world famous old Sana'a city was built at a time when households collected small quantities of water from wells and there was no piped sewerage system. Recent decades have witnessed vastly increased use of water through piped supply as well as 'improved' sewerage systems. However, both the leaks and the accumulation of damp at ground level and below are causing significant deterioration to the structure of the buildings thus undermining their stability and endangering their future.

---

11 World Bank indicators accessed 29 August 2017.

Other water related problems

Worsening water scarcity in the highlands has already led to population movements towards the coastal areas, on a temporary as well as more permanent basis. This trend is likely to accelerate in coming decades: when local wells dry up, people first purchase water from tankers which travel increasingly long distances at higher and higher costs. When this water runs out or they can no longer afford it, people move, initially temporarily to stay with relatives where water is still available, returning home after good rains when the wells have filled. Eventually they move permanently; villages have already been abandoned in Amran, al-Baidha, Dhala' and Sa'dah governorates.[12] The major coastal cities are likely to experience increased populations following such movements, causing additional stress on their water supplies.

Saline intrusion into coastal aquifers used both for human consumption and for agriculture is another problem. Three of Yemen's major cities (Hodeida, Aden and Mukalla) are on the coast and their populations are increasing rapidly. The over-exploitation of aquifers in the hinterland is already causing serious problems for life and agriculture. Rural-urban water transfers cause conflicts between their respective populations: the case of Taiz city has been discussed above and is an early example of problems which are likely to spread further.[13]

Rising sea levels are predicted and will have a deep impact on the country's population. First, the three main coastal cities and other smaller towns (such as Shihr, Mokha, Ahwar) will be affected, in addition to the smaller fishing communities and villages along the 1900 kilometres of the country's coastline. About 10% of the country's population lives in these areas and, with the worsening water situation in the highlands, this percentage is likely to increase in the next few decades. Hence significant investment will be essential to mitigate this problem, involving both coastal protection and the movement of people to higher ground, something which is particularly difficult in the case of Hodeida which is on the coastal Tihama plain. In addition, the fishing resources are likely to be transformed by changes in water temperature leading to different availability of species. This may have a further negative impact on the fishing communities and the exhaustion of species – both high and low value – as many species are already overfished to the point of extinction.

---

12 See Lackner, 'Water scarcity', p. 177.

13 M. Moench, *Yemen: Local Water Management in Rural Areas: A Case Study*, World Bank, Washington, DC 1999; and M. Moench and H. Lackner, *Decentralized Management Study*, World Bank, Sana'a 1997.

In addition to the differences between highland and coastal areas, it is also important to note that the areas under greatest water stress and with least water reserves are those with the highest population density, namely the western highlands, whereas the main large fossil aquifer with long-term potential, the Umm al-Rudhuma is located primarily under the Hadramaut governorate, extending west into Shabwa, north into Saudi Arabia and east as far as Oman and the UAE. This creates the potential for additional social and political conflict.

Weather events

As I discuss in an earlier paper,[14] one of the most common symptoms of climate change has been changing rainfall patterns. Some of the implications of this phenomenon have been discussed above as they obviously are water related. Yemen is on the edge of the monsoon zone, and its rainy seasons in the highlands – the only areas with regular rainfall – are determined by the monsoons. Rainy seasons used to systematically take place in March-April and July-August.[15] Recent decades have seen greater unpredictability of both timing and intensity. The unpredictability of rains seriously affects people's livelihoods and the extent to which rural families can be self-sufficient agriculturally, though holding size is obviously another extremely relevant factor here. Violent and sudden rainfall damages crops and washes away the topsoil, shrinking cultivable areas and reducing the amount of water available to replenish the water table.

After not having been hit by a single full cyclone for many decades, in November 2015 the country suffered not one, but two unprecedented extremely violent cyclones – Chapala and Megh – within a single month. Chapala brought hurricane force winds of over 120km/h, 610mm of rain in 48 hours, seven times the annual average, and displaced some 45,000 people, causing massive destruction mostly on the ecologically unique Socotra island and in Hadramaut and Shabwa governorates. Barely a week later, after causing further destruction in Socotra, Megh weakened but hit western areas and even reached the highlands in Ibb governorate.

Data on weather events are not easily accessible. Table 1 gives an indication of major floods in the past two decades.

Data on droughts for recent years are not available, but there have been records of droughts every few years and particularly in 2008 and 2014 in some areas and almost everywhere in the country in 2009. In Yafaʻ, a major coffee growing area,

---

14 Lackner, 'Climate Change and Security', p. 108.
15 GOY government website.

Table 1: Major Floods, 1990–2014

Year	Location/ governorate
1991	Socotra
1993	Lahej, Abyan, Aden
1996	Taiz, Hodeida, Shabwa, Mareb, Hadramaut, Abyan, Jawf
1998	Tihama, Hodeida, Taiz
1999	Socotra
2001	Saʻdah, Amran, Hodeida, Hadramaut,
2002	Tihama, Taiz, Hadramaut, Rayma
2003	Hajja, Taiz
2005	Sanaʻa, Hodeida
2006	Dhamar, Hodeida, Sanaʻa, Taiz, Saʻdah
2007	Hadramaut, Ibb, Raymah, Dhamar
2008	Hadramaut, Mahara, Taiz, Lahej, Mahweet,
2010	Sanaʻa, Ibb, Dhamar,
2013	Taiz, Dhamar, Mahweet, Sanaʻa, Ibb, Hajja, Hodeida, Shabwa, Abyan
2015	Socotra, Hadramaut, Shabwa, Abyan, Lahej
2016	Hodeida, Amran, Hajja, Sanaʻa, Mahweet, Aden, Mareb

Sources: all data from EM-DAT (2017) the International Disaster Data Base, Belgium

there was a drought lasting almost 10 years in the first decade of the century which killed off most of the coffee bushes.

Other phenomena

Only 3% of Yemen is suitable for agricultural use. Hence the loss of any culti-vable land has a direct impact on people's economic situation. Soil erosion and desertification are both problems which worsen as a result of climate change and lack of mitigating interventions. Increasing periods of drought make land more susceptible to wind blasts which then blow away topsoil. This has multiple nega-tive consequences: first, reducing fertility as there is less soil for plants to settle in; second, reducing cultivable surfaces; and third, reducing the ability of the soil to retain water when rain falls. The last point also has a cumulative effect in making flash flows more violent and greater in size. In addition, violent storms and flash floods sweep away the banks of *wadis,* thus widening *wadi* beds and destroying agricultural land, homes and infrastructure. This also increases the intensity of flash floods further downstream and additional destruction of a similar nature when the banks are unable to withstand the violence of the flows.

Desertification particularly affects those areas which are most arid. It is esti-mated that this process results in the loss of 3–5% of agricultural land annual-ly.[16] Archaeological sites which today are deep in the deserts (Mareb, Shabwa, al-Jawf) used to be irrigated agricultural areas and major cities many centuries ago. Increasing areas of the governorates bordering the Rub' al-Khali desert first experience a shift from cultivation to grazing land and eventually become com-pletely desertified. This has happened in parts of al-Jawf, Mareb, Shabwa, Had-ramaut and al-Mahra. All these factors reduce food production through lower yields and loss of growing areas, thus exacerbating the need for importing staples and for food aid. Concurrently people's ability to be self-sufficient either through their own crop production or the sale of their produce diminishes, they become more impoverished and more dependent on casual labour to survive. The increased stress and poverty induced by these changes are contributing factors to social ten-sions and dissent which, in some cases, can lead to political and military uprisings.

These phenomena also affect the country's cultural assets: ancient buildings and archaeological sites are damaged by both the impact of violent winds and rainfall, causing erosion and deterioration of the stones and, of course, the detailed outlines of reliefs and carvings. Buried in sand, sites are somewhat protected from wind erosion, but not necessarily from water damage, while those that are exposed are more likely to be looted by local people who have lost their economic resources. Cultural sites have also suffered over the centuries from the impact of earthquakes, in particular those of 1941 in Razeh and of 1982 in Dhamar.

Environmental challenges and the state

Political strategies

The Republic of Yemen was established in May 1990 by the merger between two previous states, the 'market economy' Yemen Arab Republic with its capital in Sana'a and the socialist People's Democratic Republic of Yemen with its capital in Aden. In 1994, a short civil war took place which led to the defeat of the south-ern separatists and marked the formal end of any of the socialist and welfarist policies which had been implemented in that part of the country. Thereafter, and until 2012, the entire country was ruled by President Ali Abdullah Saleh with his General People's Congress (GPC) and was a formal democracy insofar as it

16 World Bank, *Climate Investment Funds, Strategic Program for Climate Resilience for Yemen*, Meeting of the PPCR sub-committee, 17 April 2012, p. 42, para. 79.

had a multiplicity of parties and parliamentary and presidential elections, all of which systematically returned the GPC as largest party in parliament and Saleh as president. The 2011 uprisings, although encouraged by events elsewhere in the Arab world, were a direct response to years of autocracy and neoliberal economic policies which resulted in worsening poverty for the majority of the population and the emergence of a very small group of super wealthy kleptocrats.

The regime prioritised its short-term objectives of political control and capital accumulation over any other considerations. With respect to environmental issues, until the recent descent into civil war, state policies shifted from complete denial to gradual recognition of their importance and initial but weak attempts to address them. Once again, the war has allowed these issues to be completely ignored. A parallel trajectory took place in the most influential of Yemen's international partners: in 1992 the World Bank's only reference to water was to state that 'land and water shortages will continue to severely constrain agriculture' while there was no reference to any other environmental issues.[17] With the adoption of the Structural Adjustment programme in 1995, the government announced half-hearted reforms which were partially implemented, including modest increases in fuel prices explicitly intended to reduce overexploitation of groundwater for irrigation.

Government lack of concern for environmental protection or sustainability of the country's limited water supply is illustrated by the fate of the Ministry of Water and the Environment (MWE). Prior to 2003 water was linked to electricity in the administrative structure, thus emphasising the issue of supply to mostly urban consumers rather than any conservation or environmental considerations, and water extraction was unregulated. Established in 2003, within months of the final passing of the long-debated Water Law in 2002, the Ministry of Water and Environment was initially attributed full responsibility for the management, control and regulation of water for all uses. This officially gave it authority to address competition between different types of uses and in particular of ensuring priority to domestic use in areas of greatest stress, such as the Sana'a, Amran and Sa'dah basins, as well as Taiz which was already suffering from acute water crisis.

This did not sit well with the wealthy and powerful agricultural landowners, much of whose wealth derived from unregulated irrigation of high value cash crops (including qat, grapes, mangoes and other crops demanding considerable water). They extracted water from shallow renewable aquifers as well as fossil aquifers, deepening their wells frequently and thus depriving smaller and poorer

17 World Bank, *Republic of Yemen: A Medium-Term Economic Framework Report 99172-Yem*, 1992, p. 58.

farmers of the irrigation water essential for their crops. The wealthy landowners were used to paying nothing for their water except the cost of fuel and well construction and they used water at will, only constrained by the cost of deepening wells as the resource became more scarce and harder to reach. Agriculture accounts for about 90% of water usage in Yemen. These powerful individuals, particularly those situated in the highland Sanaʻa basin and surrounding areas were providing significant support to Saleh's presidency and thus had little difficulty persuading him to amend the responsibilities of the Ministry of Water and Environment. Within weeks, agricultural water was once again allocated to the authority of the Ministry of Agriculture and Irrigation whose priority concerns were not the protection of the environment or long-term sustainability but keeping happy the landholders who were also their main constituency.

Despite this major setback, the water crisis had become so blatant by the beginning of the century that the population was already suffering noticeable shortages throughout the country well beyond Taiz. Consequently, action had to be taken by government under pressure from an increasingly aware national environmental lobby, let alone the belated awareness of the issue on behalf of the country's main development financiers – in the case of the water sector, these were the World Bank, the governments of the Netherlands and Germany. So, in addition to passing the well-meaning, but with limited enforcement authority toothless, Water Law (its bylaws were issued in 2011, only 9 years later) and the establishment of the MWE, the first decade of this century saw increased official recognition of the water problem as well as of environmental issues in general. The National Water Sector Strategy and Investment Programme (NWSSIP) was approved in 2005 and updated in 2008, while the 2009 National Adaptation Programme of Action (NAPA) for the environment identified seven sectors particularly vulnerable to climate change, appropriately listing water and agriculture as the first two, followed by biological diversity and coastal environment and communities.[18]

After considerable lobbying by the MWE and international financiers involved in the water sector, January 2011 witnessed the long-awaited National Conference for the Conservation and Management of Water Resources in Yemen,[19] which was sponsored by the president. Summarised in the Sanaʻa Declaration, its recommendations largely reasserted those of the NWSSIP and were based on the belief that

18 Republic of Yemen, *National Adaptation Programme of Action*, Environmental Protection Authority 2009, p. 5.
19 C. Ward, N. Abu-Lohom and S. Atef, eds., *Management and Development of Water Resources in Yemen*, proceedings of the conference, Sanaʻa, Sheba Centre for Strategic Studies, 2011.

the few beneficiaries of the unregulated system would be willing to change their behaviour and adopt more socially conscious and humanitarian approaches to water management, all the while limiting their profits and advantages. The proposed 'community' based approaches to addressing the problem assumed shared interest and concerns within large social groups, ignoring the power relations within these groups or pre-existing conflicts, let alone conflicts arising from competition over increasingly scarce resources which are essential to survival, as is the case of water.

Subsequent events prevented the possible implementation of the recommendations listed in official declarations. From 2014 onwards, as the transition unravelled, implementation of all social and economic policies, even those addressing environmental urgency, moved to the remotest back burner of decision-making processes while politics took an increasingly military turn and the power struggle took precedence over all other issues.

Other than issues of the management and distribution of scarce water sources between the competing sectors of domestic, agricultural and industrial use, the search for alternative sources is an essential feature of planning; desalination is an obvious option, particularly since the cost of the operation has dropped considerably in recent decades. It is the main source of sweet water for all other Arabian Peninsula states which are also suffering severe fresh water scarcity. Surprisingly, desalination has barely featured in Yemeni planning to date. The National Water Sector Strategy and Investment Programme[20] (NWSSIP) of 2005 barely mentions desalination, with as little as US$500,000 allocated to studies of desalination, solar and wind energy! Since then a proposed public-private project to supply Taiz has not proceeded beyond the planning stage and has been shelved since the war started.[21]

Development policies

International funding agencies have played a major role in determining Yemeni government policies, including those addressing environmental issues, and their influence cannot be ignored. Given that 70% of the population is rural and 80% of the poor live in rural areas, agricultural and rural development policies are

---

20 Republic of Yemen, Ministry of Water and Environment, *National Water Sector Strategy and Investment Program, 2005–2009*, Sanaʿa 2005. The update in 2008 is the latest official policy statement.
21 See J. Firebrace, 'Yemen urban water: extreme challenges, practical solutions and lessons for the future. The case of Taiz', *Yemen to 2020: Political, Economic and Social Challenges*, eds. S. Al-Sarhan and N. Brehony, Berlin 2015.

of prime importance in addressing environmental challenges and improving food and water security. Until the end of the 20th century, international agencies focused their support on financing irrigated agriculture (large scale spate irrigation projects in the Tihama, Tuban and Abyan areas) and agricultural research on high-value, export-oriented and irrigated crops, following the neoliberal policies that were implemented worldwide. The policies they promoted fitted neatly within the worldwide promotion of neoliberal economic development philosophy. Lack of investment in either research on rain-fed and low-water demanding high-value crops for agriculture or economic support for other low-water use activities indicates complete ignorance and lack of concern for Yemen and its future. The level of neglect certainly demonstrates that priorities were not based on the actual agro-ecological circumstances prevailing in Yemen, or the needs of Yemenis. Other than water related investments, very little has been done with respect to environmental protection by any funding agency; in the 1970s and 1980s, *prosopis juliflora* was introduced in Yemen and elsewhere as a sand retention strategy, which became a scourge and a problem throughout the country in later decades when it contributed to flooding by obstructing water courses and damaging cropped areas.

Despite the NWSSIP and NAPA, since the turn of the century policy changed only marginally in favour of rain-fed agriculture, with the only significant investment consisting of the jointly funded World Bank and International Fund for Agricultural Development (IFAD), Rainfed Agriculture and Livestock Project (RALP) completed in 2013. However, only US$3.4 million out of US$22 million World Bank funding (and US$43 million total cost) was devoted to a 'farmer-based system of seed improvement and management'.[22] Most funding went to 'community development' investments. Although activities such as *wadi* bank protection and terrace rehabilitation have positive environmental and production outcomes, foreign investment should have concentrated on innovative and essential research and extension on drought resistant and fast maturing varieties of both staple and cash crops.

Since RALP, there has been little new investment in any projects capable of addressing the country's environmental challenges. Out of the US$423 million approved by the World Bank for Yemen between 2011, and the suspension of operations in 2015, only about 10% has been allocated to explicitly climate related investments, and hardly any of this allocated to agriculture and rural development, though some money has gone to windfarms and other energy related factors.

---

22 World Bank, *Implementation Status and Results*, December 2013, and *Project Appraisal Document*.

Since 2017, when the procedure was changed to permit investments despite the ongoing war, the Bank has predictably focused its resources primarily on urgent emergency support for health and basic income generation.

Implications of the environmental challenges

Water management

To mitigate effects of climate change, a number of issues need to be addressed. Yemen's limited and diminishing water resources need to be managed with extreme care. Water scarcity requires the creation of a new economy that concentrates on low water use. Exhaustion of water resources in the highlands and the consequent migration of the residents to coastal areas demands a major desalination programme, as well as effective water management in the highlands prioritising basic human needs, followed by livestock, and irrigated agriculture only once the two latter needs have been satisfied. Given that 90% of Yemen's water is used in agriculture, clearly people will be able to continue living in the country if this amount is significantly reduced, something which can be reasonably easily achieved by an effective and strong government. Hopefully such an entity will emerge from the current war in order to ensure that the interests of the majority prevail and the transfer of water use from agriculture to basic human needs is implemented effectively, thus enabling an even larger population to continue living in Yemen.

This scenario certainly asks for a considerable reduction of water use in agriculture in order to enable enough water being made available for domestic consumption, as well as livestock, and also for industry use insofar as more employment and income could be generated per m^3 of water in that sector. A modern low-water consuming economy is dependent on the presence of highly-educated people able to initiate enterprises suited to the 21st century. This requires a fundamental, urgent and rapid transformation of the country's education system to produce such people who are able to operate both in urban and rural areas, and would thus make it possible for many to continue living in the beautiful landscapes of Yemen's highlands, despite their water scarcity.

In addition, coastal areas must be prepared to cope with rising sea water levels, and this will demand major infrastructural protective works for the cities, as well as other measures for the fishing communities. Cyclone Chapala has demonstrated the vulnerability of coastal populations to the new events which are likely to increase in frequency due to climate change. As coastal populations grow, they need to be able to maximise benefits from their location while being protected from extreme weather events which are likely to occur more frequently.

Erosion control

Damage from wind and water erosion is a further constraint for a population that already has to survive in an extremely difficult environment. Reducing erosion from wind and water will be important to retain agricultural land and control, if not reverse, desertification. This objective will require innovative approaches which should take into consideration lessons learned from earlier mistakes. The social and economic side-effects of technical interventions should be carefully examined prior to their introduction, as there is a possibility that they can produce negative results. For instance, the spread of *prosopis juliflora* which caused considerable environmental difficulties was clearly not the original intention of those who sought to control sand movements, but took place due to neglecting implications of planting the bush in a kind of environment where it could spread well beyond the desired area.

Solar power and alternative energies

If the disastrous war in Yemen can be said to have had any positive outcome, the emergence of solar power as the main supplier of electricity throughout the country is one. In both rural and urban areas, Yemenis have rushed to acquire access to domestic solar power which is now widely used, though figures are not available; reduced price of solar equipment has certainly helped. In remote and isolated rural areas solar power is a novelty, often providing 24-hour electricity access for the first time ever, while in urban areas it replaces the national grid which has effectively stopped functioning. At the very least, people are able to operate a few lamps, their televisions, and charge their mobile devices. Those with more funds can also operate refrigerators and fans.

In earlier decades, the IMF partly justified their policy of increasing diesel prices as an environmentally positive measure intended to reduce water use, particularly through pumping water for irrigation. Farmers resisted and responded first by resorting to using electric pumps; as a result of the worsening crisis in electricity supply, Yemeni landowners have taken the lead in introducing solar pumps to irrigate their crops, to some extent with the support of the state through subsidised equipment.

Yemen is a clear case where solar and wind energy could be developed to solve local energy shortage problems and even possibly produce enough energy for export to neighbouring countries. The Mokha wind farm project which was designed in the early years of this decade should, hopefully, be implemented when military activities end. Such investments could provide environmentally friendly and cheap power, paving the way for other economic activities.

Protecting Yemen's cultural environment

Even prior to the war, Yemen's well-known urban architectural assets suffered enormously from environmental change and the introduction of modern facilities which would have been otherwise extremely welcome, such as house-delivered domestic water and sanitation systems. Improving the quality of construction and design will in future be essential if the positive aspects of modern life are to be implemented, while ensuring the conservation and preservation of what is left of the country's urban heritage. Yemen's architecture, as well as its numerous archaeological sites, are important cultural markers not only for the people of Yemen and the Peninsula, reflecting their history, but they are also potential economic resources. Cultural tourism could be a major source of income, creating thousands of jobs, while helping to promote knowledge of the country and its people.

Conclusion

Overall, in Yemen as elsewhere, those most exposed and vulnerable to environmental hazards are the rural poor and the coastal populations. While Yemenis have proved their resilience for centuries, this attribute is now weakening, particularly in poor people who have no protective buffer either in the form of savings or in stronger bodies. It is always the poor who suffer first and most from disasters. Considering a poverty rate of 54% in the 2010s, which increased to over 60% two and a half years into the war in 2017, we can deduce that in Yemen poverty is not only the result of war. Earlier inappropriate state and international funding agencies' development policies have played a major part in promoting development strategies and investments which have contributed to worsening the environmental challenges.

Although the correlation is not direct, there is little doubt that climate related events, and water shortage in particular, have contributed to deteriorating living conditions in Yemen and thus, indirectly, to the crisis which has brought the country to civil war. Therefore, in Yemen at least, in the past half century we have seen more movement from cooperation to conflict than the other way around.

However, a reversal of this situation will be essential both within Yemen and in the relationship between Yemen and its neighbours if environmentally based disaster is to be avoided for the coming generation. Addressing the country's environmental challenges is an absolute necessity if Yemenis are to continue living within its borders. This will require the implementation of serious and effective measures by a strong state committed to the welfare of all its people, and able to resist the pressures of those who have been exploiting the resources for their short-term profit at the expense of everyone else's future. Such a government will ensure that providing access to domestic water supply takes priority and that agricultural investments prioritise rain-fed crops, while ensuring that water used for irrigation is restricted, reduced and used with maximum efficiency. Protection against rising sea levels and addressing frequent and violent weather events will also have to be a part of their priority policies.

Cooperation between an effective Yemeni state with its neighbours, mainly Saudi Arabia and Oman, but also the UAE and countries across the Red Sea is essential to address the many environmental challenges faced by Yemen, including the management of joint aquifers, exhaustion of the water supply and extremely high unemployment. Yemen's population is likely to reach 50 million well before the middle of the century. Cooperation is in everyone's interest: it will make it possible for these millions to live, and ideally flourish, at home and in the region, contributing to a post-oil economy in the Arabian Peninsula. The alternative will be for many of these millions to force their way in desperation into other countries as climate refugees, overcoming all physical or administrative constraints.

So, while responsibility for the current lasting political, military, economic and social crises in Yemen cannot be attributed exclusively to environmental factors, there is little doubt that these factors have contributed to bringing about the profound crisis which has engulfed the country in the second decade of the 21st century. The factors leading to the crisis include decades of autocratic rule, neoliberal economic policies focused on short-term returns for the few at the expense of the population at large, and environmental sustainability, rapid population growth, severe limitations on labour migration to other states, water scarcity, a weak economic base and low educational standards. In addition, unfortunately, support from Yemen's international partners has been designed in such a manner as to serve their own interests rather than to solve the problems and challenges faced by Yemenis.

Bibliography

Firebrace, J., 'Yemen urban water: extreme challenges, practical solutions and lessons for the future. The case of Taiz', *Rebuilding Yemen: Political, Economic and Social Challenges*, eds. S. Al-Sarhan and N. Brehony, Berlin 2015, pp. 123–48.

Lackner, H., *Understanding the Yemeni Crisis: The Transformation of Tribal Roles in Recent Decades*, Durham Middle East Papers, Luce Fellowship paper no 17, 2016.

Lackner, H., ed., *Why Yemen Matters*, London 2014.

Lackner, H., *Yemen in Crisis: Autocracy, Neo-Liberalism and the Disintegration of a State*, London 2017.

Moench, M. and H. Lackner, *Decentralized Management Study*, World Bank, Sana'a 1997.

Republic of Yemen, Environmental Protection Authority, *National Adaptation Programme of Action*, Sana'a 2009.

Republic of Yemen, Ministry of Water and Environment, *National Water Sector Strategy and Investment Program, 2005–2009*, Sana'a 2005.

Sternberg, T., ed., *Climate Hazard Crises in Asian Societies and Environments*, London 2017.

Ward, C., *The Water Crisis in Yemen*, London 2015

Ward, C., N. Abu-Lohom and S. Atef, eds., *Management and Development of Water Resources in Yemen,* Sheba Centre for Strategic Studies 2011.

Weiss, M., 'A perfect Storm: the causes and consequences of severe water scarcity, institutional breakdown and conflict in Yemen', *Water International* 40, 2015, pp. 251–72.

World Bank, *Beyond Scarcity, Water Security in the Middle East and North Africa*, Washington, DC 2017.

World Bank, *Climate Investment Funds, Strategic Program for Climate Resilience for Yemen,* Meeting of the PPCR sub-committee, April 17th, 2012.

World Bank, *Rainfed Agriculture and Livestock Project Implementation Status and Results*, Washington, DC 2013.

World Bank, *Republic of Yemen: A Medium-Term Economic Framework Report 99172-Yem*, Washington, DC 1992.

World Bank, *Yemen: Assessing the Impacts of Climate Change and Variability on the Water and Agricultural Sectors and the Policy Implications*, Washington, DC 2010.

8

Do Virtual Water Flows Actually Flow? A Political Ecology of Agricultural Virtual Water (non)Flows in Palestine during the Post-Oslo Period[1]

María J. Beltrán

The Oslo Agreement: the economic dimension of peace

The controversial application of the Peace Agreement signed in Oslo between the Palestinian Territories and Israel in 1993, initially planned for five years and subsequently extended, marked a crucial turning point in Palestine's history. Analyses of this framework which has since governed Israeli-Palestinian relations have shown the vital role trade has played in the survival of the Palestinian economy as well as the latter's long-term dependence on Israeli policies.[2] The economic effects of restricted access to land in the West Bank and of restrictions on Palestinian water sector development have, furthermore, been significant.[3] These studies, alongside those looking at Israeli-imposed movement restrictions

---

1 Based on M. J. Beltrán and G. Kallis, 'How Does Virtual Water Flow in Palestine? A Political Ecology Analysis', *Ecological Economics* 142, 2018, pp. 17–26, copyright 2017 with permission from Elsevier.
2 A. Arnon and S. Bamya, 'Twenty Years after Oslo and the Paris Protocol', *Economics and Politics in the Israeli Palestinian Conflict Jerusalem*, ed. AIX Group, Jerusalem 2015, pp. 11–39.
3 World Bank, 'Assessment of Restrictions on Palestinian Water Sector Development, Sector Note for West Bank and Gaza', Washington, DC 2009.

within the West Bank,[4] illustrate the importance of Palestine's agricultural sector for socio-economic development and poverty reduction within complex Israeli regulations and procedures that have ultimately undermined the development of Palestinian agriculture.

Academic literature has analysed the distinct factors affecting the performance of the Palestinian agricultural sector, especially the role of water politics and trade relations.[5] The role of water in the Palestinian-Israeli conflict has been analysed by many authors,[6] who argue that the asymmetric position of Palestine in the negotiations of Oslo II arrangement has ensured Israel's domination over water allocation in Palestine. Studies have also shown how Israel-Palestine trade relations have influenced the deterioration of Palestine's agricultural productive capacities, resulting in the decline of the agricultural sector's contribution to the economy.[7] There is thus no doubt that the link between water, agriculture and trade is central to understanding contemporary social and environmental challenges in the occupied Palestinian Territories.

Studying the concept of virtual water[8] is extremely useful in making the water-agriculture-trade relationship visible, as it sheds light on agricultural trade flows in terms of water. Virtual water (VW) refers to the amount of water required for the production of a good or service. VW reaches its full potential in relation to trade, which effectively identifies VW flows between countries or regions. The

---

4 United Nations Office for the Coordination of Humanitarian Affairs occupied Palestinian territory (OCHA), 'West Bank movement and access. Update 2011', Jerusalem 2011, http:// www.ocha.org.
5 United Nations Office for the Coordination of Humanitarian Affairs occupied Palestinian territory (OCHA), 'Humanitarian Fact Sheet on the Jordan Valley and Dead Sea Area', Jerusalem 2012, http://www.ocha.org.
6 S. Lonergan and D. Brooks, *Watershed: The Role of Fresh Water in the Israeli-Palestinian Conflict*, Ottawa 1994; J. Selby, 'Dressing up domination as "cooperation": The case of Israeli-Palestinian water relations', *Review of International Studies* 29, 2003, pp. 21–38; J. Selby, 'Dependence, Independence and Interdependence in the Palestinian water sector', *Birzeit University Working Paper* 45, 2011, http://ssrn.com/abstract=2127973; J. Selby, 'Cooperation, domination and colonisation: The Israeli-Palestinian Joint Water Committee', *Water Alternatives* 6, 2013, pp. 1–24; J. Trottier, 'A wall, water and power: the Israeli "separation fence"', *Review of International Studies* 33, 2007, pp. 105–27.
7 M. Haj Khalil, *Guide to Palestine-Israel Economic and Trade Relations*, Czech Representative Office, Jerusalem 2009, http://www.mzv.cz/file/806096/Guide_to_ Palestine___Israel_Economic_and_Trade_Relations___Czech_Rep_Office.pdf; S. Taghdisi-Rad, *The Political Economy of Aid in Palestine: Relief from Conflict or Development Delayed?*, London 2011.
8 J. Allan, *The Middle East Water Question: Hydropolitics and the Global Economy*, London 2001.

term 'virtual water' was promoted to underline how Middle Eastern countries' water requirements have exceeded available resources since 1970. In other words, water scarcity in these countries has been managed by importing VW in the form of agricultural products available on the international market. While VW was defined as a theoretical indicator, the term water footprint (WF) emerged from the methodological attempt to estimate VW, defined as the 'volume of water needed for the production of the goods and services consumed by the inhabitants of the country'.[9] Amidst many other methodologies,[10] calculating WF remains the most widespread. Suffice to say that VW and WF have been popularised and numerous studies on virtual water flows of economies worldwide have shown the increase in virtual water trade across the world.[11]

In the case of Palestine, previous studies have implemented methodologies capable of estimating VW flows in the West Bank and quantifying the effects of VW trade on water management in Palestine.[12] However, there is an ongoing debate over the contradictions generated by the VW indicator when it comes to providing information for implementing water and trade policies.[13] Perhaps most critically, in terms of the objectives of this chapter, most analyses on VW flows are undertaken from a quantitative perspective while a consideration of the wider socioeconomic and environmental context is absent.[14]

In view of these epistemological gaps, I propose that a political ecology approach

9 A. Chapagain and A. Hoekstra, 'Water footprints of nations', *Value of Water Research Report Series* 16, 2004, pp. 11, UNESCO: IHE, Institute for Water Education.

10 For an overview see E. Velázquez, C. Madrid and M. J. Beltrán, 'Rethinking the concepts of virtual water and water footprint in relation to the production-consumption binomial and the water-energy nexus', *Water Resources Management* 25, 2011, pp. 743–61.

11 Chapagain and Hoekstra, 'Water footprints of nations'; A. Hoekstra and A. Chapagain, *Globalization of Water: Sharing the Planet's Freshwater Resources*, Oxford 2008.

12 D. Nazer, M. Siebel, P. Van der Zaag, Z. Mimi and H. Gijzen, 'Water Footprint of the Palestinians in the West Bank', *Journal of the American Water Resources Association* 44, 2008, pp. 449–58; Y. Nassar, 'Virtual water trade as a policy instrument for achieving water security in Palestine', *Water Resources in the Middle East. Israeli-Palestinian water issues – From Conflict to Cooperation*, eds. H. I. Shuval and S. Dweik, Berlin 2007, pp. 141–6; P. Hamdi, 'The effects of virtual water trade on the future water management in Palestine', Master Thesis, An-Najah National University, Palestine 2014.

13 D. Wichelns, 'Virtual water and water footprints offer limited insight regarding important policy questions', *International Journal of Water Resources Development* 26, 2010, pp. 639–51; D. Wichelns, 'Virtual water and water footprints: Overreaching into the discourse on sustainability, efficiency, and equity', *Water Alternatives* 8, 2015, pp. 396–414.

14 J. Chenoweth, M. Hadjikakou and C. Zoumides, 'Quantifying the human impact on water resources: A critical review of the water footprint concept', *Hydrology and Earth System Science* 18, 2014, pp. 2325–42.

to VW offers a powerful theoretical basis for contextualising and politicising environmental knowledge.[15] Political ecologists recognise the biophysical roots of environmental problems, but also focus on the political dimensions of ecological problems, showing how socio-ecological conditions are sustained by and organised through both social and metabolic-ecological processes.[16] I argue that the estimation of VW flows should be complemented with a consideration of the political, social and territorial implications of these flows – that is, who benefits and who suffers from VW flows, or non-flows. This approach means that VW flows are not just the flow of a resource, but the manifestation of the political and social relations that exist between water, agricultural production and trade in the Palestinian Territories.

The purpose of this chapter is thus twofold. Firstly, I examine the social and political mechanisms that coexist with and affect the flow of agricultural VW in Palestine during the Post-Oslo period. Secondly, I quantify these VW flows and connect them to a broader social and political context. The analysis reveals that virtual water flows evolve within the (geo)political-economic context in which they are embedded, bringing to light Israel's control over the flow of Palestinian agricultural virtual water.

This chapter hence explores the relevance of combining biophysical analyses with the examination of institutional and political relations that coexist with and affect virtual water flows. Following this introduction, the second section describes key elements in the Oslo Protocol affecting water, land governance and agricultural trade. The third section unpacks VW and the methodology I use to produce an estimate from a political ecology perspective. The fourth section presents the quantitative analysis of Palestinian agricultural VW flows from 1997 to 2013 and examines how the political and social context has conditioned these flows. Finally, I draw conclusions from my research.

Creating Palestinian dependence: tying together the elements of the Oslo Agreement

The Paris Protocol, as part of the Oslo Agreement, was designed to serve as a temporary protocol on economic relations between Palestine and Israel. More than twenty years after the implementation of this protocol, the overarching objective

---

15 T. Forsyth, *Critical Political Ecology, The politics of environmental science*, London 2003.
16 E. Swyngedouw, 'Circulations and Metabolisms: (Hybrid) Natures and (Cyborg) Cities', *Science as Culture* 2, 2006, pp. 105–21.

of the Israeli Authorities to ensure control over the Palestinian Territories has taken the form of an imposed trade integration between these two regions. By ensuring that Israeli exports flow smoothly to Palestine, while Palestinian exports to Israel and other countries are controlled, Israel preempts any possible competition between Palestinian and Israeli producers.[17]

The agricultural sector has not been an exception; restrictions imposed on land and water resources as a result of Israeli policies have had long-term implications for Palestinian agricultural production in general and for agricultural trade in particular. The creation of administrative areas (A, B and C) in the West Bank dictating Israeli and Palestinian authority powers under the Oslo process and import-export policy have led to significantly increased trading costs and reduced mobility for Palestinians; these realities have a comparatively greater impact on agricultural trade due to its time-sensitive nature. To lay bare these issues, I briefly examine three different aspects of the Oslo Accords: 1) Israeli-Palestinian agricultural trade relations; 2) Palestinians' land access and movement; and 3) Israeli-Palestinian water governance relations. I will then illustrate how these three aspects influence the performance of the Palestinian agricultural sector, moving to explore how these factors influence agricultural VW flows.

Israel-Palestine trade relations: the Paris Protocol

The Palestinian trade structure has been heavily dependent on Israel since 1967 as the source or channel for exports and imports. Official statistics suggests that Israel is the source or channel for about 80% of imports and absorbs about 90% of Palestinian exports.[18] Since its signing in 1994, the Protocol of Economic Relations, also called the Paris Protocol and considered a part of the Oslo Accords, has ensured the long-term dependence of Palestinian trade on Israeli policies. The element of interest in the Paris Protocol regarding agricultural trade (article VIII of the Protocol) is import and export policy.

The Paris Protocol, beyond its 'temporary' (five-year) framework, continues to serve as the governing framework for economic relations between the PA and Israel.[19] The Paris Protocol covered a range of economic sectors and established

---

17 Taghdisi-Rad, *The Political Economy of Aid in Palestine*.
18 United Nations Conference on Trade and Development (UNCTAD), 'Report on UNCTAD assistance to the Palestinian people: Developments in the economy of the occupied Palestinian territory', Jerusalem 2011, http://www. unctad.org.
19 Office of the Quartet Representative, 'Back to the Future: Integrating the Political and Economic Tracks', Brussels 2013, http://unispal.un.org/pdfs/AHLC_OQR-PolicyRpt.pdf.

a mechanism for Palestinian-Israeli economic and financial relations. The model established in the Protocol for Palestinian-Israeli trade is known as a 'customs union', the main characteristic of which is the absence of economic borders between the two countries.[20] As a result, the Palestinian economy is integrated in, and dependent on, the Israeli economy.

The reality of this dependence becomes very visible upon understanding how exports and imports operate in theory and in practice. In terms of exports, the Protocol stipulates that Palestinians have the right to export their agricultural products to external markets *without restrictions*, on the basis of certificates of origin issued by the PA. However, Palestinian trade with other countries is handled through Israeli sea and air ports, or through border crossings between the PA, Jordan and Egypt, which are also controlled by Israel. With respect to imports, the PA has all powers and responsibilities over imports, customs policy and procedures related to the goods itemised on lists A1, A2 (agricultural products) and B (industrial products) of the Paris Protocol. These lists specify the quantities of goods Palestinians are allowed to import and determine the rates of customs and other import charges, the regulation of licensing requirements and procedures, and regulation of standard requirements.

In practice, however, Israeli authorities apply different procedures for imports to Israel and imports to the PA. In many cases, the difference favours Israeli importers who can clear their goods more quickly and cheaply (e.g. storage and handling) and receive support services (e.g. issuing of telecommunication import licenses). In addition, Israeli laws, regulations and procedures surrounding import-export are available only in Hebrew. This practice results in higher transaction costs for the Palestinian importer.[21] Furthermore, the Israeli government imposes restrictions on Palestinian goods being transported into or out of the occupied Palestinian territory, whereby in commercial crossings goods must be unloaded from the Palestinian vehicle, checked extensively, then reloaded onto an Israeli vehicle on the other side. Such realities mean that Palestinian imports and exports can cost twice those of Israeli imports and exports: average export cost and time for Israel are $670 and 11 days, whereas for Palestine they are $1310 and 23 days. Regarding imports, trading costs and time are $650 and 10 days for Israel and $1225 and 40 days for Palestine.[22]

---

20 Haj Khalil, *Guide to Palestine*.
21 Office of the Quartet Representative, 'Back to the Future'.
22 Palestinian Ministry of Economy and the Applied Research Institute Jerusalem, *The Economic Costs of the Israeli Occupation for the Occupied Palestinian Territory*, Jerusalem 2011, http://www.arij.org/.

Under the current circumstances, the structural difficulties in importing products to Palestine from countries other than Israel have led Palestinian traders to buy products through Israeli importers. Both Palestinian and Israeli importers have a clear incentive not to specify Palestine as a final destination, due to the stricter security and clearance procedures detailed above. Indeed, a significant share of the goods sold from Israel to Palestine are indirect imports, with 58% of the total Palestinian imports from Israel produced in a third country.[23] This fictitious enormous weight of Israeli imports on the Palestinian economy has been defined as the 'hidden distortion' of the Palestine trade structure.[24]

Palestinian mobility and land access: the administrative areas in the West Bank

The Oslo Accords, signed in 1993 and 1995, were intended to temporarily divide the West Bank into three administrative zones, called areas A, B, and C. Area A, which contains 18% of the West Bank land area, consists mostly of the main towns of Ramallah, Hebron, Bethlehem and Jericho under full Palestinian Authority (PA) civil and security control. In Area B, around 22% of the West Bank, the PA has control over civilian services such as planning, but only joint security control with the Israeli military. Area C is the largest administrative area of the West Bank, comprising 60% of the territory, and is under full control of the Israeli Civil Administration. Part of the Coordinator of Government Activities in the Territories, the Civil Administration was established by the Government of Israel in 1981 as a unit of the Ministry of Defence in order to carry out practical bureaucratic functions within the territories occupied in 1967. In Area C, the Israeli government has control over Palestinian land and imposes restrictions to the construction of water infrastructure and agricultural expansion.

During the Second Intifada (2000–2004), the Palestinian uprising against Israel also known as the Al-Aqsa Intifada,[25] Israel tightened movement policies and built the West Bank wall, severely restricting the Palestinians' land access. The creation

---

23 Bank of Israel, 'Recent economic developments', August 2010, http://www.boi.org.il.
24 Taghdisi-Rad, *The Political Economy of Aid in Palestine*.
25 The Second Intifada broke out at the end of September 2000, following a visit by Israel's then-opposition leader Ariel Sharon to Jerusalem's Temple Mount. After seven years of the Oslo peace process, negotiations had failed to deliver a Palestinian state and Palestinian discontent was intensified by the collapse of the Camp David summit in July 2000. No definitive ending date can be assigned to the Second Intifada, though some would suggest February 2005.

of the wall, Israeli settlements and road barriers have led to the requisition of 7884 dunums[26] (788 hectares) of land throughout the West Bank from 2005–2006 alone.[27]

The impact produced by the administrative areas on the Palestinians' land access and movement is exemplified in the Jordan Valley. Almost 45% of total Palestinian irrigated areas in the West Bank are concentrated in the Jordan Valley region.[28] It is considered one of the areas of highest agricultural potential in the Palestinian Territories and also one of the most restricted areas on earth. Ninety-four per cent of the Jordan Valley is off limits for Palestinian development.[29] Access to the Jordan Valley is controlled through numerous checkpoints and the West Bank barrier, restricting the movement of Palestinian vehicles. Within the Jordan Valley there are 37 Israeli settlements with a population of 9,500 inhabitants; these settlements contravene international law.[30]

Domination dressed up as cooperation? Israeli-Palestinian water governance

While the Peace Agreement signed in Oslo in 1993 offers only a brief treatment of water issues, the Israeli-Palestinian interim arrangement for the development and use of Palestinian water resources signed in 1995, known as Oslo II, established an elaborate framework for the allocation and management of shared water resources (Article 40). The implications of Oslo II on the availability of water resources to Palestinians have been thoroughly examined,[31] showing principally that this framework has failed to ensure efficient, equitable, and sustainable management of water over the long term.

The Jordan River is the main source of surface water in the area, but the river is currently an Israeli military zone and Palestinians have no access to water from Jordan River. In the case of groundwater, Article 40 established that the requirements for fresh water would be divided between immediate and future needs of

---

26 Dunum is a traditional unit of land area in the Middle East, still commonly used today in Israel and Palestine. The dunum is a metric unit equal to 0.1 hectare.
27 Taghdisi-Rad, *The Political Economy of Aid in Palestine*.
28 Palestinian Central Bureau of Statistics (PCBS), 'Land Use Statistics in the Palestinian Territory, 1997–2008', http://www.pcbs.gov.ps/.
29 OCHA, 'Humanitarian Fact Sheet on the Jordan Valley'.
30 Ibid.
31 Lonergan and Brooks, *Watershed*; World Bank, *Assessment of Restriction*; Selby, 'Dependence, Independence and Interdependence'; Selby, 'Cooperation, domination and colonisation'; Selby, 'Dressing up domination as "cooperation"'.

the occupied Palestinian Territories. Immediate needs, for example, allocate 29 cubic hectometres (hm^3) for Palestinians, 23.6 hm^3 for the West Bank, and the rest for Gaza Strip. Regarding future needs, according to the projections done in 1995 as part of the Oslo Agreement, the Palestinian supply should increase 70–80 hm^3 per year above 1995 consumption levels.[32]

During the five-year 'interim arrangement', which is still in place over fifteen years later, water-related decisions had to be made with Israeli and PA consent. An Israeli-Palestinian Joint Water Committee (JWC) was established and given the authority to regulate the use of water resources in the Palestinian territory. However, despite the existence of Palestinian representatives on the JWC, Israel has been able to veto or delay water-related projects, resulting in the rejection and delay of dozens of water projects submitted by the PA.[33] Furthermore, the agreement established that JWC had the right to control water quotas on Palestinian wells, imposing the quota as the maximum consumption level of the wells in 1995.

Among the many criticisms this agreement has received, Jan Selby argues for the complete restructuring of the Israeli-Palestinian water 'cooperation' pact, because it involves 'domination dressed up as "cooperation"'.[34] He furthermore concludes that under the terms of the Oslo II agreement Israel has achieved large absolute and per capita increases in water supply, including increases in both domestic and agricultural use, facilitating Israel's expansionist territorial and settlement interests within the West Bank.[35] In contrast, Palestinian water production in the West Bank has dropped overall by 20 hm^3 per year since 1995. This absolute decline in internal water production has been partially compensated by an increase in water purchases from Israel of over 100%.[36]

The decline in internal water production, combined with increased dependency on water supplies from Israel and the land requisition policies mentioned above, has undermined Palestine's agricultural production capacities, resulting in the decline of the Palestinian agricultural sector's contribution to the economy. Between 1995 and 2008 the share of agriculture in GDP declined from 12% to a mere 5%.[37] Agricultural growth is limited by land and water availability, as well as

---

32 D. Brooks and J. Trottier, 'A modern agreement to share water between Israelis and Palestinians: the FoEME proposal', Bethlehem 2012.
33 Selby, 'Cooperation, domination and colonisation'.
34 Selby, 'Dressing up domination as "cooperation"'.
35 Selby, 'Cooperation, domination and colonisation'.
36 Ibid.
37 United Nations Conference on Trade and Development (UNCTAD), *Report on UNCTAD*

the expansion of Israeli settlements. Although from 1997 to 2008 the population of the Palestinian territories increased by 72%, the total cultivated land area remained fairly constant in size.[38] Agricultural intensification was also limited mainly due to lack of access to markets as a result of inefficient and high production costs caused by lack of access to pesticides, equipment and agricultural subsidies.[39]

The Paris Protocol, Administrative Areas and Oslo II Accords: engineering Palestinian dependence

An examination of these aspects of the Oslo Agreement shows the significant link between land access, mobility, water access, agriculture and trade; all are equally important to the Palestinian economy, are cross-linked and strategically reinforce each other. As the implementation of the Oslo Agreement on the ground has shown, Palestine is materially and politically dependent on the Israeli economy. Dependence, as defined by Selby, is a state of affairs where a society is heavily constrained by, and requires the material support of other societies that are neither constrained by nor dependent on the material support of the society in question.[40] I have shown so far that Palestinian dependence is produced, first, by the constriction of society expressed by declining internal water production, land access, movement, and internal and external trade, and second, through the reduced material support that is the result of this threefold decline.

Figure 13 visualises how contemporary Palestinian dependency is rooted in relations of dependency between water, trade and agriculture. On the one hand, Israel's domination over water allocation and agricultural land in Palestine, together with control over Palestinian trade relations, have undermined Palestine's agricultural production capacity. On the other hand, Israel's movement restrictions on people and goods within the Territories and to the outside world have stifled the trade of agricultural products. This means that Palestinians are mainly dependent on Israel for importing the agricultural products that for the aforementioned reasons – among many others – they are not able to produce.

The material dimension of these dependency relations between water, trade and agriculture can be examined through the analysis of the agricultural trade flows in terms of water. The next section examines how, using a political ecology

assistance to the Palestinian people: Developments in the economy of the occupied Palestinian territory, Jerusalem 2012, http://www.unctad.org.
38 PCBS, 'Land Use Statistics in the Palestinian Territory'.
39 Taghdisi-Rad, *The Political Economy of Aid in Palestine*.
40 Selby, 'Dependence, Independence and Interdependence'.

approach, the concepts of virtual water and water footprint can be used critically, and presents the methodologies used to estimate virtual water flows of the Palestinian Territories in order to contextualise these flows.

Virtual water: exploring the link between water, trade and agriculture from a political ecology perspective

Political ecologists have shown how water management is not merely a technical question that can be addressed through scientific expertise. It is the social nature of water that is at stake, involving human values, behaviour and political-economic organisation.[41] Water is a biopolitical resource,[42] which means that there is a link between the constitution and consolidation of political and economic power on the one hand, and the control of aquatic socionatures on the other. This, in turn, 'implies a shift from regarding water as the object of social processes, to a nature that is both shaped by, and shapes, social relations, structures and subjectivities'.[43] Society shapes and is shaped by water, both materially and discursively, and water flows are embedded in all institutional and political processes that coexist with them and affect them.[44]

Both VW and WF approaches shed light on the material dimension of water circulation and offer metrics for a deeper analysis of water production and consumption, as well as water trade flows. Nevertheless, it is noteworthy the proliferation of studies with the objective of quantifying VW and WF indicators which do not refer to the power relations associated with the circulation of these physical flows.[45] Numerous critiques of VW and WF have also been launched both at the methodological and normative levels, largely pointing to the contradictions generated by these indicators when it comes to providing relevant information for the implementation of water and trade policies.[46] Barnes shows that virtual

41 J. Linton and J. Budds, 'The hydrosocial cycle: Defining and mobilizing a relational-dialectical approach to water', *Geoforum* 57, 2014, pp. 170–80.

42 K. Bakker, 'Water: political, biopolitical, material', *Social Studies of Science* 42, 2012, pp. 616–23.

43 Linton and Budds, 'The hydrosocial cycle', p. 170.

44 E. Swyngedouw, 'The Political Economy and Political Ecology of the Hydro-Social Cycle', *Journal of Contemporary Water Research & Education* 142, 2009, pp. 56–60.

45 M. J. Beltrán and E. Velázquez, 'The political ecology of virtual water in southern Spain', International Journal of Urban and Regional Research 39, 2015, pp. 1020–36.

46 Velázquez *et al*, 'Rethinking the concepts'; Wichelns, 'Virtual water and water footprints offer'; Wichelns, 'Virtual water and water footprints: Overreaching'; Chenoweth *et al*, 'Quantifying'.

water models abstract water from the material context of its use,[47] while Wichelns argues that 'virtual water and water footprint calculations are essentially silent on the most important aspects of water allocation and use'.[48] From a political ecology perspective, disembedded from its institutional and political processes, the VW metaphor is distorting how we understand socio-ecosystems, shifting our attention from complex systems of thinking toward simplified flow analysis.[49] The combined approach of the political ecology of VW, therefore, goes beyond the estimation of water flows and explains how methodological efforts should be complemented by the consideration of political, social and territorial drivers and implications of VW flows.

Estimating VW flows through a political ecology perspective

The studies undertaken to date on WF and VW in Palestine[50] do not present VW estimations within the wider institutional and political framework in which Palestine is immersed. In order to refute critiques of VW and WF approaches, I mobilise quantitative and qualitative data analysis to show that VW flows are not just the flow of a resource, but the manifestation of the political and social relations that are organised around trade in the Palestinian Territories. This approach enables me to shed light on the power relations hidden behind VW flows and to question who controls the flow of VW and how, and whether VW flows actually flow or not, and why.

To estimate the agricultural VW flows of Palestinian territories since the signature of Oslo Agreements, I took data on agricultural production and crop yield from the FAOSTAT database from 1997–2013.[51] Crops included in the calculations were the main crops produced in the Palestinian Territories by area and production, analysing the Palestinian Central Bureau of Statistics (PCBS) agricultural production database:[52] tomato, potato, cucumber, eggplant, wheat, citrus (oranges and lemon), banana, olives (exported as olive oil), and dates. Crop water

---

47 J. Barnes, 'Water, water everywhere but not a drop to drink: The false promise of virtual water', Critique of Anthropology 33, 2013, pp. 371–89.
48 Wichelns, 'Virtual water and water footprints offer', p. 649.
49 Beltrán and Velázquez, 'The political ecology of virtual water'.
50 Nazer et al, 'Water Footprint'; Nassar, 'Virtual water trade'; Hamdi, 'The effects of'.
51 FAOSTAT is a data base for the statistic division of the Food and Agriculture Organization of the United Nations (FAO), http://faostat.fao.org/.
52 Palestinian Central Bureau of Statistics (PCBS), 'Agricultural Statistics 1993–2008', http://www.pcbs.gov.ps/.

requirements were estimated using CROPWAT.[53] Import and export data production of the selected crops was taken from the FAOSTAT database from 1997–2013.

Since the purpose is to estimate the evolution of VW agricultural flows, I focus on the volume of water (blue and green[54]) used in agriculture (internal agricultural water use) compared to the volume of water imported and exported through agricultural products. I draw a temporal picture, estimating the agricultural VW flows of Palestinian territories since the signature of Oslo Agreements (1997–2013).

To integrate these VW estimations with the wider Palestinian institutional and political framework, the analysis is based on information from different primary and secondary sources to corroborate findings and allow a process of triangulation. I conducted fieldwork over five months (in 2012 and 2013), with the support of the European Network of Political Ecology and Friends of the Earth Middle East. Quantitative and qualitative social research methodology consisted of anthropological direct observation, semi-structured interviews, surveys, and two focus groups with farmers in Auja Ecocenter (Friends of the Earth Middle East). Twelve relevant stakeholders' representatives from different research institutes, NGOs and Palestinian government institutions were interviewed. Field notes were used to record the observations during the fieldwork period in a narrative, descriptive way. Finally, I systematically reviewed secondary data including policy documents, statistics and the reports of NGOs and international bodies.

I now show how the flow of VW has been conditioned by the evolution of the political and social relations between Israel and Palestine during the Post-Oslo period, presenting the agricultural virtual water estimations in Palestine framed within the institutional and political context of the Post-Oslo Agreement.

Do virtual water flows actually flow? Results and discussion

Figure 14 demonstrates the evolution of the VW agricultural flows in Palestine during Post-Oslo trade regime (1997–2013), divided into three phases. The first is from 1997 to 2000, the years subsequent to the signing of the Oslo Agreement

---

53 CROPWAT is a free software for the calculation of crop water requirements and irrigation requirements based on soil, climate and crop data. See: http://www.fao.org/nr/water/infores_databases_cropwat.html.

54 Falkenmark and Rockström 2006's characterisation of water according to its origin (blue and green water) helps in specifying the different types of water contained in produced or consumed goods and services. Blue water refers to surface and groundwater from rivers and aquifers, while green water is the water contained in the soil (rainwater that does not become run-off).

and before the outbreak of the Second Intifada. The second is from 2001 to 2009, where the impact of the Second Intifada from 2001–2005 is clear and then from 2006–2009 when Palestinian-Israeli relations become more stable. The third phase is from 2010 to 2013, when a significant shortage of rain affected the area. Overall the figure captures the effects of the Oslo agreement on trade, evident in the remarkable increase in VW imports. During the Second Intifada, Palestinian VW exports and imports declined. The end of the Second Intifada meant a gradual recovery in trade and VW imports. From 2009–2010, both internal water use and VW imports decline, suggesting that perhaps they were affected by the prolonged absence of rainfall. Overall, during the analysed period, Israel has been Palestine's main VW trade partner,[55] with the exception of the Second Intifada years, in which trade relations between Israel and Palestine declined significantly.[56]

Prior to the Oslo Accords, the Israeli Administration controlled the affairs of the occupied Palestinian territory through direct military rule.[57] Following the Oslo Accords – i.e. the first phase of Figure 14 – this was institutionalised under the terms of the Paris Protocol. After the signature of Oslo Agreement in 1993, up to 1999, we can observe a significant increase in trade activities between Israel and the Palestinian Territories reflected in the increase of agricultural VW imports (Figure 14).

Agricultural VW exports have not experienced substantial growth, despite the fluctuation in the value of exports, with an initial increase after the Oslo Agreement (Figure 14). This can be attributed to Israel's system of complex trade regulations and procedures and its impact on exports of time-sensitive goods, such as agricultural products.[58] Overall, the agricultural VW exports during the entire analysed period remained at an average of 3% of the agricultural water use. This might seem a low percentage, but it is comparable to the export/import percentages computed for other Middle Eastern countries.[59] In this vein, the data shows that Palestinian exports of food products – and subsequently VW – to Israel is insignificant in contrast to the Palestinian market for Israeli food products exports.

---

55 US Agency for International Development (USAID), *Sector Report: Agriculture in West Bank/Gaza,* September 2002, http://pdf.usaid.gov/pdf_docs/Pnacu074.pdf.
56 Observatory of Economic Complexity (OEC), 'Trade balance statistics from Palestine', http://atlas.media.mit.edu/en/profile/country/pse/#Trade_Balance.
57 UNCTAD, *Report on UNCTAD Assistance.*
58 S. Djankov, C. Freund and C. Pham, 'Trading on time', *Review of Economics and Statistics* 92, 2010, pp. 166–73.
59 Chapagain and Hoekstra, 'Water footprints of nations'.

From 1997 to 2008, both the internal agricultural water use and the total cultivated area in the Palestinian Territories remained fairly constant.[60]

Trade relations between Israel and Palestine declined significantly during the Second Intifada (2000–2005). This decline was the result of severe border restrictions and the discriminatory treatment that Palestinian products received at Israeli ports.[61] The decrease in trade activities is reflected in the evolution of agricultural VW imports from 1999 to 2003, when we observe a decreasing trend in the process of agricultural VW imports, until 2004 when they gradually started to grow again.

In the third phase, from 2009 to 2010, internal agricultural use dropped by 50%. This significant decline is coupled with the fact that although from 1997 to 2008 the total cultivated area in the Territories remained fairly constant, the total cultivated area in Palestine decreased from 1,853,951 dunums (185,395 hectares) in the 2007/2008 season to 1,034,900 dunums (103,490 hectares) in the 2010/2011 season.[62] The reason for this decline is that following the shortfall in precipitation during several years, in 2009 the shortage of rain became a chronic event that compounded the water shortage situation in the Palestinian Territories[63] and resulted in the emergency decision of the European Commission to provide €6 million for food assistance to victims of water shortage in the occupied Palestinian territory.[64] In the rainy seasons during 2007–2011, the amount of rainfall in the West Bank was between 354 mm and 500 mm, compared to an average annual rainfall of 532 mm,[65] which constitutes only about 74% of the average annual rainfall in the West Bank.[66] In the year 2010, decreasing annual rainfall

---

60 PCBS, 'Land Use Statistics in the Palestinian Territory'.

61 Taghdisi-Rad, *The Political Economy of Aid in Palestine.*

62 Palestinian Central Bureau of Statistics (PCBS) and Palestinian Ministry of Agriculture, 'Agricultural Statistics Survey, 2010/2011', http://www.pcbs.gov.ps/pcbs-metadata-en-v4.2/index.php/catalog/159.

63 Food and Agriculture Organization of the United Nations (FAO) and United Nations Office for the Coordination of Humanitarian Affairs occupied Palestinian territory (OCHA), 'Drought Update in Rural West Bank 2009', http://www.fao.org/emergencies/resources/documents/resources-detail/en/c/173550/.

64 European Commission Aid Office, 'Occupied Palestinian territory and Syria: Commission allocates €6 million for drought victims. Report IP/09/923', Brussels 2009.

65 Palestinian Ministry of Agriculture, 'Rainfall Seasonal Report 2011', http://www.moa.gov.ps.

66 The analysed period includes several years with low rainfall (1999, 2001, 2004; see Gilmont, 2014). However, the only year in the entire analysed period that the shortage of rain is coupled with a significant decline in both the internal agricultural water use and total cultivated area in Palestine is 2010. In fact, Gilmont (2014, p. 79) suggests for Israel that

forced Palestinian farmers to intensify their use of available water resources.[67] Of course, droughts do not have a physical impact only; they also have social and political repercussions. The fact that Palestine's water use and agriculture, for example, are so vulnerable to natural water availability has to do with the limited irrigation infrastructure and reservoirs governed by Palestine, which in turn has to do with its economic and geographical isolation, and the control of regional infrastructures by Israel.

The noteworthy decline in internal agricultural water use during this third phase was initially compensated by VW imports (see Figure 14). Indeed, in 2010 the agricultural VW imports represented 90% of the internal agricultural water use, its maximum figure during the post-Oslo regime. Contrary to what could have been expected, from 2010 onwards the VW imports have continued to fall until 2013, the final year of data analysis. This reduction could be ascribed to the increase in the amount of international food aid received in Palestine during the drought years (which does not fall into the category of trade, and hence does not count as VW).

In summary, a contextualised analysis of the evolution of agricultural virtual water flows offers two key results. First, virtual water flows have not remained constant over time but have been profoundly affected by the political and social relations between Palestine and Israel. Environmental conditions also play a role, affecting the Palestinian agricultural sector that is already vulnerable and relies on limited water resources. The case of the 2009 shortage of rain illustrated Palestinian dependence on virtual water imports from Israel. Second, the controversial application of the Oslo Agreement has resulted in Israeli control over Palestinian trade and hence over virtual water flows, especially in agricultural products. The imposed trade integration between Israel and Palestine implies that Israel has remained the main virtual water trade partner for Palestine in the post-Oslo years, and that its position has been reinforced. The fact that from 1993 to 1999 an average of 80% of agricultural Palestinian imports came from Israel[68] confirms that from the signing of Oslo Accords to the beginning of Second Intifada in 2000 Israel was Palestine's main VW trade partner.

'by 2009–10, natural water supply had been reduced to the levels of the early 1960s'. This reduction in natural water supplied in the region has probably affected this decline.
67 F. Dweik, 'Changes of the Palestinian agricultural Land use under Drought', Applied Research Institute, Jerusalem 2011.
68 USAID, *Sector Report*.

Palestine: an emblematic place for studying the relationship between water and power

My analysis of the Oslo Agreement has shown that both the fictitious and enormous weight of Israel imports on the Palestinian economy is the result of trade restriction policies set by Israel, revealing an existing interest in halting the flow of agricultural virtual water exports and in diverting the flow of agricultural virtual water imports towards Israel. Paradoxically, the Oslo Accord was defined as the 'peace of markets', based on the idea that other aspects of the conflict (Palestinian refugees, the situation in Jerusalem or the settlements) would fall into place eventually.[69] Other voices, such as Naomi Klein, were more sceptical, claiming that 'when there will finally be peace between us (the Israelis) and the Palestinians, there will be a situation of dependence, of a structured lack of equality between the two entities'.[70] As this analysis has shown, Palestine's high level of dependency on trade with Israel reveals a continuation of the 'imposed integration' strategy that characterised the post-1967 economic regime.[71]

Ultimately, through contextualising the agricultural VW flows in Palestine, my research demonstrates that Palestinian dependence on VW imports is sustained by and organised through a combination of social processes on the one hand, and metabolic-ecological processes on the other. The different aspects of the institutional framework of the Oslo Accords that were examined – the administrative areas, the Oslo II Accords and the Paris Protocol – are embedded within the unequal power relations between Israel and Palestine that constitute critical institutional and political processes. The environmental conditions, such as the average annual rainfall in Palestine, also play a key role in understanding the complex processes that structure the water-agriculture-trade relationship that a study of agricultural VW flows brings to light. Only by considering the two dimensions together can we begin to understand the socio-natural relations that underpin and create flows, or non-flows, of virtual water in Palestine.

Bibliography

Allan, J., *The Middle East Water Question: Hydropolitics and the Global Economy*, London 2001.

---

69 N. Klein, *The Shock Doctrine,* London 2007.
70 Klein, *The Shock*, p. 430.
71 Arnon and Bamya, 'Twenty Years'.

Arnon, A. and S. Bamya, 'Twenty Years after Oslo and the Paris Protocol', *Economics and Politics in the Israeli Palestinian Conflict Jerusalem*, eds. Aix Group, Jerusalem 2015.

Bakker, K., 'Water: political, biopolitical, material', *Social Studies of Science* 42, 2012, pp. 616–23.

Barnes, J., 'Water, water everywhere but not a drop to drink: The false promise of virtual water', *Critique of Anthropology* 33, 2013, pp. 371–89.

Bank of Israel, 'Recent economic developments', August 2010, http://www.boi.org.il.

Beltrán, M. J. and E. Velázquez, 'The political ecology of virtual water in southern Spain', *International Journal of Urban and Regional Research* 39, 2015, pp. 1020–36.

Brooks, D. and J. Trottier, 'A modern agreement to share water between Israelis and Palestinians: the FoEME proposal', Bethlehem 2012, http://ecopeaceme.org/uploads/13411307571~%5E$%5E~Water_Agreement_FINAL.pdf.

Chapagain, A. and A. Hoekstra, 'Water footprints of nations', *Value of Water Research Report Series* 16, 2004, pp. 11, UNESCO: IHE, Institute for Water Education.

Chenoweth, J., Hadjikakou, M. and C. Zoumides, 'Quantifying the human impact on water resources: A critical review of the water footprint concept', *Hydrology and Earth System Science* 18, 2014, pp. 2325–42.

Djankov, S., Freund, C. and C. Pham, 'Trading on time', *Review of Economics and Statistics* 92, 2010, pp. 166–73.

Dweik, F., 'Changes of the Palestinian agricultural Land use under Drought', Applied Research Institute, Jerusalem 2011.

European Commission Aid Office, 'Occupied Palestinian territory and Syria: Commission allocates €6 million for drought victims. Report IP/09/923', Brussel 2009.

Falkenmark, M. and J. Rockström, 'The New Blue and Green Water Paradigm: Breaking New Ground for Water Resources Planning and Management', *Journal of Water Resources Planning and Management* 132, 2006, pp. 129–32.

Food and Agriculture Organization of the United Nations (FAO), 'Occupied Palestinian Territory. Water Use', 2016, http://www.fao.org/nr/water/aquastat/countries_regions/Profile_segments/PSE-WU_eng.stm.

Food and Agriculture Organization of the United Nations (FAO) and United Nations Office for the Coordination of Humanitarian Affairs in occupied Palestinian territory (OCHA), 'Drought Update in Rural West Bank 2009',

February 2009, http://www.fao.org/emergencies/resources/documents/
resources-detail/en/c/173550/.

Forsyth, T., *Critical Political Ecology. The Politics of Environmental Science*,
London 2003.

Gilmont, M., 'Decoupling dependence on natural water: reflexivity in the
regulation and allocation of water in Israel', *Water Policy* 16, 2014, pp.
79–101.

Haj Khalil, M., *Guide to Palestine-Israel Economic and Trade Relations*, Czech
Representative Office, Jerusalem 2009, http://www.mzv.cz/file/806096/
Guide_to_Palestine___Israel_Economic_and_Trade_Relations___Czech_
Rep_Office.pdf.

Hamdi, P., 'The effects of virtual water trade on the future water management in
Palestine', Master Thesis, An-Najah National University Palestine 2014.

Hoekstra, A. and A. Chapagain, *Globalization of Water: Sharing the Planet's
Freshwater Resources,* Oxford 2008.

Klein, N., *The Shock Doctrine,* London 2007.

Linton, J. and J. Budds, 'The hydrosocial cycle: Defining and mobilizing a
relational-dialectical approach to water', *Geoforum* 57, 2014, pp. 170–80.

Lonergan, S. and D. Brooks, *Watershed: The Role of Fresh Water in the Israeli-
Palestinian Conflict*, Ottawa 1994.

Nassar, Y., 'Virtual water trade as a policy instrument for achieving water
security in Palestine', *Water Resources in the Middle East. Israeli-
Palestinian Water Issues – From Conflict to Cooperation*, eds. H. I. Shuval
and S. Dweik, Berlin 2007, pp. 141– 6.

Nazer, D., M. Siebel, P. Van der Zaag, Z. Mimi and H. Gijzen, 'Water Footprint
of the Palestinians in the West Bank', *Journal of the American Water
Resources Association* 44, 2008, pp. 449–58.

Observatory of Economic Complexity (OEC), 'Trade balance statistics from
Palestine', http://atlas.media.mit.edu/en/profile/country/pse/#Trade_Balance.

Office of the Quartet Representative, 'Back to the Future: Integrating the
Political and Economic Tracks', Brussels 2013, http://unispal.un.org/pdfs/
AHLC_OQR-PolicyRpt.pdf.

Palestinian Central Bureau of Statistics (PCBS), 'Agricultural Statistics 1993–
2008', http://www.pcbs.gov.ps/.

Palestinian Central Bureau of Statistics (PCBS), 'Land Use Statistics in the
Palestinian Territory, 1997–2008', http://www.pcbs.gov.ps/.

Palestinian Central Bureau of Statistics (PCBS) and Palestinian Ministry of Agriculture, 'Agricultural Statistics Survey, 2010/2011', http://www.pcbs. gov.ps/pcbs-metadata-en-v4.2/index.php/catalog/159.

Palestinian Ministry of Agriculture, 'Rainfall Seasonal Report 2011', http://www.moa.gov.ps.

Palestinian Ministry of Economy and the Applied Research Institute Jerusalem, *The Economic Costs of the Israeli Occupation for the Occupied Palestinian Territory*, Jerusalem 2011, http://www.arij.org/.

Selby, J., 'Cooperation, domination and colonisation: The Israeli-Palestinian Joint Water Committee', *Water Alternatives* 6, 2013, pp. 1–24.

Selby, J., 'Dependence, Independence and Interdependence in the Palestinian water sector', *Birzeit University Working Paper* 45, 2011, http://ssrn.com/ abstract=2127973.

Selby, J., 'Dressing up domination as "cooperation": The case of Israeli-Palestinian water relations', *Review of International Studies* 29, 2003, pp. 21–38.

Swyngedouw, E., 'Circulations and Metabolisms: (Hybrid) Natures and (Cyborg) Cities', *Science as Culture* 2, 2006, pp. 105–21.

Swyngedouw, E., 'The Political Economy and Political Ecology of the Hydro-Social Cycle', *Journal of Contemporary Water Research & Education* 142, 2009, pp. 56–60.

Taghdisi-Rad, S., *The Political Economy of Aid in Palestine: Relief from Conflict or Development Delayed?*, London 2011.

Trottier, J., 'A wall, water and power: the Israeli "separation fence"', *Review of International Studies* 33, 2007, pp. 105–27.

United Nations Conference on Trade and Development (UNCTAD), 'Report on UNCTAD assistance to the Palestinian people: Developments in the economy of the occupied Palestinian territory', Jerusalem 2011, http://www.unctad.org.

United Nations Conference on Trade and Development (UNCTAD), 'Report on UNCTAD assistance to the Palestinian people: Developments in the economy of the occupied Palestinian territory', Jerusalem 2012, http://www.unctad.org.

United Nations Office for the Coordination of Humanitarian Affairs in occupied Palestinian territory (OCHA), 'West Bank movement and access. Update 2011', Jerusalem 2011, http://www.ocha.org.

United Nations Office for the Coordination of Humanitarian Affairs in occupied Palestinian territory (OCHA), 'Humanitarian Fact Sheet on the Jordan Valley and Dead Sea Area', Jerusalem 2012, http://www.ocha.org.

US Agency for International Development (USAID), 'Sector Report: Agriculture in West Bank/Gaza', September 2002, http://pdf.usaid.gov/pdf_docs/Pnacu074.pdf.

Velázquez, E., C. Madrid and M. J. Beltrán, 'Rethinking the concepts of virtual water and water footprint in relation to the production-consumption binomial and the water-energy nexus', *Water Resources Management* 25, 2011, pp. 743–61.

Wichelns, D., 'Virtual water and water footprints offer limited insight regarding important policy questions', *International Journal of Water Resources Development* 26, 2010, pp. 639–51.

Wichelns, D., 'Virtual water and water footprints: Overreaching into the discourse on sustainability, efficiency, and equity', *Water Alternatives* 8, 2015, pp. 396–414.

World Bank, 'Assessment of Restrictions on Palestinian Water Sector Development, Sector Note for West Bank and Gaza', Washington, DC 2009.

9

Renewable Deployment in the MENA Region: Growth Effects and Explaining Factors

Philipp Dees and Georgeta Vidican Auktor

Renewables in the MENA

Because of its geographical location, the MENA region has high potential for electricity generation from renewable energy sources.[1] Yet, electricity generation from renewable sources remains at a low level across the region, with only Morocco, Syria and Turkey generating ten per cent or more of their total electricity production from renewables in recent years; for Syria, the high share is a consequence of the civil war, the last pre-war value was far below ten per cent. Among the renewable energy sources, hydropower has the highest share in generation. Only ten MENA countries reported electricity generation from other renewable sources than hydro in 2014, and Morocco was the first country in the region to pass the threshold of five per cent of electricity generation from non-hydro renewables in 2013; Turkey followed in 2014.

---

1 Our definition of the MENA region includes the following countries: Algeria, Bahrain, Egypt, Iran, Iraq, Israel, Jordan, Kuwait, Lebanon, Libya, Morocco, Oman, Palestine (West Bank and Gaza), Qatar, Saudi Arabia, Syria, Tunisia, United Arab Emirates, Yemen. Following the definition of the US Energy Information Administration, 'renewable sources' include biomass, hydro, geothermal, solar, wind, ocean thermal, wave action and tidal action.

Meanwhile, MENA countries face rising energy demand, calling for a rapid expansion of their electricity generation capacity. The rich endowment with renewables opens opportunities for using local resources to cover increasing demand. This might be advantageous for two reasons: first, dependency on fossil fuels makes the economy of energy-importing countries vulnerable, for example due to rising energy prices, while for the energy exporting countries, higher domestic consumption means lower revenues from oil and gas exports; second, abundant renewable energy resources could offer an opportunity for MENA countries to meet COP21 targets in a cost-effective way.[2]

Until now, however, deployment of renewables has been rather low in the MENA region. One major reason for this underperformance relates to the potential trade-offs between the high investment costs for renewable energy generation and economic growth.[3] The effects of renewable electricity generation on growth have been widely discussed in academic literature in recent years, as one aspect of the energy-growth literature. However, only limited research on this relationship exists within the regional context of MENA (see the next section for an overview of the literature).

Our analysis seeks to contribute to the debate on the renewables-growth nexus with a specific focus on the MENA region. In contrast to earlier research, we consider not only electricity generation from renewables, but also generation capacity. Our reason for this choice is the potential negative impact on economic growth caused by shifting investments away from other sectors to renewables. As increasing generation capacity is highly capital intensive, the economic effect – if

---

2 Several studies exploring decarbonisation strategies in the region point out that the use of renewables means that 'a near complete decarbonization of the power sector can be achieved at moderate costs' (M. Haller, S. Ludig and N. Bauer, 'Decarbonization scenarios for the EU and MENA power system: Considering spatial distribution and short term dynamics of renewable generation', *Energy Policy* 47, 2012, pp. 282–290, doi:10.1016/j. enpol.2012.04.069); see, as well, C. Karakosta and J. Psarras, 'Understanding CDM potential in the Mediterranean basin: A country assessment of Egypt and Morocco', *Energy Policy* 60, 2013, pp. 827–39, doi:10.1016/j.enpol.2013.05.078; N. Supersberger and L. Führer, 'Integration of renewable energies and nuclear power into North African Energy Systems: An analysis of energy import and export effects', *Energy Policy* 39.8, 2011, 4458–65, doi:10.1016/j.enpol.2010.12.046; and German Aerospace Center, 'Concentrating Solar Power for the Mediterranean Region. Final Report', Stuttgart 2005, http://www.dlr.de/Portaldata/1/Resources/portal_news/newsarchiv2008_1/algerien_med_csp.pdf.
3 One example that points to the high initial investments is M. El Fadel *et al*, 'Emissions reduction and economic implications of renewable energy market penetration of power generation for residential consumption in the MENA region', *Energy Policy* 52, 2013, pp. 618–27, doi:10.1016/j.enpol.2012.10.015.

it exists – should appear when capacity is expanded, and not when generation increases while capacity is constant.

We begin inquiry into the renewables-growth nexus by applying panel estimation methods on a panel of 12 MENA countries over a period from 1990 to 2014. We did not have all necessary data to add the remaining eight MENA countries to the panel. Our main finding in this phase is that capacity expansion has no negative impact on growth, and that an increase of generation from renewables even appears to impact growth positively. Next, we assess the factors which explain differences in the deployment of renewable electricity technologies in the MENA region. We have identified that countries with larger oil reserves show a slower progress in renewable energy deployment, while countries with a higher GDP per capita, larger gas reserves, stronger legal rights and a more autocratic regime show a faster progress.

The general outline of the chapter is as follows: in the next section, we provide an overview of the literature relevant for our research, followed by an overview of our data and methodology, before presenting the results on the renewable-growth nexus. We then turn to the factors explaining renewables deployment in the region and finish with a conclusion and a short discussion on policy implications.

Literature review

Energy-growth literature has expanded rapidly during the last decades. An overview of various papers and their results on the energy-growth nexus can be found, for example, in Iyke,[4] and a recent meta-study was conducted by Menegaki.[5]

The nexus between renewable energy and growth has become an important branch of the energy-growth literature during the last years. In his meta-analysis, Sebri found 40 studies with 153 settings examining this topic up to December 2013, including working papers and some grey literature. He shows that the studies come to different conclusions with respect to the renewables-growth nexus and the direction it is taking. These differences are due to model specification, time frame and the level of development in the countries considered. With regard to the latter, he shows how for both developed and developing countries the probability

---

4 B. N. Iyke, 'Electricity consumption and economic growth in Nigeria: A revisit of the energy-growth debate', *Energy Economics* 51, 2015, pp. 166–76, doi:10.1016/j. eneco.2015.05.024.
5 A. N. Menegaki, 'On energy consumption and GDP studies; A meta-analysis of the last two decades', *Renewable and Sustainable Energy Reviews* 29, 2014, pp. 31–6, doi:10.1016/j. rser.2013.08.081.

of discovering a positive trend that indicates a correlation between renewables and growth is higher when countries are grouped into different panels with respect to their stage of development, as opposed to panels including countries in various stages of development.[6]

One of the most recent studies on the energy-growth nexus in the MENA region is Kayıkçı and Bildirici, which assesses the connection between output, electricity consumption and oil rents. They find that higher electricity consumption leads to higher GDP growth for most resource-rich countries in their sample, while the causality is reversed for most of the countries with low natural resources.[7] Tang and Abosedra also show a positive correlation between energy consumption and economic growth, with tourism, gross capital formation and political stability as explanatory variables besides energy consumption. Their results hold for different estimation techniques (pooled OLS, random and fixed effects, fixed effects with panel corrected standard errors and one- and two-step dynamic GMM).[8] Farhani focusses on the links between renewable energy consumption, growth and CO_2 emissions. He finds no causal linkage between renewables and GDP in the short run, while GDP growth has influence on renewable energy consumption in the long run; the sign, however, differs within countries and is not significant for the overall panel.[9] We reviewed several other studies focusing on individual countries, panels including some MENA countries, and some that used other energy or environmental variables than renewable electricity. We will not discuss these findings here as their results do not differ much from the papers discussed above.[10]

6 M. Sebri, 'Use renewables to be cleaner: Meta-analysis of the renewable energy consumption–economic growth nexus', *Renewable and Sustainable Energy Reviews* 42, 2015, pp. 657–65, doi:10.1016/j.rser.2014.10.042.
7 F. Kayıkçı and M. E. Bildirici, 'Economic Growth and Electricity Consumption in GCC and MENA Countries', *South African Journal of Economics* 83.2, 2015, http://onlinelibrary.wiley.com/doi/10.1111/saje.12061/epdf.
8 C. F. Tang and S. Abosedra, 'The impacts of tourism, energy consumption and political instability on economic growth in the MENA countries', *Energy Policy* 68, 2014, pp. 456–64, doi:10.1016/j.enpol.2014.01.004.
9 S. Farhani, 'Renewable Energy Consumption, Economic Growth and CO2 Emissions: Evidence from Selected MENA Countries', *Energy Economics Letters* 1.2, 2013, http://ssrn.com/abstract=2294995.
10 M. Abid and R. Mraihi, 'Disaggregate Energy Consumption Versus Economic Growth in Tunisia: Cointegration and Structural Break Analysis', *Journal of the Knowledge Economy* 6.4, 2015, pp. 1104–22, doi:10.1007/s13132-014-0189-4; A. Omri *et al*, 'Financial development, environmental quality, trade and economic growth: What causes what in MENA countries', *Energy Economics* 48, 2015, pp. 242–52, doi:10.1016/j.eneco.2015.01.008; H. Hamdi and R. Sbia, 'The Dynamic Relationship between CO2 Emissions, Energy Usage and Growth in Gulf Cooperation Council (GCC) Countries: An Aggregated Analysis', *Economie Appliquee*

None of the mentioned studies include capital and labour as explanatory variables for growth, although economic theory counts them as important variables, which is the reason why we have included these factors in our model.[11] Most often they replace energy consumption in the growth function by a renewable energy variable, but do not consider energy and renewables.[12] We consider this to be potentially misleading: if an increase of energy consumption would have a positive impact on growth, the renewable variable could proxy this and a potentially negative effect running from renewables on growth might then be discovered. For this reason, we decided to add energy and renewable electricity to our model.

The studies we reviewed do not offer in-depth explanations for why or whether MENA countries use renewable energy resources. They normally focus on assessing if there is a positive impact from renewables on growth or not. Although there are some papers that discuss development factors concerning energy systems and the use of renewable energy in the MENA region,[13] none identifies the components

---

67.2, 2014; A. A. Naji Meidani and M. Zabihi, 'Energy Consumption and Real GDP in Iran', *International Journal of Energy Economics and Policy* 4.1, 2014, pp. 15–25; H. Mohammadi and S. Parvaresh, 'Energy consumption and output: Evidence from a panel of 14 oil-exporting countries', *Energy Economics* 41, 2014, pp. 41–6, doi:10.1016/j.eneco.2013.11.002; M. I. Shahateet, K. A. Al-Majali and F. Al-Hahabashneh, 'Causality and Cointegration between Economic Growth and Energy Consumption: Econometric Evidence from Jordan', *International Journal of Economics and Finance* 6.10, 2014, doi:10.5539/ijef.v6n10p270; U. Al-Mulali and C. N. C. Sab, 'Energy consumption, pollution and economic development in 16 emerging countries', *Journal of Economic Studies* 40.5, 2013, pp. 686–98, doi:10.1108/JES-05-2012-0055; A. Omri, 'CO_2 emissions, energy consumption and economic growth nexus in MENA countries: Evidence from simultaneous equations models', *Energy Economics* 40, 2013, pp. 657–64, doi:10.1016/j.eneco.2013.09.003; B. Ozcan, 'The nexus between carbon emissions, energy consumption and economic growth in Middle East countries: A panel data analysis', *Energy Policy* 62, 2013, pp. 1138–47, doi:10.1016/j.enpol.2013.07.016; M. E. H. Arouri *et al*, 'Energy consumption, economic growth and CO_2 emissions in Middle East and North African countries', *Energy Policy* 45, 2012, pp. 342–9, doi:10.1016/j.enpol.2012.02.042; H. Abbasinejad, G. F. Yazdan and E. Asghari Ghara, 'The Relationship between Energy Consumption, Energy Prices and Economic Growth: Case Study (OPEC Countries)', *OPEC Energy Review* 36.3, 2012; and O. D. Sweidan, 'Energy Consumption and Real Output: New Evidence from the UAE', *OPEC Energy Review* 36.3, 2012.
11 Some studies focusing on other regions use capital and labour. For example, N. Apergis and J. E. Payne, 'Renewable energy consumption and economic growth: Evidence from a panel of OECD countries', *Energy Policy* 38, 2010, doi:10.1016/j.enpol.2009.09.002.
12 See, for example, M. S. Ben Aïssa, M. Ben Jebli and S. Ben Youssef, 'Output, renewable energy consumption and trade in Africa', *Energy Policy* 66, 2014, pp. 11–18, doi:10.1016/j.enpol.2013.11.023; Farhani, 'Renewable Energy Consumption, Economic Growth and CO_2 Emissions: Evidence from Selected MENA Countries'; and Apergis and Payne, 'Renewable energy consumption and economic growth: Evidence from a panel of OECD countries'.
13 Such as I. Ruble and P. Nader, 'Transforming shortcomings into opportunities: Can

of renewable deployment using econometric methods. We see this as a gap in the literature and we emphasise the need for further research.

When analysing other regions, countries or groups of countries, some studies employ econometric methods to explain renewable energy deployment. Among these are Ackah and Kizys, who investigate oil-producing countries in Africa;[14] Pfeiffer and Mulder, with a focus on 108 developing countries' deployment of non-hydro renewable energy technologies;[15] and Eyraud *et al* who study 35 developed and emerging countries and focus on renewables, but also on energy efficiency.[16] The variables used in these studies differ, but their results are to a certain degree aligned. Eyraud *et al* argued that, among other variables considered, a sound financial system resulting in low interest rates, high prices for fossil fuels and feed-in-tariffs stimulates deployment of renewable energy and energy efficiency technologies. For Pfeiffer and Mulder (2013), per capita income, regulatory instruments, democratic and stable regimes and schooling has a positive influence on renewable deployment, while among others a high fossil fuel production hinders it. Ackah and Kizys confirm the findings of Pfeiffer and Mulder on income and energy prices and to a certain extent fossil fuel production, and they further maintain that depletion of fossil fuel resources is a driving factor behind renewable energy deployment.

---

market incentives solve Lebanon's energy crisis?', *Energy Policy* 39.5, 2011, pp. 2467–74, doi:10.1016/j.enpol.2011.02.011, for Lebanon; A. Boudghene Stambouli, 'Algerian renewable energy assessment: The challenge of sustainability', *Energy Policy* 39.8, 2011, pp. 4507–19, doi:10.1016/j.enpol.2010.10.005, for Algeria; and Z. Abdmouleh, R. A. Alammari and A. Gastli, 'Recommendations on renewable energy policies for the GCC countries', *Renewable and Sustainable Energy Reviews* 50, 2015, pp. 1181–91, doi:10.1016/j.rser.2015.05.057; D. Reiche, 'Energy Policies of Gulf Cooperation Council (GCC) countries – possibilities and limitations of ecological modernization in rentier states', *Energy Policy* 38.5, 2010, pp. 2395–2403, doi:10.1016/j.enpol.2009.12.031; and K. D. Patlitzianas, H. Doukas and J. Psarras, 'Enhancing renewable energy in the Arab States of the Gulf: Constraints & efforts', *Energy Policy* 34.18, 2006, pp. 3719–26, doi:10.1016/j.enpol.2005.08.018, for the GCC countries.

14 I. Ackah and R. Kizys, 'Green growth in oil producing African countries: A panel data analysis of renewable energy demand', *Renewable and Sustainable Energy Reviews* 50, 2015, pp. 1157–66, doi:10.1016/j.rser.2015.05.030.

15 B. Pfeiffer and P. Mulder, 'Explaining the diffusion of renewable energy technology in developing countries', *Energy Economics* 40, 2013, pp. 285–96, doi:10.1016/j.eneco.2013.07.005.

16 L. Eyraud *et al*, 'Who's going green and why? Trends and Determinants of Green Investment', IMF Working Paper 11/296, Washington, DC 2011, http://www.imf.org/external/pubs/ft/wp/2011/wp11296.pdf.

Data and methodology

Table 1 lists the variables we have used, data sources and their range and units. Our dataset covers the years 1990 to 2014, but data is missing for some countries and some years, making our panel unbalanced.

For the energy-renewables-growth nexus, we estimate a variation of the neoclassical growth model, explaining the output (Y) by a Cobb-Douglas function of the input factors, which are here energy (E), capital (C), labour (L) and electricity generated from renewable sources (RE_G) and the capacity available for this generation (RE_C); in addition, there is a factor measuring total productivity (B_0):

$$Y = B_0 C^{\beta C} L^{\beta L} E^{\beta E} RE^{\beta RE}$$

RE ('renewable electricity') implies our use of either RE_G or RE_C, depending on the specification.

For the estimations, we transform the equation to logarithms, obtaining therefore a linear function. Moreover, as unit-root testing shows that the logged variables are integrated of order 1, we use the first differences to obtain the equation below where lower-case letters indicate logs and Δ indicates the first differences:

$$\Delta y = \beta_0 + \beta_c \Delta c + \beta_L \Delta l + \beta_E \Delta e + \beta_{RE} \Delta re$$

The use of first differences due to the non-stationarity of our variables means that we are explaining the GDP growth rate through the growth of inputs into the production function, so we are not estimating elasticities.[17] However, using logarithms and first differences leads to loss of data: for all countries reporting a value of zero for one of the variables (most often for renewable electricity), using the logarithm transformation creates a missing value, as the logarithm of zero is not defined. In addition, gaps greater than one year in data reporting (which occurs in the MENA region particularly with respect to gross fixed capital formation) excludes those countries from the panel, as first differences obviously need two consecutive data points in order to be calculated. This results in only 12 countries remaining on the panel: Algeria, Bahrain, Egypt, Iran, Israel, Jordan, Lebanon, Morocco, Saudi Arabia, Tunisia, Turkey and the United Arab Emirates (UAE).

---

17 The first difference, $\ln(x_t) - \ln(x_{t-1})$, can be transformed to $\ln(xt: x_{t-1})$, where $xt: x_{t-1}$ is the growth rate of x, and moreover, for growth rates between 0.9 and 1.1, the natural logarithm of the growth rates equals approximately the percentage change of x. Elasticities would be the resulting percentage change of the output, if one input factor is changed by one per cent; this would be the result if we use the logged variables in levels and not in first differences.

Table 1: Used Variables and data sources

Variable	Description	Source	Range/Unit
Y	GDP	World Development Indicators (WDI)	Constant 2010 US$
C	Gross fixed capital formation	WDI	Constant 2010 US$
L	Total labour force	WDI	Number of people
E	Energy use	WDI	kt of oil equivalent
RE_G	Electricity generation from renewable sources	US Energy Information Administration (EIA)	TWh
RE_C	Available capacity for electricity generation from renewable sources	EIA	GW
$Y:N$	GDP per capita	WDI	Constant 2010 US$
E_{imp}	Share of Energy Imports	WDI	Percentage of energy use (negative values for energy exporting countries)
FIT	Existence of a feed-in-tariff scheme	International Energy Agency	0 or 1
Res_{Oil}	Proved oil reserves	EIA	Billion barrels
Res_{Gas}	Proved reserves of natural gas	EIA	Billion barrels
p_{Oil}	Spot price of crude oil	[a]	US$ per million btu
p_{Gas}	Spot price of Natural gas	[a]	US$ per million btu
$p_{fuel}:p_{Oil}$	Relation between pump price for gasoline (US$ per litre) and spot price of crude oil (US$ per million btu) – as proxy for fossil fuel subsidies	Own calculation with data from WDI (gasoline price)[a]	
Reg	Regime	(recoded)[b]	0 (autocratic) to 100 (democratic)
$Right$	Property Rights	[c]	Index from 0 to 100 (best)
$Free_{Cor}$	Freedom from Corruption	[c]	Index from 0 to 100 (best)
$Free_{Bus}$	Business Freedom	[c]	Index from 0 to 100 (best)
$Free_{Fin}$	Financial Freedom	[c]	Index from 0 to 100 (best)
$Free_{Inv}$	Investment Freedom	[c]	Index from 0 to 100 (best)
N	Population	WDI	Number of people
β_0	Constant		

a) BP, 'BP Statistical Review of World Energy 2015', London 2015, http://www.bp.com/content/dam/bp/pdf/energy-economics/statistical-review-2015/bp-statistical-review-of-world-energy-2015-full-report.pdf.
b) Marshall, Gurr and Jaggers, 'Polity IV project. Political Regime Characteristics and Transistions, 1800-2013'.
c) Miller and Kim, '2015 Index of Economic Freedom'.

We estimate equation 2 for the panel, using country fixed effects and robust standard errors clustered on the country level. We set up several subpanels: as Sebri,[18] or for example Kahsai *et al*,[19] indicate in their research the growth effect of renewables may depend on level of development, hence we set up a panel that only includes countries classified as middle-income countries by the World Bank (combining the upper middle and the lower middle-income category of the World Bank); due to data restrictions, we cannot show results for the high-income countries in the region, and no country in the region is classified as 'low income'. One other aspect discussed in the literature is that the impact of renewable electricity on growth might depend on the country's resources, particularly oil.[20] For this reason, in our subpanels we differentiate between oil exporting and non-oil exporting countries. And a third instrumental aspect might be geography, so we set up subpanels to separate the North African countries from the Middle Eastern countries.

To identify factors for renewable energy deployment, we again use a model with country-fixed effects and robust, clustered standard errors. As we want to explain success in renewable energy deployment, we use the increase of capacity available for electricity generation from renewable sources as a dependent variable, measured as the first difference of the logarithmised renewables capacity. This dependent variable is explained by several factors that are part of the vector X (with β as the corresponding vector of coefficients):

$$\Delta re_c = \beta X$$

For X, we considered numerous variables in different combinations, mostly following how those variables were used in the literature (see section 2). We excluded those variables that did not have a significant effect on one of our (sub-) panels and did not improve the quality of the model. The remaining variables included in our model, their respective sources and units are listed in Table 1. Variables that we considered but finally dropped, as they did not improve the model, consisted of FDI inflows (as proxy for the openness of the economy), CO_2

---

18 Sebri, 'Use renewables to be cleaner'.

19 M. S. Kahsai *et al*, 'Income level and the energy consumption–GDP nexus: Evidence from Sub-Saharan Africa', *Energy Economics* 34.3, 2012, pp. 739–46, doi:10.1016/j.eneco.2011.06.006.

20 See, for example, Mohammadi and Parvaresh, 'Energy consumption and output'; and O. Damette and M. Seghir, 'Energy as a driver of growth in oil exporting countries?', *Energy Economics* 37, 2013, pp. 193–99, doi:10.1016/j.eneco.2012.12.011.

emissions (absolute and per capita), the consumer price index, interest rates (all from the World Development Indicators database), solar irradiation, wind full load hours,[21] and World Heritage Foundation's Economic Freedom indices, including the overall score.[22]

Two groups of variables need further explanation as their use and structure is not common knowledge:

1. Our regime variable (Reg) is the polity variable of Marshall *et al.*[23] It combines several indicators for institutionalised democracy and institutionalised autocracy. This combination is reflected on a scale from -10 to $+10$, with -10 indicating a strong autocratic and $+10$ indicating a strong democratic regime (see the codebook in Marshall *et al* for further explanations on the construction and the underlying indices). For an easier interpretation, we recoded the variable at a range from 0 to 100.

2. The indices for economic freedom from Miller and Kim,[24] Right, $Free_{Bus}$, $Free_{Cor}$, $Free_{Fin}$ and $Free_{Inv}$, are all constructed similarly. By exploring several resources, Miller and Kim place the countries on a scale running from 0 to 100, with 100 indicating perfect freedom. For example, for the strength of property rights, they consider 'the extent to which a country's legal framework allows individuals to freely accumulate private property, secured by clear laws that are enforced effectively by the government'.[25] A score of 100 would mean that those rights are guaranteed perfectly for all the five dimensions they consider in this context, which consist of: physical property rights, intellectual property rights, strength of investor protection, risk of expropriation and quality of land administration. Further explanation on the construction of the economic freedom variables and the underlying data sources can be found in the 'About the index' section of Miller and Kim.[26]

---

21 Both from German Aerospace Center, 'Concentrating Solar Power for the Mediterranean Region. Final Report', p. 57.
22 T. Miller and A. B. Kim, '2015 Index of Economic Freedom', The Heritage Foundation, *The Wallstreet Journal*, Washington, DC 2015, http://heritage.org/index/explore.
23 M. G. Marshall, T. R. Gurr and K. Jaggers, 'Polity IV project. Political Regime Characteristics and Transitions, 1800–2013', (Center for Systematic Peace, Vienna, Virginia 2014), http://www.systemicpeace.org/inscrdata.html.
24 Miller and Kim, '2015 Index of Economic Freedom'.
25 Ibid.
26 Ibid.

A better availability of data allows us to include two more countries in the panel (Libya and Qatar), while the time span is shortened, as some data is only available from 1995 onwards. Our consideration for setting up subpanels is the same as discussed above for the renewables-growth model. We present an additional subpanel for the high-income countries, as we have sufficient data here.

Results: renewables and growth

Table 3 shows the results for estimations of the growth function (equation 2) for our MENA panel and the subpanels. For the sake of comparison, we estimated the same function for a worldwide panel and two subpanels, non-OECD countries and middle-income countries (Table 2). As mentioned earlier, in our analysis we differentiate between renewable electricity generation (RE_G) and installed renewable capacity (RE_C).

Table 2: Renewables-growth estimates for a worldwide setting

	All Countries		Non-OECD		Middle-income	
	Δre_G	Δre_C	Δre_G	Δre_C	Δre_G	Δre_C
Δc	***0.1401	***0.1383	***0.1310	***0.1289	***0.1443	***0.1441
Δl	*0.1085	**0.1191	0.0807	0.0940	0.0327	0.0316
Δe	***0.1808	***0.1831	***0.1836	***0.1870	***0.1899	***0.1880
Δre_G	***0.0079		**0.0073		***0.0117	
Δre_C		**0.0058		*0.0065		*0.0066
β_0	***0.0227	***0.0226	***0.0260	***0.0065	***0.0260	***0.0262
Observations	2,505	2,514	1,819	1,828	1,429	1,436
Number of countries included in the model	130	130	107	107	74	74

*** indicates significance on a 1 per cent level, ** on 5 per cent and * on 10 per cent.

In our estimations we did not identify any negative effects on growth from either an increase of generation using renewable sources (Δre_G) or from an expansion of renewable capacity (Δre_C). On the contrary, there is evidence for a positive relationship between renewable generation and growth, as the estimated coefficient is significantly positive for the overall panel, the oil-exporting and the middle-income subpanel. This effect is remarkably higher than the worldwide estimates.

We do not address causality in a more in-depth manner and hence emphasise that the positive linkage between renewables and growth might be bi-directional or reverse. But some basic tests which we have conducted point to a causality existing between renewables and growth.

Regarding the other input factors, only the estimates for capital are significant for our MENA panels, and they tend to be higher than worldwide estimates. The estimates for the labour force fluctuate, but do not significantly go above zero (other than in the worldwide panel, where the estimates are significantly positive for the all-countries estimation), and energy use is not significant either (in contrast to the worldwide panel, where it is positive for the overall panel and all subpanels).

As mentioned in the introduction, one concern is that the relatively high investments for renewable capacity might divert capital from other profitable investments in the region. The insignificant influence of renewable capacity expansion on growth does not confirm this hypothesis. Renewable capacity expansion is neutral with respect to growth.

Expanding renewable generation might even enhance growth as renewable generation and GDP are positively linked in the MENA region. This raises the question as to why deployment of renewables remains low in the region. We discuss this in the next section.

Results: factors affecting renewable deployment in the MENA region

Table 4 shows the results of our estimation for factors influencing renewable deployment in the MENA region and its different subpanels. We now focus on increasing renewable capacity (Δre_c), since deployment is measured better as an increase in capacity rather than changes in generation (the latter might fluctuate between years merely because of different weather conditions). Our main interest is to identify which variables are significant and to discuss their signs. The size of the estimated coefficients should be interpreted with great care as it strongly depends on the values and ranges of the underlying variables that are partly not metric.

For the overall panel, we can identify GDP per capita, the proved gas reserves and the strength of property rights as variables with a positive impact on RE deployment. The first factor indicates that investing in renewables might be easier for wealthier countries, as they have more capital available for the high initial investments. The last point suggests that those high investments will only be undertaken by private actors if they can be guaranteed to earn returns on their investments and do not have to fear expropriation. The significantly positive coefficient for gas resources interacts with the significantly negative coefficient for oil reserves. The latter coefficient is higher than the first, so that in total resource rich

Table 3: Renewables-growth estimates for the MENA region

	MENA[a]		Oil Exporting[b]		Non-oil Exporting[c]		Middle-income[d]		North Africa[e]		Middle East[f]	
	Δre_G	Δre_C	Δre_G	Δre_C	Δre_G	Δre_C	Δre_G	Δre_C	Δre_G	Δre_C	Δre_G	Δre_C
Δc	***0.1887	***0.1872	**0.1733	**0.1618	***0.1924	***0.2029	***0.1974	***0.2013	**0.1291	**0.1065	***0.2088	***0.2081
Δl	−0.0537	−0.0058	0.0075	0.1046	−0.0802	−0.1003	−0.0953	−0.0820	−0.2001	−0.2231	0.0111	0.0739
Δe	0.0679	0.0628	−0.0523	−0.0456	0.1113	0.0946	0.0565	0.0568	0.1009	0.1149	0.0497	0.0452
Δre_G	*0.0156		*0.0122		0.0184		*0.0180		0.0173		0.0085	
Δre_C		0.0069		0.0118		0.0017		0.0040		−0.0004		0.0071
β_0	***0.0295	***0.0290	***0.0302	***0.0278	***0.0303	***0.0320	***0.0303	***0.0304	***0.0316	***0.0335	***0.0301	***0.0281
Observations	216	219	82	85	134	134	187	187	95	95	121	124
Number of countries included in the model	12	12	6	6	6	6	8	8	4	4	8	8

*** indicates significance at a 1 per cent level, ** at 5 per cent and * at 10 per cent.

a)   Included countries: Algeria, Bahrain, Egypt, Iran, Israel, Jordan, Lebanon, Morocco, Saudi Arabia, Tunisia, Turkey, United Arab Emirates.

b)   Algeria, Bahrain, Egypt, Iran, Saudi Arabia, United Arab Emirates.

c)   Israel, Jordan, Lebanon, Morocco, Tunisia, Turkey.

d)   Algeria, Egypt, Iran, Jordan, Lebanon, Morocco, Tunisia, Turkey.

e)   Algeria, Egypt, Morocco, Tunisia.

f)   Bahrain, Iran, Israel, Jordan, Lebanon, Saudi Arabia, Turkey, United Arab Emirates.

Table 4: Factors for renewable electricity deployment in the MENA region

	MENA[a]	Oil Exporting[b]	Non-oil Exporting[c]	High-income[d]	Middle-income[e]	North Africa[f]	Middle East[g]
Y/N	**$6.720 \cdot 10^{-5}$	$1.939 \cdot 10^{-4}$	*$6.370 \cdot 10^{-5}$	$1.275 \cdot 10^{-4}$	$1.060 \cdot 10^{-5}$	$9.460 \cdot 10^{-5}$	$7.250 \cdot 10^{-5}$
E_{imp}	$4.548 \cdot 10^{-4}$	$4.307 \cdot 10^{-4}$	$9.075 \cdot 10^{-4}$	$7.321 \cdot 10^{-3}$	$1.949 \cdot 10^{-4}$	$5.568 \cdot 10^{-4}$	$-1.364 \cdot 10^{-3}$
FIT	$9.459 \cdot 10^{-2}$	$-6.210 \cdot 10^{-2}$	$2.072 \cdot 10^{-1}$	***$1.884 \cdot 10^{0}$	*$6.325 \cdot 10^{-2}$	**$1.193 \cdot 10^{-1}$	$1.742 \cdot 10^{-1}$
Res_{Oil}	***$-8.722 \cdot 10^{-3}$	**$-1.238 \cdot 10^{-2}$	$-4.846 \cdot 10^{-1}$	$5.902 \cdot 10^{-1}$	**$-4.216 \cdot 10^{-3}$	**$-4.384 \cdot 10^{-2}$	$-1.907 \cdot 10^{-2}$
Res_{Gas}	****$9.757 \cdot 10^{-4}$	$1.230 \cdot 10^{-3}$	$-3.231 \cdot 10^{-2}$	$2.453 \cdot 10^{-2}$	$3.023 \cdot 10^{-4}$	$3.087 \cdot 10^{-4}$	*$2.609 \cdot 10^{-3}$
p_{Oil}	$-1.220 \cdot 10^{-4}$	$2.146 \cdot 10^{-3}$	$-6.143 \cdot 10^{-4}$	$6.757 \cdot 10^{-4}$	$8.160 \cdot 10^{-5}$	$-1.856 \cdot 10^{-4}$	$-1.157 \cdot 10^{-3}$
p_{Gas}	$1.078 \cdot 10^{-2}$	$1.990 \cdot 10^{-2}$	$-5.354 \cdot 10^{-3}$	*$1.711 \cdot 10^{-1}$	$3.852 \cdot 10^{-3}$	$1.255 \cdot 10^{-2}$	$1.625 \cdot 10^{-2}$
$p_{fuel}{:}p_{Oil}$	$2.039 \cdot 10^{0}$	$1.364 \cdot 10^{1}$	$-1.436 \cdot 10^{0}$	$-5.701 \cdot 10^{0}$	$-1.610 \cdot 10^{-2}$	$1.632 \cdot 10^{0}$	$3.420 \cdot 10^{0}$
Reg	**$-3.847 \cdot 10^{-3}$	$-8.010 \cdot 10^{-5}$	***$-3.934 \cdot 10^{-3}$	*$-2.538 \cdot 10^{-1}$	**$-3.549 \cdot 10^{-3}$	$-3.412 \cdot 10^{-3}$	$-3.172 \cdot 10^{-2}$
$Right$	**$1.957 \cdot 10^{-3}$	$1.248 \cdot 10^{-3}$	$-1.011 \cdot 10^{-3}$	$1.189 \cdot 10^{-1}$	**$1.416 \cdot 10^{-3}$	$1.100 \cdot 10^{-3}$	$-2.339 \cdot 10^{-4}$
$Free_{Cor}$	$1.647 \cdot 10^{-4}$	$3.308 \cdot 10^{-3}$	$9.554 \cdot 10^{-4}$	$1.292 \cdot 10^{-2}$	$9.248 \cdot 10^{-4}$	$2.371 \cdot 10^{-3}$	$1.546 \cdot 10^{-3}$
$Free_{Bus}$	$7.895 \cdot 10^{-4}$	$-1.530 \cdot 10^{-3}$	$-9.010 \cdot 10^{-5}$	$2.687 \cdot 10^{-3}$	$-7.896 \cdot 10^{-4}$	$-1.087 \cdot 10^{-3}$	$1.367 \cdot 10^{-3}$
$Free_{Fin}$	$2.472 \cdot 10^{-3}$	$-1.655 \cdot 10^{-4}$	*$4.845 \cdot 10^{-3}$	$-2.000 \cdot 10^{-2}$	$1.431 \cdot 10^{-3}$	$2.980 \cdot 10^{-3}$	$3.072 \cdot 10^{-3}$
$Free_{Inv}$	$1.853 \cdot 10^{-3}$	$2.247 \cdot 10^{-3}$	$8.120 \cdot 10^{-5}$	$8.001 \cdot 10^{-3}$	$5.787 \cdot 10^{-4}$	$1.193 \cdot 10^{-4}$	**$4.821 \cdot 10^{-3}$
N	*$-8.030 \cdot 10^{-9}$	$-1.170 \cdot 10^{-8}$	$-2.730 \cdot 10^{-8}$	$-1.190 \cdot 10^{-6}$	$-1.320 \cdot 10^{-9}$	$-3.000 \cdot 10^{-9}$	*$-1.710 \cdot 10^{-8}$
β_0	*$-7.312 \cdot 10^{-1}$	$-1.624 \cdot 10^{0}$	$-7.411 \cdot 10^{-2}$	$-2.500 \cdot 10^{1}$	$-1.028 \cdot 10^{-1}$	$-2.191 \cdot 10^{-1}$	$-1.017 \cdot 10^{0}$
Observations	187	77	110	36	151	84	103
Number of countries included in the model	14	8	6	5	9	5	9

*** indicates significance at a 1 per cent level, ** at 5 and * at 10 per cent.

a) Included countries: Algeria, Bahrain, Egypt, Iran, Israel, Jordan, Lebanon, Libya, Morocco, Qatar, Saudi Arabia, Tunisia, Turkey, United Arab Emirates.
b) Algeria, Bahrain, Egypt, Iran, Libya, Qatar, Saudi Arabia, United Arab Emirates.
c) Israel, Jordan, Lebanon, Morocco, Tunisia, Turkey.
d) Bahrain, Israel, Qatar, Saudi Arabia, United Arab Emirates.
e) Algeria, Egypt, Iran, Jordan, Lebanon, Libya, Morocco, Tunisia, Turkey.
f) Algeria, Egypt, Morocco, Tunisia.
g) Bahrain, Iran, Israel, Jordan, Lebanon, Qatar, Saudi Arabia, Turkey, United Arab Emirates.

countries show a lower increase in renewable energy capacity, which confirms the results arrived at by Acquaah and Kizys,[27] and Pfeiffer and Mulder.[28] The negative impact of oil resources on renewable energy deployment suggests that oil-rich countries might be late-movers in renewable energy investments.

The significantly negative sign of the regime variable suggests that renewable energy deployment is higher in more autocratic countries. This may be due to three reasons: first, with the exception of Israel, the countries with the highest GDP per capita in the region tend to be more autocratic, so that there might be some collinearity with the GDP per capita variable; second, the more autocratic countries are the ones with higher oil reserves, which has a significantly negative impact on renewable energy deployment; and third, it might be easier for autocratic regimes to direct governmental spending towards investments on renewables once a high-level commitment for diversifying the energy mix has been made.

We can show the effect of feed-in tariffs only in several subpanels, but not in the overall panel. In cases in which the impact is significant, the estimated coefficient is positive, implying that feed-in tariffs enhance renewable energy deployment.

One important non-significant variable is the pump gasoline-oil price ratio that we have used as proxy for fossil fuel subsidies. This element is insignificant in all panels, suggesting that such subsidies might not matter much for investments in renewables, even if they create various market distortions.[29]

The subpanels mainly confirm our results in the overall panels. The fact that some coefficients that were significant in the overall panel are insignificant in several subpanels might be a result of the fewer number of observations in the subpanels.

Policy implications and conclusion

Our results concerning the energy-growth nexus show that renewable capacity expansion does not have a significant effect on growth, and we can reject our initial hypothesis that renewable capacity expansion might slow growth down. In contrast, our results suggest that there could be a positive impact on growth from

---

27 Ackah and Kizys, 'Green growth in oil producing African countries'.
28 Pfeiffer and Mulder, 'Explaining the diffusion of renewable energy technology in developing countries'.
29 When we did the same estimations with the increase of renewable generation as the dependent variable, this variable became significant with a negative sign, suggesting that fuel subsidies might matter for the effective use of renewable technologies.

electricity generation from renewable sources. Therefore, increasing investments in renewable energy technologies and expanding their deployment (i.e. enlarging the market for renewable energy) might enhance economic growth in the MENA region. Increasingly studies have also shown that sizable socio-economic effects can also be captured as a result, in the form of employment status and private sector development.[30]

Regarding renewable energy deployment, our results show that up to now, investing in additional renewable capacity has been much more attractive for countries with smaller or no oil reserves. For such countries it has been primarily important to address energy security concerns by reducing dependency on fossil fuel imports. Given that the worldwide demand for oil and gas is increasing and the costs for further resource exploration are rising, it seems that additional investments in renewable generation capacity might entail a positive contribution to the future economic of these countries by reducing their vulnerability when faced with changing fossil fuel prices on the world market. The fact that currently oil prices have stabilised at a low level and are not expected to increase to previous levels is not expected to undermine current investments in alternative energy technologies. Increasing energy demand, expected to reach an average yearly rate of five to six per cent in the MENA region in the coming two decades,[31] will call for further solutions in diversifying the energy mix.

Moreover, our results show positive effects from renewable electricity generation on growth in oil-exporting countries. The impact is higher in the oil-exporting countries in the MENA region compared to the impact recorded in the worldwide panel, suggesting that investing in renewable electricity generation is profitable for oil-exporting countries. Therefore, it is not surprising to see that fossil-fuel rich countries, such as Saudi Arabia, the UAE, or Qatar, have started to invest heavily in renewable energy generation and in knowledge development since 2007.[32] For these countries, investing in renewables may be a way to reduce

---

30 See for example C. P. Kost, *Renewable energy in North Africa: Modeling of future electricity scenarios and the impact on manufacturing and employment*, Schriften des Lehrstuhls für Energiewirtschaft, TU Dresden 7, Dresden 2015; R. de Arce *et al*, 'A simulation of the economic impact of renewable energy development in Morocco', *Energy Policy* 46, 2012, pp. 335–45, doi:10.1016/j.enpol.2012.03.068; and Supersberger and Führer, 'Integration of renewable energies and nuclear power into North African Energy Systems'.
31 International Energy Agency, *Morocco 2014: Energy policies beyond IEA countries*, Paris 2014.
32 Y. Al-Saleh and G. Vidican, 'Innovation dynamics of sustainability journeys for hydrocarbon-rich countries', *International Journal of Innovation and Sustainable Development* 7.2, 2013, pp. 144–71, doi:10.1504/IJISD.2013.053320; G. Vidican *et al*, 'An

domestic fossil fuel consumption – or to meet increasing energy demand without an increase in domestic fuel consumption – and to increase fuel exports for higher revenues. Renewable electricity generation also reduces the costs of domestic energy consumption and increases welfare. By investing in renewable energy, the Gulf countries are seeking to maintain their global competitive advantage in the energy sector.

Another relevant finding from our analysis is that countries with stronger property rights show a faster increase in renewable capacity, and that for some subpanels other variables measuring economic freedom are significantly positive as well. This suggests that an economic environment that encourages private investments might help to attract investments in renewable energy technologies. This would lead to an expansion of the market for these energy technologies, thus creating opportunities for potentially positive growth effects.

The policy implications of these results are vast. We would like to point to one specific aspect that relates to renewable electricity generation and growth effects, specifically the need for expanding regional cooperation efforts in the area of energy generation. Electricity generation from renewables is more volatile (as it is subject to weather conditions) and thus cannot be as easily controlled (or integrated into the existing grid) as generation from conventional technologies. It is more complicated to guarantee a reliable power supply from systems relying significantly on renewable technologies. One way to deal with this problem is a larger regional coverage of the power sector, as it opens additional possibilities in that unfavourable conditions in one region can be balanced by better conditions in another region, or that one technology can be balanced with another (for example, by increasing hydro generation during calm wind periods). As Haller *et al* has pointed out, the limited transmission capacity in the region might lead to higher storage requirements, higher curtailments and power prices when the share of renewables increases in the MENA region.[33] Expanding the transmission capacity and using a common balancing system might further enhance renewable deployment in the region. But one should keep in mind that achieving a greater level of cooperation in the power sector is not a simple task due to, for example, political issues and the fact that a more integrated power system means also a loss in autonomy as far as the power sector is concerned. This dichotomy remains a

empirical examination of the development of a solar innovation system in the United Arab Emirates', *Energy for Sustainable Development* 16.2, 2012, doi:10.1016/j.esd.2011.12.002.
33 Haller, Ludig and Bauer, 'Decarbonization scenarios for the EU and MENA power system'.

challenge for the deployment of renewables, particularly in the power sector in the MENA region.

Bibliography

Abdmouleh, Z., R. A. Alammari and A. Gastli, 'Recommendations on renewable energy policies for the GCC countries', *Renewable and Sustainable Energy Reviews* 50, 2015, pp. 1181–91, doi:10.1016/j.rser.2015.05.057.

Abid, M. and R. Mraihi, 'Disaggregate Energy Consumption Versus Economic Growth in Tunisia: Cointegration and Structural Break Analysis', *Journal of the Knowledge Economy* 6.4, 2015, pp. 1104–22, doi:10.1007/s13132-014-0189-4.

Ackah, I. and R. Kizys, 'Green growth in oil producing African countries: A panel data analysis of renewable energy demand', *Renewable and Sustainable Energy Reviews* 50, 2015, pp. 1157–66, doi:10.1016/j.rser.2015.05.030.

Al-Mulali, U. and C. N. C. Sab, 'Energy consumption, pollution and economic development in 16 emerging countries', *Journal of Economic Studies* 40.5, 2013, pp. 686–98, doi:10.1108/JES-05-2012-0055.

Al-Saleh, Y. and G. Vidican, 'Innovation dynamics of sustainability journeys for hydrocarbon-rich countries', *International Journal of Innovation and Sustainable Development* 7.2, 2013, pp. 144–71, doi:10.1504/IJISD.2013.053320.

Apergis, N. and J. E. Payne, 'Renewable energy consumption and economic growth: Evidence from a panel of OECD countries', *Energy Policy* 38, 2010, pp. 656–60, doi:10.1016/j.enpol.2009.09.002.

Arce, R. de, R. Mahía, E. Medina and G. Escribano, 'A simulation of the economic impact of renewable energy development in Morocco', *Energy Policy* 46, 2012, pp. 335–45, doi:10.1016/j.enpol.2012.03.068.

Arouri, M. E. H., A. Ben Youssef, H. M'Henni and C. Rault, 'Energy consumption, economic growth and CO2 emissions in Middle East and North African countries', *Energy Policy* 45, 2012, pp. 342–49, doi:10.1016/j.enpol.2012.02.042.

Ben Aïssa, M. S., M. Ben Jebli and S. Ben Youssef, 'Output, renewable energy consumption and trade in Africa', *Energy Policy* 66, 2014, pp. 11–8, doi:10.1016/j.enpol.2013.11.023.

Boudghene Stambouli, A., 'Algerian renewable energy assessment: The challenge of sustainability', *Energy Policy* 39.8, 2011, pp. 4507–19, doi:10.1016/j.enpol.2010.10.005.

BP, 'BP Statistical Review of World Energy 2015', London 2015, http://www.bp.com/content/dam/bp/pdf/energy-economics/statistical-review-2015/bp-statistical-review-of-world-energy-2015-full-report.pdf.

Damette, O. and M. Seghir, 'Energy as a driver of growth in oil exporting countries? ', *Energy Economics* 37, 2013, pp. 193–9, doi:10.1016/j.eneco.2012.12.011.

El Fadel, M., G. Rachid, R. El-Samra, G. Bou Boutros and J. Hashisho, 'Emissions reduction and economic implications of renewable energy market penetration of power generation for residential consumption in the MENA region', *Energy Policy* 52, 2013, pp. 618–27, doi:10.1016/j.enpol.2012.10.015.

Eyraud, L., A. Wane, C. Zhang and B. Clements, 'Who's going green and why? Trends and Determinants of Green Investment', IMF Working Paper 11/296, Washington, DC 2011, http://www.imf.org/external/pubs/ft/wp/2011/wp11296.pdf.

Farhani, S., 'Renewable Energy Consumption, Economic Growth and CO2 Emissions: Evidence from Selected MENA Countries', *Energy Economics Letters* 1.2, 2013, pp. 24–41, http://ssrn.com/abstract=2294995.

German Aerospace Center, 'Concentrating Solar Power for the Mediterranean Region. Final Report', Stuttgart 2005, http://www.dlr.de/Portaldata/1/Resources/portal_news/newsarchiv2008_1/algerien_med_csp.pdf.

Haller, M., S. Ludig and N. Bauer, 'Decarbonization scenarios for the EU and MENA power system: Considering spatial distribution and short term dynamics of renewable generation', *Energy Policy* 47, 2012, pp. 282–90, doi:10.1016/j.enpol.2012.04.069.

Hamdi, H. and R. Sbia, 'The Dynamic Relationship between CO2 Emissions, Energy Usage and Growth in Gulf Cooperation Council (GCC) Countries: An Aggregated Analysis', *Economie Appliquee* 67.2, 2014, pp. 161–82.

Hossein, A., G. F. Yazdan and E. Asghari Ghara, 'The Relationship between Energy Consumption, Energy Prices and Economic Growth: Case Study (OPEC Countries)', *OPEC Energy Review* 36.3, 2012, pp. 272–86.

International Energy Agency, *Morocco 2014: Energy policies beyond IEA countries*, Paris 2014.

Iyke, B. N., 'Electricity consumption and economic growth in Nigeria: A revisit of the energy-growth debate', *Energy Economics* 51, 2015, pp. 166–76, doi:10.1016/j.eneco.2015.05.024.

Kahsai, M. S., C. Nondo, P. V. Schaeffer and T. G. Gebremedhin, 'Income level and the energy consumption–GDP nexus: Evidence from Sub-Saharan Africa', *Energy Economics* 34.3, 2012, pp. 739–46, doi:10.1016/j. eneco.2011.06.006.

Karakosta, C. and J. Psarras, 'Understanding CDM potential in the Mediterranean basin: A country assessment of Egypt and Morocco', *Energy Policy* 60, 2013, pp. 827–39, doi:10.1016/j.enpol.2013.05.078.

Kayıkçı, F. and M. E. Bildirici, 'Economic Growth and Electricity Consumption in GCC and MENA Countries', *South African Journal of Economics* 83.2, 2015, pp. 303–16, http://onlinelibrary.wiley.com/doi/10.1111/saje.12061/ epdf.

Kost, C. P., *Renewable energy in North Africa: Modeling of future electricity scenarios and the impact on manufacturing and employment*, Schriften des Lehrstuhls für Energiewirtschaft, TU Dresden 7, Dresden 2015.

Marshall, M. G., T. R. Gurr and K. Jaggers, 'Polity IV project. Political Regime Characteristics and Transistions, 1800–2013', Center for Systematic Peace, Vienna, Virginia 2014, http://www.systemicpeace.org/inscrdata.html.

Menegaki, A. N., 'On energy consumption and GDP studies; A meta-analysis of the last two decades', *Renewable and Sustainable Energy Reviews* 29, 2014, pp. 31–6, doi:10.1016/j.rser.2013.08.081.

Miller, T. and A. B. Kim, '2015 Index of Economic Freedom', The Heritage Foundation; The Wallstreet Journal, Washington, DC 2015, http://heritage. org/index/explore.

Mohammadi, H. and S. Parvaresh, 'Energy consumption and output: Evidence from a panel of 14 oil-exporting countries', *Energy Economics* 41, 2014, pp. 41–6, doi:10.1016/j.eneco.2013.11.002.

Naji Meidani, A. A. and M. Zabihi, 'Energy Consumption and Real GDP in Iran', *International Journal of Energy Economics and Policy* 4.1, 2014, pp. 15–25.

Omri, A., 'CO2 emissions, energy consumption and economic growth nexus in MENA countries: Evidence from simultaneous equations models', *Energy Economics* 40, 2013, pp. 657–64, doi:10.1016/j.eneco.2013.09.003.

Omri, A., S. Daly, C. Rault and A. Chaibi, 'Financial development, environmental quality, trade and economic growth: What causes what in

MENA countries', *Energy Economics* 48, 2015, pp. 242–52, doi:10.1016/j. eneco.2015.01.008.

Ozcan, B., 'The nexus between carbon emissions, energy consumption and economic growth in Middle East countries: A panel data analysis', *Energy Policy* 62, 2013, pp. 1138–47, doi:10.1016/j.enpol.2013.07.016.

Patlitzianas, K. D., H. Doukas and J. Psarras, 'Enhancing renewable energy in the Arab States of the Gulf: Constraints & efforts', *Energy Policy* 34.18, 2006, pp. 3719–26, doi:10.1016/j.enpol.2005.08.018.

Pfeiffer, B. and P. Mulder, 'Explaining the diffusion of renewable energy technology in developing countries', *Energy Economics* 40, 2013, p. 285–96, doi:10.1016/j.eneco.2013.07.005.

Reiche, D., 'Energy Policies of Gulf Cooperation Council (GCC) countries – possibilities and limitations of ecological modernization in rentier states', *Energy Policy* 38.5, 2010, pp. 2395–403, doi:10.1016/j.enpol.2009.12.031.

Ruble, I. and P. Nader, 'Transforming shortcomings into opportunities: Can market incentives solve Lebanon's energy crisis?', *Energy Policy* 39.5, 2011, pp. 2467–74, doi:10.1016/j.enpol.2011.02.011.

Sebri, M., 'Use renewables to be cleaner: Meta-analysis of the renewable energy consumption-economic growth nexus', *Renewable and Sustainable Energy Reviews* 42, 2015, pp. 657–65, doi:10.1016/j.rser.2014.10.042.

Shahateet, M. I., K. A. Al-Majali and F. Al-Hahabashneh, 'Causality and Cointegration between Economic Growth and Energy Consumption: Econometric Evidence from Jordan', *International Journal of Economics and Finance* 6.10, 2014, doi:10.5539/ijef.v6n10p270.

Supersberger, N. and L. Führer, 'Integration of renewable energies and nuclear power into North African Energy Systems: An analysis of energy import and export effects', *Energy Policy* 39.8, 2011, pp. 4458–65, doi:10.1016/j. enpol.2010.12.046.

Sweidan, O. D., 'Energy Consumption and Real Output: New Evidence from the UAE', *OPEC Energy Review* 36.3, 2012, pp. 287–300.

Tang, C. F. and S. Abosedra, 'The impacts of tourism, energy consumption and political instability on economic growth in the MENA countries', *Energy Policy* 68, 2014, pp. 458–64, doi:10.1016/j.enpol.2014.01.004.

Vidican, G., L. McElvaney, D. Samulewicz and Y. Al-Saleh, 'An empirical examination of the development of a solar innovation system in the United Arab Emirates', *Energy for Sustainable Development* 16.2, 2012, pp. 179–88, doi:10.1016/j.esd.2011.12.002.

and upgrade the electric grids. The domestic demand hike may also cause Algeria's energy exports to decline and thus reduce public spending and job creation, eventually risking civil unrest as one of the useful roles of hydrocarbon revenues is to avoid public discontent.[3] Moreover, the country is highly vulnerable to climate change effects such as heat waves and severe desertification besides existing water scarcity, and the threat will continue further with serious impacts on economy and development in the future.

All the considerations mentioned above make a strong case for the development and integration of renewable energy in the national mix. If the government expects to maintain its hydrocarbon export revenue, cope with the domestic consumption – that is expected to reach 75TWh to 80TWh in 2020, and 130TWh to 150TWh by 2030 – and take action to mitigate climate change, a sustainable approach in the form of promoting renewable power generation naturally becomes a top priority.[4]

The national Renewable Energy and Energy Efficiency Program (REEE) and the Arab League's International Renewable Energy Agency's Pan-Arab Renewable Energy Strategy 2030 have been the main points of reference in this chapter, as well as academic paper sources evaluating the different renewable technologies applicable to the region. An understanding of the local socioeconomic situation is arrived at through studying articles prepared by think tanks such as the Carnegie Middle East Center.

Algeria's intended nationally determined contribution at the COP21 meeting was pretty ambitious for a hydrocarbon rich MENA country.[5] Promoting renewable energy is a great step towards achieving sustainability, but are the current measures effective enough to bring these ambitious projects to life?[6]

---

3 B. Brand and J. Zingerle, 'The renewable energy targets of the Maghreb countries: Impact on electricity supply and conventional power markets', *Energy Policy* 39.8, 2011, pp. 4411–9, http://www.sciencedirect.com/science/article/pii/S0301421510007603.
4 Algerian Ministry of Energy and Mines, 'Renewable Energy and Energy Efficiency Program', January 2016, http://www.energy.gov.dz/francais/uploads/2016/Projets_du_Secteur/Programme_EnR_2016/Plaquette_PNEREE_2016_Fr.pdf.
5 Algerian Ministry of Energy and Mines, 'Intended Nationally Determined Contribution – Algeria', for the UNFCCC UN Framework Convention on Climate Change, 3 September 2015, http://www4.unfccc.int/Submissions/INDC/Published%20Documents/Algeria/1/Algeria%20-%20INDC%20(English%20unofficial%20translation)%20September%2003,2015.pdf.
6 IRENA, Arab League and RCREEE, 'Pan-Arab Renewable Energy Strategy 2030: Roadmap of Actions for Implementation', International Renewable Energy Agency (IRENA), League of Arab States and the Regional Centre for Renewable Energy and Energy

Methodology

This research has been conducted on a qualitative basis through reading academic papers, official publications from Algerian governmental organisations and reports from international bodies such as IRENA and the United Nations. The authors of said material are experts on the subject of socioeconomic and renewable development in North Africa and Algeria in particular. Through literature review, we can establish the legal, financial and geographical opportunities for renewable energy development as well as the existing barriers. Eventually, the results are compiled into a SWOT analysis – the internal strengths and weaknesses and the external opportunities and threats – making the case for 'Renewables in Algeria'.

Strengths

- High potential for renewable energy resources: solar radiation, geothermal and wind in the Sahara, and biomass in the north.
- Clear green commitments through legislation and national programmes and agencies: the COP21 meeting INDC and ratification, NEAL (Algeria New Energy Agency) and the REEE programme.
- Ambitious green targets: 6% of electricity production by 2015, 15% by 2020, and 40% by 2030.
- Vast land space available to build projects without disturbing people's livelihood and properties contrary to shale gas drilling that is widely protested by the locals.
- Oil wealth and account surplus can be used, as well as local and international banks willing to invest.

Weaknesses

- Fossil fuel subsidies prevent growth of renewable energy technologies by making them less attractive.
- Consumer and environmental groups are not consulted by policymakers to create better measures and regulations in order to activate the process and initiate more projects.
- Institutions and government agencies are not prepared to deal with renewable energy related affairs.

Efficiency, 2014, rena.org/DocumentDownloads/Publications/IRENA_Pan- Arab_Strategy_ June%202014.pdf.

- Lack of courses on renewable energy in the education system which leads to lack of knowhow.
- Lack of policy to provide financial guarantee for foreign or private investors to ensure they will receive payment under power purchase agreement with Sonelgaz.

Opportunities

- Renewable energy technologies prices are decreasing especially for PV and wind which are at the heart of the REEE.
- Green electricity could feed some loads during electricity shortages, as power cuts have prompted the people to protest in the past.
- Soaring energy demand has to be met without compromising fossil fuel destined for export and thus prevent loss of earnings.
- People's awareness: unemployment and power cuts are only some of the issues the Algerian people are facing. People are also aware of climate change concerns due to the heat waves that have hit the country in the past few summers, and finally there are multiple ongoing protests in the south against shale gas fracking.
- In rural areas streets and public facilities could be powered by solar PV which would show the benefits of renewables to the people and involve them in future sustainable development projects.
- Promotion of local manufacturing which leads to job creation and knowhow benefits.
- Most local investors are willing to enter into partnership with international investors.
- Support and cooperation from international banking organisations, such as World Bank CSP Project and DESERTEC.

Threats

- Low share of local financing schemes will lead to full dependency on international loans, which have lengthy procedures.
- The discovery of new sources of energy that could threaten the future of renewable energy – Algeria has the third largest shale gas reserves in the World.
- Political uncertainty: Almost every law and programme mentioned has been reviewed and amended at some point. Changes can be drastic like,

for instance, the very crucial hydrocarbon law that opened the way for foreign exploration and exploitation of oil and gas, before being recognised as a hostile investment and business framework.

Results and discussion

Legislation and financing

As mentioned earlier, a difficult business framework in the country may deter consumers and investors to engage in the process of integrating renewables in the country's energy mix. Fortunately, Algeria is one of the only six Arab countries – along with Jordan, Morocco, Palestine, Tunisia and Syria – that has taken the steps to address this issue by introducing legislation, and encouraging and regulating future renewables development in its territory.

The Algerian government has created different bodies to effectively deal with the challenges of a sustainable future, notable among them are APRUE, SKTM and NEAL. APRUE is an agency in charge of the promotion and rationalisation of energy use, and NEAL (Algeria New Energy Agency). SKTM, which stands for Sharikat Kahraba Takate Moutajadida, a subsidiary of Sonelgaz is an agency dedicated to renewable energy. Several legislations have been introduced to facilitate the development of renewable energy. It is worth mentioning a few key legislations at this point.

Act 99-09 (July 1999) on energy control establishes the National Program for Energy Control (PNME), which promotes renewable energy and its use. A national fund for energy control (FNME) was put in place to finance PNME's actions and projects.

Act 02-01 (February 2002) on electricity and public pipeline gas distribution ensures the purchase of renewables and related extra-cost compensation. This act endorses a special scheme for electricity generation from renewables which seeks to diverge from the common system. Under the provisions of article 26 of this act, decree 04-92 on electricity diversification costs prescribes preferential rates for renewable electricity generation, provision of installation connection costs and the grant of a green premium varying between 100% and 300% of the cost per kWh.

Act 04-09 (August 2004) on the promotion of renewable energy for the purpose of sustainable development enacts a national programme for the promotion of renewable energy technologies and the tools required to achieve that objective. The act includes the creation of a national monitoring body to promote the development and use of renewable energy.

Then in 2004, the 04-92 decree on electricity generation diversification was enacted with the purpose of creating incentives towards the use of renewables rather than traditional energy sources. Unique in Africa at the time, the decree determined a detailed compensation system for renewable electricity. Following the ratification of the market liberalisation act, 35% of electricity is being generated by private foreign-owned plants which is then sold to Sonelgaz, the national electricity and gas distribution company and the only buyer. However, the incentive measures for renewable energy put in place are said to be insufficient in attracting private investors, which has prompted the government to review the law.[7]

It is worth to mention the executive decree 06-428 of article 26 (November 2006) which grants renewable energy priority grid access.

Finally, we come to the Renewable Energy and Energy Efficiency Program, launched in 2011 and updated in 2015. The REEE consists of three phases: phase 1 (2011–2013) was a trial for testing different available technologies through pilot projects; phase 2 (2014–2015) started the deployment of the programme; and phase 3 (2016–2020) realised the deployment of the programme at a large scale. By 2020, sixty solar photovoltaic and concentrating solar power plants, wind farms and hybrid power plants will have been deployed.

The REEE consists of installing up to 22,000 MW of renewable power generating between 2011 and 2030, of which 12,000 MW is allocated for domestic demand and 10,000 MW intended for export. Indeed, Algeria's ambition is to become a major solar energy player in the future, as illustrated in the DESERTEC project aiming to export renewable electricity from North Africa to the European Union. The end goal is that 40% of electricity produced for domestic consumption will be from renewable energy sources by 2030. The plan looks at different renewable sources including solar, wind, geothermal and biomass. The development of renewables is thought to be at the heart of the country's economic and development objectives, through offering energy security, and even water and food security as it would benefit not only the power sector but also agriculture and water desalinisation plants already widely used in the country.[8]

As regards to financing, the law dedicates a specific funding scheme for renewables. According to the 2009 and later 2011 reviewed Supplementary Finance Act

7 M. Navhmany *et al*, 'Climate Change Legislation in Algeria: An Excerpt from the 2015 Global Climate Legislation Study A Review of Climate Change Legislation in 99 Countries', *The London School of Economics and Political Science and Grantham Research Institute on Climate Change and the Environment*, 2015, e.ac.uk/GranthamInstitute/wp-content/uploads/2015/05/ALGERIA.pdf.
8 Algerian Ministry of Energy, 'Renewable Energy and Energy Efficiency Program'.

(LFC), the percentage of oil royalties dedicated to financing renewable energy projects and cogeneration is increased from 0.5 to 1%. That same year, the LFC predicted that oil revenues would amount to 1529.4 billion dinars. The oil royalties will be reserved for national renewable energy schemes and energy efficiency funds.[9]

In terms of fiscal incentives, contrary to the petroleum fiscal system, which is one of the most hostile incentives in the world, Algeria has taken measures to welcome investors in the renewable energy field. Feed-in-Tariffs (FIT) were adopted by Act 02-01 (2002) as a price support incentive. As well as customs duties and import VAT reductions for components, raw materials and semi- finished products used in the manufacturing of renewable energy equipment. Another opportunity is the availability of regional funding such as the national fund mentioned above but also provided by private Arab and international banks. In terms of energy market structure, it is important to know that Algeria has liberalised power generation activities in 2002, clearing the way for private renewable energy companies to compete with foreign fossil fuel companies. Regarding the important issue of subsidies, the government plans to grant subsidies to cover additional costs for electricity generation and drinking water desalinisation, but the details remain unclear.[10]

Renewable energy potential

The main renewable source that has been active in Algeria is hydropower, but the government decided in 2014 to gradually stop this activity and close plants in order to save the water supply for the population's domestic use when water scarcity became an urgent issue – and because hydropower was fairly insignificant in terms of the total power generation. The national focus is now primarily on solar power, followed by wind, geothermal and biomass.

Solar

This energy source is the major focus of the REEE. By 2030, solar energy is set to become a major contributor to the national electricity production at a rate of 37%.[11] The Maghreb region, and Algeria in particular, has a high solar potential.

---

9 IRENA, 'Pan-Arab Renewable Energy'.
10 Algerian Ministry of Energy, 'Renewable Energy and Energy Efficiency Program'.
11 Algerian Ministry of Energy, 'Renewable Energy and Energy Efficiency Program'.

According to a study by the German Aerospace Centre on Europe and the MENA, Algeria shows exceptional irradiation levels: 1200 kWh/m2 per year in the northern grand Sahara compared to 800 kWh/m2 per year to southern Europe. Algeria has the best records in all of the Mediterranean basin; and one of the highest in the world with a national average of sunshine duration of 2000 hours, and 3900 in the highlands and Sahara. The energy equivalent received per year is illustrated in Figure 15.

The study concluded that the potential is measured at 169,000 TWh per year for solar thermal and 13.9 TWh per year for solar photovoltaic. The country's annual sunshine exposure is equivalent to 2,500 kWh/m2. Daily solar energy potential varies from 4.66 kWh/m2 in the north to 7.26 kWh/m2 in the south.

Algeria aims to become a manufacturing base in the solar industry. By implementing a national training programme, the REEE could use the engineering and technical skills of the country's youth. Such a programme would help to develop a local technology knowhow and create thousands of direct and indirect jobs that are well needed in the current domestic economic situation – Algeria has a high rate of educated youth unemployment. The aim is also not only to produce clean electricity for the domestic market, but to supply the European market through the long-time and well-studied DESERTEC project, which consists of a group of politicians, economists and scientists who have planned an EU-MENA network of CSP, PV, wind, hydro, biomass and geothermal plants.[12] A successful existing project is implemented in Hassi R'Mel, Algeria's largest gas field, integrating solar combined cycle power station since 2011. A hybrid power station and world's first, with a 120 MW SIEMENS gas turbine and steam cycle fired by natural gas – the steam turbine receives additional solar-generated steam on a 180,000 m2 area – the project is capable of cutting down carbon emissions.

Wind

Wind energy has a relatively low potential in Algeria; even so, it comes second in the REEE programme, the reason for which is that it constitutes the second best potential renewable source with a share expected to reach about 3% of the electricity production in 2030. Wind potential varies a lot in the country depending on the area due to a very diverse climate and topography. Algeria is divided into two geographic zones, the northern Mediterranean coast of 1,200 kilometres that includes a mountainous relief with a continental climate, and the desertic south

---

12 Desertec Foundation, 'Our Vision', http://www.desertec.org.

with a Saharan climate where the wind potential is higher with a wind speed of 4 to 6 m/s. This is a pretty good potential, especially in the southwest of the country, where it could be beneficial in water pumping.[13] According to the same German Aerospace Agency study, the wind potential is 35 TWh per year.

Geothermal

This renewable energy source is abundant but not put to effective use as of yet. Jurassic limestones in the northern coast constitute important geothermal reservoirs with over 200 thermal sources. These sources often have temperatures above 40°C, with the highest at 96°C, and are often used for balneology and greenhouse heating. In the south a much larger reservoir, called 'the Albian groundwater table', at an average temperature of 57°C covers several square kilometres. The northern and southern reservoirs are exploited at a flow rate of 2 m^3/s and 4 m^3/s respectively. However today their use is focused in the north where the generated heat discharge is 240 megawatts thermal (MWt). Even though these three zones are clearly known already as seen in blue in Figure 16, there is a need for further engineering studies to determine their energy potential.

Biomass

The recovery of organic waste, mainly animal manure, for biogas production could be considered an economic and ecological solution with the advantage of being decentralised and offering energy independence to the country's rural areas. Municipal waste is an important source as well; Algeria produces annually more than 10 million tons of solid waste.[14] As for vegetal sources – just 10% of the country's surface – potential is thought to be found in maritime pine and eucalyptus from Algerian forestry residue.[15]

13 Algerian Ministry of Energy and Mines, 'New Renewable Energy Development Program 2015–2030', 15 February 2015, http://portail.cder.dz/spip.php?article4446.
14 S. Zafar, 'Renewable Energy in Algeria', *EcoMena*, 10 March 2016, ecomena.org/renewables-algeria.
15 Y. Himri, A. Malik, A. Boudghene Stambouli, S. Himri and D. Belkacem, 'Review and use of the Algerian renewable energy for sustainable development', *Renewable ad Sustainable Energy Reviews* 13.6–7, 2009, pp. 1584–91, http://www.sciencedirect.com/science/article/pii/S1364032108001391.

Local R&D

Several research centres have been created for renewable technology development, among them the Center for the Development of Renewable Energy (CDER) and the Center for Research and Development of Electricity and Gas (CREDEG). The Algerian government is interested in manufacturing renewable energy technologies locally. Renewable technologies are an opportunity for job creation, especially for the qualified educated youth who cannot be absorbed into the job market due to low oil prices and production. Algeria, along with Egypt, Jordan, Morocco, Libya and Tunisia, is part of an investment project called MENA CSP. This project is supported by the World Bank which can offer strategic concessional loans from the Clean Technology Fund (CTF) to accelerate Concentrated Solar Power expansion. Algeria and its Arab neighbours could eventually become major suppliers and consumers of CSP-generated electricity.[16] Local energy manufactories and foreign partnerships have worked in the past with successful General Electric projects in petroleum and water desalinisation sectors, for instance.

Barriers to renewable energy development

Renewable energy development could be hindered by the same institutional or fiscal barriers that are affecting the petroleum industry, such as unfavourable regulations for foreign companies who cannot own more than a 49% minority of a venture, or unclear and few project bidding opportunities. Moreover, such conditions can vary at any given time due to the unstable local legislative environment. Algeria has a lot of human, economic and energy potential but robust reforms are needed to address the root problems that today cause delays for both hydrocarbon and renewable projects.[17]

There is also the issue of fossil fuel subsidies that deters potential investors and consumers. Electricity and fuel are very cheap in Algeria due to being heavily subsidised. Subsidies for fossil fuel products reached $22.2 billion (11% of GDP).[18]

16 World Bank, 'Middle East and North Africa (MENA) Region Assessment of the Local Manufacturing Potential for Concentrated Solar Power (CSP) Projects', *The World Bank Energy Sector Management Assistance Program*, 2011, iteresources.worldbank.org/INTMENA/Resources/CSP-Job-Study-Eng-Sum.pdf
17 L. Achy, 'Algeria's Financial Surplus and Socioeconomic Struggles', *Carnegie Middle East Center*, 15 May 2012, http://carnegieendowment.org/2012/05/15/algeria-s-financial-surplus-and-socioeconomic-struggles-pub-48276.
18 C. Nakhle, 'Middle East and North Africa Oil Producers Are Facing a New Price Reality', *Carnegie Middle East Center*, 30 June 2015, carnegieendowment.org/2015/06/30/middle-east-and-north-africa-oil-producers-are-facing-new-price-reality-pub-60605.

Regulated by Commission de Régulation de l'Electricité et du Gaz (CREG), the power sector that sets the tariffs, residential electricity prices – residential and construction being the most energy intensive sectors – are heavily subsidised at US\$0.03 per kWh. The tariff structure is flat.[19]

Even with the lowering cost of renewable energy technologies, fossil fuel plants remain the most attractive option. On top of that, the petroleum infrastructure in place is old but still operative and the new pipeline projects launched in the past few years are obviously seen as justifiable in maintaining the revenue and health of the country; on the other hand, renewable energy technologies require high upfront costs while providing variable generation.

Foreign investors need to have a guarantee of high premiums in view of security issues, such as the In Salah attack on foreign workers of international oil companies, and political uncertainty when it comes to measures and regulations, such as the existing difficulties to access the land where the potential for renewable energy development exists.[20]

Finally, a few other local barriers exist such as the lack of knowhow, lack of coordination and communication between governmental institutions, lack of management transparency for the monopolistic national power company Sonelgaz and the slow bureaucracy. Unfortunately besides FiT – which is thought to be more compatible with small-size rather than large-scale projects since it is not capable of rewarding investors – there is no other assurance for investors in terms of fixed long-term prices for generated electricity.[21]

Conclusion

Although the contribution of renewable energy to the national primary energy consumption mix is rather poor today, hydrocarbon rich Algeria is well on the road to renewable energy and sustainable development for tomorrow.

The current legal initiatives are ambitious but still need to be reviewed and amended in order to meet the challenges that are slowing down the development of renewable energy. It has become a matter of urgency to reform the subsidy system which is counter effective, causing public deficit and higher consumption instead of focusing on offering better incentives for consumers to seek out green energy and better investment opportunities and fiscal benefits for green energy

19 IRENA *et al*, 'Pan-Arab Renewable Energy Strategy'.
20 IRENA *et al*, 'Pan-Arab Renewable Energy Strategy'.
21 IRENA *et al*, 'Pan-Arab Renewable Energy Strategy'.

producers. The fall of oil price should be exploited as an opportunity to reform the system, since even if it were to rise again the system would still incur losses for the government. The way forward is to take advantage of the geographic qualities of the country by making use of renewable energy resources and stimulating different sectors of the economy such as agriculture and manufacturing in order to diversify the economy and lead it away from fossil fuels.

Climate change is an imminent threat that has already affected the country and the phenomenon will only worsen if no action is taken. The public must be educated and renewable energy – and efficiency – has to be stressed as the pre-eminent solution.

Bibliography

Achy, L., 'Algeria's Financial Surplus and Socioeconomic Struggles', *Carnegie Middle East Center*, 15 May 2012, http://carnegieendowment.org/2012/05/15/algeria-s-financial-surplus-and-socioeconomic-struggles-pub-48276.

Achy, L., 'Algeria Needs More Than Hydrocarbon Law Amendments', *Carnegie Middle East Center*, 22 January 2013, http://carnegieendowment.org/2013/01/22/algeria-needs-more-than-hydrocarbon-law-amendments-pub-50726.

Achy, L., 'On the Algerian Economy: A Widening Gap Between Resources and Achievements', *Carnegie Middle East Center*, 22 November 2013, http://carnegieendowment.org/2013/11/12/on-algerian-economy-widening-gap-between- resources-and-achievements-pub-53716.

Algerian Ministry of Energy and Mines, 'Intended Nationally Determined Contribution – Algeria', for the UNFCCC UN Framework Convention on Climate Change, 3 September 2015, http://www4.unfccc.int/Submissions/INDC/Published%20Documents/Algeria/1/Algeria%20-%20INDC%20(English%20unofficial%20translation)%20September%2003,2015.pdf.

Algerian Ministry of Energy and Mines, 'New Renewable Energy Development Program 2015–2030', 15 February 2015,

Algerian Ministry of Energy and Mines, 'Renewable Energy and Energy Efficiency Program', January 2016, http://www.energy.gov.dz/francais/uploads/2016/Projets_du_Secteur/Programme_EnR_2016/Plaquette_PNEREE_2016_Fr.pdf.

Bentouba, S., A. Slimani, M. Boucherit and H. M. Seghir, 'L'energie renouvelable en Algerie et l'impact sur l'environnement', paper presented at the 10th International Meeting on Energetical Physics, University of

Bechar, Algeria, 3–4 November 2010, http://www.univ-bechar.dz/jrs/articles/
A0.1.2010.10.pdf.

Brand, B. and J. Zingerle, 'The renewable energy targets of the Maghreb
countries: Impact on electricity supply and conventional power markets',
Energy Policy 39.8, 2011, pp. 4411–9, http://www.sciencedirect.com/science/
article/pii/S0301421510007603.

Boudghene Stambouli, A., 'Algerian renewable energy assessment: The
challenge of sustainability', *Energy Policy* 39.8, 2011, pp. 4507–19,
ciencedirect.com/science/article/pii/S0301421510007378.

CDER Publications, 'The wind deposit map in Algeria', https://www.cder.dz/
spip.php?article1765.

Desertec Foundation, 'Our Vision', http://www.desertec.org.

Elliot, S., M. Geller Maurice and L. Sahar, 'ANALYSIS: Algeria's draft
amended oil, gas law offers new tax breaks', *S&P Global Platts*, 2 January
2013.

Fekroui A. and M. Abouriche, 'Algeria Country Update Report', *Proceedings of
the World Geothermal Congress* 1, 1995, pp. 31–4.

German Aerospace Center, 'Concentrating Solar Power for the Mediterranean
Region', DLR, commissioned for Federal Ministry for the Environment,
Nature Conservation and Nuclear Safety Germany, 16 April 2005, r.de/
Portaldata/1/Resources/portal_news/newsarchiv2008_1/algerien_med_csp.
pdf.

Ghanem-Yazbeck, D., 'Algeria on the Verge: What Seventeen Years of
Bouteflika Have Achieved', *Carnegie Middle East Center*, 28 April 2016,
carnegieendowment.org/2016/04/28/algeria-on-verge-what-seventeen-
years-of- bouteflika-have-achieved-pub-63438.

Ghanem-Yazbeck, D., 'Algeria, the Sleeping Giant of North Africa', *Carnegie
Middle East Center*, 4 November 2015, carnegieendowment.org/2015/11/04/
algeria-sleeping-giant-of-north-africa-pub-61875.

Himri, Y., A. Malik, A. Boudghene Stambouli, S. Himri and D. Belkacem,
'Review and use of the Algerian renewable energy for sustainable
development', *Renewable and Sustainable Energy Reviews* 13.6–7, 2009, pp.
1584–91, ciencedirect.com/science/article/pii/S1364032108001391.

IRENA, Arab League and RCREEE, 'Pan-Arab Renewable Energy Strategy
2030: Roadmap of Actions for Implementation', International Renewable
Energy Agency (IRENA), League of Arab States and the Regional Centre
for Renewable Energy and Energy Efficiency, 2014, http://www.irena.org/

DocumentDownloads/Publications/IRENA_Pan- Arab_Strategy_June%20
2014.pdf.

Lamri, R., 'Protests in Algeria intensify as shale-gas drilling continues',
OpenDemocracy, 13 November 2015, endemocracy.net/arab-awakening/
rachida-lamri/protests-in-algeria-intensify- as-shalegas-drilling-continues.

Lamri, R., 'A question of sovereignty, justice and dignity: the people
vs. the government on fracking in Algeria', *OpenDemocracy*, 4
March 2015, endemocracy.net/arab-awakening/rachida-lamri/
question-of-sovereignty- justice-and-dignity-people-vs-government-on-fra.

Mahmoudi, H., O. Abdellah and N. Ghaffour, 'Capacity building strategies and
policy for desalination using renewable energies in Algeria', *Renewable and
Sustainable Energy Reviews* 13.4, 2009, pp. 921–6, http://www.sciencedirect.
com/science/article/pii/S1364032108000257?np=y.

Menani, S., 'Algeria Renewable Energy Program Outlook and Applications',
presented at the Energy Week 2012, Vaasa, Finland, 19–23 March 2012, ei.fi/
files/pdf/694/REGIONAL_ENERGY4_Menani.pdf.

Navhmany, M., S. Fankhauser, J. Davidova, N. Kingsmill, T. Landesman,
H. Roppongi, P. Schleifer, J. Setzer, A. Sharman and S. Stolle, 'Climate
Change Legislation in Algeria: An Excerpt from the 2015 Global Climate
Legislation Study A Review of Climate Change Legislation in 99 Countries',
The London School of Economics and Political Science and Grantham
Research Institute on Climate Change and the Environment, 2015, e.ac.uk/
GranthamInstitute/wp-content/uploads/2015/05/ALGERIA.pdf.

Nakhle, C., 'Algeria's Shale Gas Experiment', *Carnegie Middle East
Center*, 23 April 2015, http://carnegieendowment.org/2015/04/23/
algeria-s-shale-gas-experiment-pub-59851.

Nakhle, C., 'Middle East and North Africa Oil Producers Are Facing a
New Price Reality', *Carnegie Middle East Center*, 30 June 2015, http://
carnegieendowment.org/2015/06/30/middle-east-and-north-africa-oil-
producers-are-facing-new-price-reality-pub-60605.

Rahmouni, S., B. Negrou, N. Settou, J. Dominguez and A. Gouareh, 'Prospects
of hydrogen production potential from renewable resources in Algeria',
International Journal of Hydrogen 42.2, 2017, pp. 1383–95.

RCREEE, 'Algeria Renewable Energy Country Profile,' *Regional Center for
Renewable Energy and Energy Efficiency*, published online, 2012. http://
www.rcreee.org/sites/default/files/algeria_fact_sheet_print.pdf.

RCREEE, 'Algeria Energy Efficiency Country Profile,' *Regional Center for Renewable Energy and Energy Efficiency*, http://www.rcreee.org/sites/default/files/algeria_ee_fact_sheet_print.pdf.

Sahar, L., 'Algeria's Silver Lining', *Carnegie Middle East Center*, 22 January 2015, carnegieendowment.org/sada/?fa=58781.

Saibi, H., 'Geothermal Resources in Algeria', Proceedings World Geothermal Congress, Melbourne, Australia, 19–25 April 2015, angea.stanford.edu/ERE/db/WGC/papers/WGC/2015/01068.pdf.

Solargis, 'Algeria Direct Normal Irradiation Map', http://solargis.com/products/maps-and-gis-data/free/download/algeria.

United Nations, 'Le secteur des énergies renouvelables en Afrique du Nord: Situation actuelle et perspectives', *UN Commission économique pour l'Afrique, Bureau pour l'Afrique du Nord*, 2012, pp. 28–34, 51–3 and 85–8, eca.org/sites/default/files/PublicationFiles/renewable_energy_sector_in_north_africa_fr.pdf.

U.S. Energy Information Administration, 'Country Analysis Brief: Algeria', 11 March 2016, eia.gov/beta/international/analysis_includes/countries_long/Algeria/algeria.pdf.

World Bank, 'Middle East and North Africa (MENA) Region Assessment of the Local Manufacturing Potential for Concentrated Solar Power (CSP) Projects', *The World Bank Energy Sector Management Assistance Program*, 2011, http://siteresources.worldbank.org/INTMENA/Resources/CSP-Job-Study-Eng-Sum.pdf.

Zafar, S., 'Renewable Energy in Algeria', *EcoMena*, 10 March 2016, ecomena.org/renewables-algeria.

11

A System of Systems (SoS) Approach to Sustainable Energy Planning: Insight for the Persian Gulf Countries

Maral Mahlooji, Ludovic Gaudard and Kaveh Madani

Energy production

Fossil fuels have been the dominant global source of energy production since the 19th century,[1] and the major source of global anthropogenic greenhouse gas emissions.[2] Their overuse and sometimes unregulated utilisation has resulted in large carbon dioxide emissions, escalating the impacts of climate change. This issue is further fuelled by rapid population growth and the consequent raise in energy demand.[3] Accordingly, the energy sector has become the area of focus for mitigation of climate change,[4] and governments have developed policies to decarbonise their energy portfolios and transition away from the use of incumbent fossil fuels towards increasing their share of renewable energies.[5]

1 U. F. Akpan and G. E. Akpan, 'The Contribution of Energy Consumption to Climate Change: A Feasible Policy Direction', *International Journal of Energy Economics and Policy* 2.1, 2012, pp. 21–33.
2 IEA, 'Annual energy outlook 2015 with projections to 2040', https://www.eia.gov/outlooks/aeo/pdf/0383(2015).pdf.
3 S. Sorrel, 'Reducing energy demand: A review of issues, challenges and approaches', *Renewable and Sustainable Energy Reviews*, 2015, pp. 74–82; EIA, 'World energy demand and economic outlook', https://www.eia.gov/forecasts/ieo/world.cfm.
4 IEA, 'Annual energy outlook 2015 with projections to 2040'.
5 J. Bryden, L. Riahi and R. Zissler, 'MENA Renewables Status Report', http://www.ren21.net/Portals/0/documents/activities/Regional%20Reports/MENA_2013_lowres.pdf.

However, a sole focus on reducing carbon emissions and implementing policies that only emphasise this importance can lead to deterioration of the environment, rendering the endeavour ineffective in achieving sustainable energy production goals.[6] Substitution of conventional energy alternatives with renewable sources could result in unintended consequences and exhaustion of other natural resources such as land and water;[7] this possibility is commonly ignored when it comes to introducing policies that involve portfolio decarbonisation. The overexploitation of our precious natural resources leads to secondary impacts that create additional hurdles in achieving a sustainable energy mix. This additional pressure on natural resources combined with the tendency to overlook existing interrelations among ecosystem components can lead to strategic failure and the eventual disintegration of the whole system. In order to achieve a sustainable future, polices should intend to resolve current issues without creating new challenges.[8]

The Persian Gulf region

This chapter investigates the most desirable energy technologies for the Persian Gulf region. The territory consists of seven Arab states, namely Iraq, Saudi Arabia, Kuwait, Oman, Qatar, United Arab Emirates (UAE), Bahrain, and the non-Arab state of Iran. All these nations except Iran and Iraq are part of the Gulf Cooperation Council (GCC).[9] This case study offer insight to the Persian Gulf countries which have a small contribution towards the global emission of greenhouse gases. The amount of this contribution is determined based on comparison to countries like China, USA, and India, who are responsible for over 50 per cent of the global emissions.[10] The highest contribution of the region comes from Iran and Saudi Arabia which are respectively ranked seventh (1.71%) and eight (1.67%) when it

---

6 S. Hadian and K. Madani, 'A system of systems approach to energy sustainability assessment: Are all renewables really green?', *Ecological Indicators* 52, 2015, pp. 194–206.
7 K. Madani and S. Khatami, 'Water for Energy: Inconsistent Assessment Standards and Inability to Judge Properly', *Current Sustainable/Renewable Energy Reports* 2.1, 2015, pp. 10–16.
8 P. Hjorth and K. Madani, 'Sustainability monitoring and assessment: new challenges require new thinking', *Journal of Water Resources Planning and Management* 140.2, 2014, pp. 133–5.
9 M. A. Awan. 'E-government: Assessment of GCC (Gulf Co-operating Council) countries and services provided', *International Conference on Electronic Government*, Berlin 2003, pp. 500–3.
10 T. A. Boden, G. Marland and R. J. Andres, *Global, Regional, and National Fossil-Fuel CO2 Emissions. Carbon Dioxide Information Analysis Center*, Oak Ridge National Laboratory, U.S. Department of Energy, Oak Ridge 2015, doi 10.3334/CDIAC/00001_V2015.

Countries	INDCs
Bahrain	*Sets out a number of policies and actions that will contribute to 'low greenhouse gas emission development'. It highlights its Economic Vision 2030, which seeks to diversify the country's economy and reduce its dependence on oil and gas.*
Iraq	–
Iran	*A 4% cut in emissions by 2030 relative to business as usual, or a 12% cut conditional on international support of $35bn. Both elements are conditional on an end to sanctions. Includes section on adaptation.*
Kuwait	*Focuses on actions that will bring about economic diversification that will also bring down emissions, though does not set a reduction target.*
Oman	*An unconditional 2% emissions cut by 2030, relative to business as usual levels. This will be achieved through an unquantified 'increase' in renewables and 'reduction' in gas flaring. Will develop climate legislation. Includes a short section on adaptation. Additional efforts would require international support.*
Qatar	*Focuses on actions that will bring about economic diversification that will also bring down emissions, though does not set a reduction target.*
Saudi Arabia	*An 'ambitious' programme of renewable energy investment and 'economic diversification', along with energy efficiency and carbon capture and storage. Expects emissions savings of up to 130 million tonnes of CO$_2$ equivalent by 2030, relative to business as usual. Includes a section on adaptation.*
United Arab Emirates	*To 'limit' emissions and increase the share of 'clean energy' in the energy mix to 24% by 2021, up from 0.2% in 2014. Includes a section on adaptation actions with mitigation co-benefits.*

Table 1: The Persian Gulf Nations' Intended Nationally Determined Contributions (INDCs). Source: Carbon Brief, Paris 2015: *Tracking country climate pledges*, 16 September 2015, https://www.carbonbrief. org/paris-2015-tracking-country-climate-pledges.

comes to total annual carbon dioxide (CO$_2$) emissions.[11] However, the position of the Persian Gulf countries changes when the CO$_2$ emission per capita is estimated as a metric for damage against climate change. In descending order, the positions are as follows: Qatar (1st), Kuwait (4th), UAE (5th), Bahrain (6th), Saudi Arabia (9th), Oman (18th), and Iran (44th). Thus, the region is home to some of the countries with the highest emissions per capita in the world.[12] It does not come as a surprise that these are the richest countries in the region, a factor that imitates similar trends seen in the West, i.e. the higher the income per capita, the higher the emissions.[13]

11 T. A. Boden, G. Marland and B. Andres, *Ranking of the world's countries by 2014 per capita fossil-fuel CO$_2$ emission rates*, Oak Ridge National Laboratory, U.S. Department of Energy, Oak Ridge 2017, doi 10.3334/CDIAC/00001_V2017.
12 Ibid.
13 H. Pouran, 'MENA, climate change ENA, climate change', *The Middle East in London* 12.3, 2016, pp. 5–6.

Governments have demonstrated their awareness of the existing climate change challenges and their desire to tackle such issues. To this effect, Persian Gulf countries have come to an agreement to limit their greenhouse gas emission. This is demonstrated through the region's establishment of Intended Nationally Determined Contributions (INDCs), provided in Table 1. Although most countries lack set targets and clear roadmaps, their commitment to fulfilling national responsibilities is apparent.

Up until now, the level of incorporation of renewables among the Persian Gulf countries and the wider Middle East and North Africa (MENA) has been quite low. Only 6% of MENA's power is generated through renewable resources and hydropower accounts for 80% of that share.[14] When specific cases in Persian Gulf countries are considered (Table 2), similar patterns emerge with regards to hydropower, where 98% of the region's renewable power generation is sourced from this energy alternative.[15] This trend is followed by small shares of solar photovoltaic (0.4%), wind energy (0.79%) and concentrated solar power (1.01%).[16] However, the increase in the number of renewable projects (Figure 17) demonstrates the coming changes in the region. More nations are focusing on investing in renewable projects at a utility scale. Over time, technological growth and advancements have resulted in cost reduction and the increased efficiency of renewable technologies.[17]

The Persian Gulf region and the wider MENA are recognised to have incomparable climatic and geographical advantages for various renewables, including geothermal, wind, and solar technologies.[18] This potential must be exploited further if a more sustainable energy mix is to be achieved.

To support decision makers in the move towards achievement of a sustainable energy mix, there is need for an assessment framework that addressees the specific resources of the Persian Gulf region and understands the complexities of the system. Dynamic interaction between each relative system must be accounted for when developing policies for a sustainable energy mix. It is important to develop a holistic understanding of the problem in order to make informed decisions that do not solely focus on one aspect. The System of System (SoS) framework allows

---

14 M. El-Khayat, A. Barghouth, M. Mahmoud and N. Myrsalieva, *Pan-Arab Renewable Energy Strategy 2030*, http://www.irena.org/DocumentDownloads/Publications/IRENA_Pan-Arab_Strategy_June%202014.pdf.
15 Bryden, Riahi, and Zissler, *MENA Renewables Status Report*, p. 9.
16 Ibid.
17 Bryden, Riahi, and Zissler, *MENA Renewables Status Report*, p. 31.
18 El-Khayat, Barghouth, Mahmoud and Myrsalieva, *Pan-Arab Renewable Energy Strategy 2030*.

	Installed Capacity (MW)						
	Solar		Wind	Biomass	Geothermal	Hydro	Total
Countries	PV	CSP		and Waste			
Bahrain	5[b]	0[b]	0.5[a]	0[b]	0[b]	0[b]	5.5
Iran	4.3[c]	17[b]	91[a]	0[b]	0[b]	9500[c]	9612.3
Iraq	3.5[d]	0[b]	0[b]	0[b]	0[b]	1864[a]	1867.5
Kuwait	1.8	0[b]	0[b]	0[b]	0[b]	0[b]	1.8
Oman	0.7	0[b]	0[b]	0[b]	0[b]	0[b]	0.7
Qatar	1.2	0[a]	0[a]	40[a]	0[a]	0[a]	41.2
Saudi Arabia	7 (2013)	0[b]	0[b]	0[b]	0[b]	0[b]	7
United Arab Emirates	22.5	100 (2013)	0[b]	0[a]	0[b]	0[b]	12.5
Total Persian Gulf countries	46	117	91.5	0	0	11364	11548.5
Total percentage exploited Persian Gulf countries	0.40%	1.01%	0.79%	0%	0%	98%	100%

[a]2012 [b]2011 [c]2010 [d]2009

Table 2: Installed Renewable Energy Capacity in the Persian Gulf
Countries for Power Generation. Source: J. Bryden, L. Riahi and
R. Zissler, *MENA Renewables Status Report*, p. 11.

the integration of numerous systems and accounts for the dynamic impact of their interaction, even if they are typically independently managed. Hadian and Madani (2015)[19] have proposed the use of this high-level approach in considering the existing trade-offs among the lower-level systems. More specifically, this chapter works to determine the desirability of eleven different energy alternatives through the analysis of four different sustainability criteria, namely carbon, water, cost and land footprints. We argue that it is vital to study the nexus of energy, land, water and economy to determine the aggregated impact of each energy option before blindly increasing the share of renewables in the energy mix of a country. The following section presents each nexus from an energy perspective across the Persian Gulf region.

The energy nexus

Water and energy are independently managed systems that are deeply interlocked.[20]

---

19 Hadian and Madani, 'A system of systems approach to energy sustainability assessment: Are all renewables really green?', p. 195.
20 Madani and Khatami, *Water for Energy: Inconsistent Assessment Standards and Inability to Judge Properly*, p. 10.

Energy is required to purify, desalinate and transport water. On the other hand, energy generation is heavily dependent on water availability, which can evolve with climate change.[21] For this reason, the correlation of energy demand and water availability cannot be ignored.[22]

This nexus is even more important in the MENA region, since all statistical indicators imply that the region is one of the hottest and most water scarce territories on Earth. All Persian Gulf countries, except Iraq and Iran, battle with acute fresh-water scarcity. The World Bank defines water scarcity as a country's access to less than 1,000 cubic metres of water a year. This factor challenges the region with new problems, such as reduction of available grazing land for livestock and competition for food.[23] The United Nations has identified a link between freshwater-starved societies and systematic problems such as poverty, unintended urbanisation and environmental deterioration. There is additional stress on fragmented institutional governing structures where shortages are particularly acute.[24]

The scarcity issue is set to worsen as freshwater demand rises with rapid population growth. In 2009, Russell projected an increase of 36% over the coming decade in water demand across the GCC states.[25] The demand for domestic water is estimated to double in the Persian Gulf region by 2025, while the demand for industrial usages will increase threefold over that period.[26] Combined with the continuous mismanagement of renewable water resources in these countries, the systematic shortage is only set to gain momentum and escalate overtime.[27] Therefore, it is important to consider the trade-off among carbon emission and energy technology and its resulting impact on water resources in order to avoid unsustainable outcomes that can aggravate the water scarcity issues of the region even further.[28]

The cost of energy generation is another crucial factor that needs to be

---

21 L. Gaudard, F. Romerio, F. Dalla Valle, R. Gorret, S. Maran, G. Ravazzani, M. Stoffel and M. Volonterio, 'Climate change impacts on hydropower in the Swiss and Italian Alps', *Science of the Total Environment* 493, 2014, pp. 1211–21.

22 L. Gaudard, F. Avanzi and C. De Michelec, 'Seasonal aspects of the energy-water nexus: The case of a run-of-the-river hydropower plant', *Applied Energy*, 2018, pp. 604–12.

23 H. Pouran, 'MENA, climate change ENA, climate change', p. 6.

24 J. A. Russell, 'Environmental Security and Regional Stability in the Persian Gulf', *Middle East Policy* 16.4, 2009, pp. 90–101.

25 Russell, 'Environmental Security and Regional Stability in the Persian Gulf', p. 91.

26 Ibid.

27 Ibid.

28 Madani and Khatami, 'Water for Energy: Inconsistent Assessment Standards and Inability to Judge Properly', pp. 10–1.

addressed when it comes to sustainable development. Traditionally, energy planners focused on implementing the cheapest possible energy portfolio. However, decision makers are now coming to the realisation that other externalities must be considered.[29] Although cheaper energy production is desirable, especially for a developing region like the Persian Gulf, however the ideal energy alternative should ensure adverse impacts on environmental resources are minimised. A trade-off between the cost of energy and its consequent effects on natural resources should be considered.[30] Investing in cheap fossil fuels with the sole intention of lowering impact on economic resources can severely exacerbate the existing pressure on environmental resources such as land and water and lead to higher overall emissions.

The Persian Gulf countries present a special case since their economic growth is heavily dependent on the international gas and oil markets. The countries bordering the Persian Gulf have benefited from the highest rate of economic growth around the world. This is mainly due to the utilisation and development of abundant oil and gas resources.[31] Since sustainable energy programmes are expensive, Persian Gulf countries require a large rent from their fossil fuel resources to fund their mitigating plans. The failure of implementing such mitigation and adaptation plans will leave a negative impact on Persian Gulf societies; as a result, regional stability can also be compromised. Nonetheless, to efficiently address climate change, carbon emissions generated from combustion of fossil fuels must be controlled and reduced, subsequently lowering demand for fossil fuels, which in turn negatively affects the market and economic resources of the region. In absence of this revenue, the Persian Gulf countries could be tackling the issue of decreasing GDP per capita, economic deterioration and political conflicts. Finding an equilibrium is therefore a complex process in the region when it comes to sustainable use of fossil fuels.[32] The economy-energy nexus has to be incorporated into the decision making process when selecting optimal energy alternatives in the region.

The rapid economic growth has been equivalent to unparalleled population

---

29 OECD, 'OECD Green Growth Studies', https://www.oecd.org/greengrowth/greening-energy/49157219.pdf.

30 X. Tang, X. Benjamin, C. McLellan, S. Snowden, B. Zhang and M. Höök, 'Dilemmas for China: Energy, Economy and Environment', *Sustainability* 7.5, 2015, pp. 5508–20.

31 N. Y. Khan, 'Multiple stressors and ecosystem-based management', *Aquatic Ecosystem Health and Management* 10, 2007, 259–67.

32 P. F. Sale, 'The Growing Need for Sustainable Ecological Management of Marine Communities of the Persian Gulf', *A Journal of the Human Environment* 40.1, 2011, pp. 4–17.

growth, specifically in Bahrain, UAE, and Qatar. Bahrain has the fastest growing population in the region. The country's population increased from 661,000 in 2001 to 1 million in 2009,[33] and to 1.4252 million in 2016,[34] making it the most densely populated country in the world. Similarly, Qatar's local population of 700,000 in 2001[35] rose to 2.6 million in 2016.[36] Qatar's oil and gas production has assisted in raising its economic growth to the point where it has the second largest per-capita income of all countries.[37]

Industrial expansion and rapid population growth have led to large ecological transformations among productive coastal habitats all over the Persian Gulf. Intertidal flats, mangrove forests, fringing coral reefs, seagrass beds, and sandy embayments, in particular, have all been impacted by coastal dredging and development for industrial, commercial, and residential use. The lack of capacity and action from environmental regulation agencies has resulted in numerous negative environmental effects.[38] Land depreciation is a major problem which can lead to the crumbling of ecological sustainability[39] through water quality deterioration, productivity corrosion in ecosystems and losses in biodiversity.[40] It is hence important to implement technologies which are land efficient and have minimum land requirement for further production. Consequently, the energy-land nexus has a key role in sustainable development.

Methodology

We evaluate the desirability of 11 different energy technologies through the use of System of Systems (SoS) framework,[41] working with four impact indicators believed to be the most relevant to issues currently faced by the region.

33 Sale, 'The Growing Need for Sustainable Ecological Management of Marine Communities of the Persian Gulf', p. 8.
34 World Bank, *Bahrain*, https://data.worldbank.org/country/Bahrain.
35 Sale, 'The Growing Need for Sustainable Ecological Management of Marine Communities of the Persian Gulf', p. 8.
36 World Bank, *Qatar*, https://data.worldbank.org/country/qatar.
37 Sale, 'The Growing Need for Sustainable Ecological Management of Marine Communities of the Persian Gulf', p. 8.
38 Ibid.
39 B. Burkhard, F. Kroll, S. Nedkov and F. Müller, 'Mapping ecosystem service supply, demand and budgets', *Ecological Indicators* 21, 2012, pp. 17–29.
40 Sale, 'The Growing Need for Sustainable Ecological Management of Marine Communities of the Persian Gulf', p. 8.
41 Hadian and Madani, 'A system of systems approach to energy sustainability assessment: Are all renewables really green?', pp. 195–9.

Existing lifecycle information on these impact indicators was gathered through extensive literature review. The indicators include water footprint,[42] land footprint,[43] carbon footprint,[44] and levelised cost. The values for cost were obtained through our own computation based on Kost *et al*'s (2013)[45] calculation of minimum and maximum oil price between 2011 and 2016 with a discount rate of 10%.

The next step involved the ranking of each technology. The compiled values are typically organised within a range. This introduced uncertainty was dealt with by the application of the Monte-Carlo approach. Five notions of optimality were selected using five multi-criteria decision-making methods and used to determine the ranking of technologies[46] – for more specific detail on the methodology refer to Hadian and Madani (2015).[47] It was anticipated that identical ranking would not be achieved under different optimality approaches, as assumptions differ from one approach to another. The rankings were aggregated to determine the relative aggregate footprint (RAF) of each technology. This index portrays the overall desirability of energy alternatives with respect to the four sustainability indicators

42 W. Gerbens-Leenes, A. Hoekstra and T. H. van der Meer, 'The water footprint of energy from biomass: A quantitative assessment and consequences of an increasing share of bio-energy in energy supply', *Ecological Economics* 68.4, 2009, pp. 1052–60; M. M. Mekonnen, P. W. Gerbens-Leenes and A. Y. Hoekstra, 'The consumptive water footprint of electricity and heat: a global assessment', *Environmental Science: Water Research & Technology* 3, 2015, pp. 285–97.

43 R. I. McDonald, J. Fargione, J. Kiesecker, W. M. Miller and J. Powell, 'Energy sprawl or energy efficiency: climate policy impacts on natural habitat for the United States of America', *PLoS One* 4.8, 2009, e6802.

44 S. Schlömer, T. Bruckner, L. Fulton, E. Hertwich, A. McKinnon, D. Perczyk, J. Roy, R. Schaeffer, R. Sims, P. Smith and R. Wiser, 'Annex III: Technology-specific cost and performance parameters', *Climate Change 2014: Mitigation of Climate Change. Contribution of Working Group III to the Fifth Assessment Report of the Intergovernmental Panel on Climate Change*, eds. O. Edenhofer, R. Pichs-Madruga, Y. Sokona, E. Farahani, S. Kadner, K. Seyboth, A. Adler, I. Baum, S. Brunner, P. Eickemeier, B. Kriemann, J. Savolainen, S. Schlömer, C. von Stechow, T. Zwickel and J. C. Minx, Cambridge 2014, p. 1333.

45 C. Kost *et al*, *Levelized cost of electricity renewable energy technologies*, https://www.ise.fraunhofer.de/content/dam/ise/en/documents/publications/studies/Fraunhofer-ISE_LCOE_Renewable_Energy_technologies.pdf.

46 S. Mokhtari, K. Madani and N. B. Chang, 'Multi-Criteria Decision Making under Uncertainty: Application to California's Sacramento-San Joaquin Delta Problem', *World Environmental and Water Resources Congress 2012: Crossing Boundaries*, Albuquerque 2012, pp. 2339–48.

47 Hadian and Madani, 'A system of systems approach to energy sustainability assessment: Are all renewables really green?', pp. 195–9.

and performance uncertainty. The higher the RAF value, the more undesirable a technology is considered to be and vice versa.

Regional resource availability

The desirability of energy technologies within a country may vary according to their resource availability. For example, a country with severe land limitations such as Bahrain would be sensitive to land intensive technologies. As a result, higher priority (weight) will be allocated to their land footprint. Consequently, the resource availability of nations would impact their optimal choice of technology. The RAF must therefore be computed by weighting the indicators, i.e. giving priority to indicators based on regional conditions.

Figure 18 presents the weights assigned to each impact indicator for each country within the Persian Gulf territory. These weights are calculated through the consideration of their position within the global benchmark values of land area per capita,[48] GDP with purchasing power parity (PPP),[49] freshwater withdrawal as a percentage of total renewable water resources,[50] and carbon emissions per capita.[51] The values for these metrics are compared against the global benchmark values to determine country specific weighting – for more information on the methodology refer to Hadian and Madani (2015).[52] If the land and economic resources of a specific country are amongst the top of the global benchmark values, it means the country assigns a lower priority (weight) to these indicators. These metrics of positive attributes signify that the country can afford to implement a higher share of land intensive or expensive technologies. Conversely, water withdrawal and carbon emissions have negative attributes. This means if their values are high in a given country, special attention must be paid to these footprints when building an energy mix. Thus, the country must steer away from water intensive and high carbon emitting technologies. The weight attributed to each indicator is set in accordance with the abundance and restrictions of the resources in each country.

As demonstrated in Figure 18, the highest weight across the region is associated with water resources and carbon emissions. This is consistent with the

---

48 FOA, *Land*, http://faostat.fao.org/beta/en/#data/RL.
49 World Bank, *GDP per capita*, http://data.worldbank.org/indicator/NY.GDP.PCAP.PP.CD.
50 AQUASTAT, *AQUASTAT database*, http://www.fao.org/nr/water/aquastat/data/query/index.html?lang=en.
51 World Bank, *CO_2 emissions*, http://data.worldbank.org/indicator/EN.ATM.CO2E.PC.
52 Hadian and Madani, 'A system of systems approach to energy sustainability assessment: Are all renewables really green?', pp. 195–9.

demographics of the region, as it is under severe water stress and home to countries with some of the highest emissions per capita in the world.

Relative desirability of energy resources

Figure 19 maps the relative desirability of each energy technology across the Persian Gulf countries. Green represents highly desirable technologies while red signifies the most undesirable technologies. The application of weights allows the identification of any disparity between the different decision-making levels and allows the allocation of the most desirable energy technology in accordance to the needs of each country.

Figure 19 demonstrates that once the resource availability of a country has been taken into account, the desirability of technologies varies from one country to another. Onshore wind is generally desirable across the region due to its small water and carbon footprint. Offshore wind's desirability drops slightly due to a higher associated cost in comparison to onshore wind.

While nuclear has a low overall relative aggregate footprint, it is not the most desirable technology in all countries, considering its cost and water footprint – nuclear requires cold water to cool down the installation.[53] This factor, combined with the region's problem of water scarcity, tends to lower this technology's desirability. Therefore, water footprint is an important indicator to consider. As a result, onshore wind energy gains in relative desirability across the region.

Concentrated solar power is associated with low water and carbon footprint but suffers from high costs in comparison to other technologies. For countries like Oman, UAE and Kuwait, with higher economic resources, this technology has medium desirability. While for a country like Iraq with a lower GDP per capita this technology becomes less desirable.

Biomass and large-scale hydropower represent the most undesirable technologies across the region. Hydropower's high land and water footprint is the main reason behind its undesirability. This technology is even more inefficient when it comes to water restricted countries. Hence for a region as water scarce as the Persian Gulf, hydropower becomes highly undesirable, contrary to its current role as the dominant renewable energy in the region. Biomass is also undesirable across the region due to its large land and water use and intermediate carbon emissions. These technologies are extremely undesirable for UAE, Bahrain, Kuwait,

---

53 World Nuclear Association, *Cooling Power Plants*, http://www.world-nuclear.org/
information-library/current-and-future-generation/cooling-power-plants.aspx.

and even more so for Iraq. Their desirability improves slightly for Iran, Saudi Arabia, and Oman, as these countries enjoy better land availability and slightly higher water availability.

Iraq is an insightful case because of its high water stress and lower economic capacity. Therefore, nuclear, concentrated solar power and hydropower are less desirable in Iraq than in the rest of the region. However, coal, oil, and natural gas are more desirable in Iraq than in the rest of the region. This is because Iraq has the lowest weight assigned to its carbon emissions compared to the rest of the Persian Gulf nations and due to its low economic capacity, the country favours cheap and less water-intensive energy technologies. In other words, it can afford to invest in more carbon-intensive technologies given they have a lower economic burden and water use. Considering the low cost and water footprint of coal, oil and natural gas and high land availability in Iraq, these technologies portray their highest desirability in this country.

Hydropower is the most exploited renewable technology throughout the region, whilst biomass's share is projected to increase in future portfolios. When the issues of water scarcity, land restrictions and carbon emission are taken into consideration, these highly popular renewable alternatives are outperformed by conventional fuels such as oil, coal and natural gas. The results obtained above offer a good insight into the impact consideration of other factors can have on the attractiveness and sustainability of technologies, demonstrating that environmental and economic capacity matter when analysing the energy situation within a given region and when planning for a sustainable energy mix.

Conclusions and policy insights

The dominant reliance on fossil fuels for energy production has led to high greenhouse gas emissions. This phenomenon is worsening the impacts of climate change and affecting natural resources. It is crucial now to address the complexity of energy planning and consider the dynamic relationship that exists between an energy system and that of other environmental and economic systems, while accounting for the uncertainties associated with a multi-attributed decision-making approach. This approach allows us to develop a holistic understanding of the secondary impacts of energy technologies on valuable natural resources and economic capacities, an essential element in developing sustainable energy pathways.

This chapter portrays the potential damage renewables can cause if they are not assessed holistically before implementation. The Persian Gulf region possesses a large potential for renewable energies,[54] such as geothermal, wind, and solar technologies which remain largely unexploited.[55] These alternatives represent immense potential for decarbonising energy portfolios without placing additional burden on natural resources of the region. It is possible for the region to diversify its supply by tapping into these highly desirable renewable energies with lower aggregated impacts, in combination with existing cheap and abundant fossil fuels. However, there is no 'one fits all' solution that can be prescribed to all countries of the region. It is important to fabricate an energy mix for each country with respect to its local resource availability conditions. As seen in Figure 17, the highest growth rates are seen in solar and wind energy within the wider MENA region, followed by biomass. Our results verify solar and wind power to be amongst the more sustainable options with respect to the four indicators considered here. However, an increasing trend in the use of biomass technology for electricity production can lead to unsustainable outcomes due to its impact on land and water resources, and its intermediate level of carbon emissions.

The implementation of an SoS perspective demonstrates that highly promoted renewable energy sources such as hydropower and biomass are not as environmentally friendly as previously believed. Hydropower is unsuitable due to its water intensive nature and large land use, and biomass because of its higher than anticipated carbon emission, combined with its high land and water consumption. These factors offset the efforts of both these renewable energies in decarbonisation of energy portfolios. Combined with other issues such as competition with the agricultural sector and impact on biodiversity in the region, the use of these technologies can lead to an immense burden on the already suffering region of the Persian Gulf. In the case of biomass technology, negative impacts on the surrounding areas can lead to a higher level of carbon emission,[56] making this technology unsustainable. In many rural areas, communities are still dependent on biomass as a source of energy. There are predictions of increase in the share of small-scale biomass in energy portfolios of countries such as Qatar and the UAE

---

54 OECD, *Renewable Energies in the Middle East and North Africa: Policies to Support Private Investment*, http://www.keepeek.com/Digital-Asset-Management/oecd/finance-andinvestment/renewable-energies-in-the-middle-east-and-north-africa_9789264183704-en#.WOQVA_krLIU..

55 M. El-Khayat, A. Barghouth, M. Mahmoud and N. Myrsalieva, 'Pan-Arab Renewable Energy Strategy 2030'.

56 I. El-Husseini, T. El-Sayed, W. Fayad and D. Zywietz, 'A New Source of Power The Potential for Renewable Energy in the MENA Region', http://www.strategyand.pwc.com/media/file/A_New_Source_of_Power-FINAL.pdf.

for electricity production.[57] This has a potential of creating further damage in the region.

Conventional technologies such as natural gas, coal and oil outperform biomass and hydropower. Policymakers and decision-makers have failed to consider the impact of these technologies on valuable natural resources in mitigating the impact of global warming and developing a green future. This is apparent in the existing high share of renewables such as hydropower and projected increase of biomass in future portfolios. A simple substitution of fossil fuels with renewable energy does not secure a sustainable future if impacts beyond carbon emission are not considered. There is therefore a need for reforming policies in the region if adverse environmental impacts are to be avoided.

Our results demonstrate a general desirability for low-carbon technologies, excluding the highly exploited technologies of hydropower and globally popular technology of biomass. Our findings show the existing potential to reduce the overall footprint through a decarbonised energy mix that would include both renewable and non-renewable technologies. Careful consideration is needed in selecting the most appropriate technologies with respect to various economic and environmental indicators. However, if the transition pathways to low-carbon energy alternatives continue to implement a high share of hydropower, biomass and conventional fossil fuels, this shift is more likely to lead to undesirable secondary impact on valuable, already scarce, and endangered natural resources. On the other hand, dominant reliance on fossil fuel resources due to abundant availability and cheaper costs can similarly lead to unsustainable outcomes.

As discussed in this research, nuclear energy has the lowest relative aggregative footprint and it is suggested to have high desirability within the region. However, among the Persian Gulf nations, Iran is the only country with nuclear share in its energy portfolio.[58] In Europe, countries such as Germany, Spain, Belgium and Switzerland are decommissioning their nuclear power plants[59] as the associated risks and the economic resource needed for risk assessment are too high. Our analysis does not consider the issues of security, risk assessment, regulation, social or political acceptance of the energy technologies considered. If Iran is to implement nuclear as a source of energy, it is crucial to fully understand

---

57 J. Bryden, L. Riahi and R. Zissler, *MENA Renewables Status Report.*
58 World Nuclear Association, *Safety of Nuclear Reactors – World Nuclear Association*, http://www.world-nuclear.org/information-library/safety-and-security/safety-of-plants/safety-of-nuclear-power-reactors.asp.
59 EEA, *Overview of electricity production and use in Europe*, https://www.eea.europa.eu/data-and-maps/indicators/overview-of-the-electricity-production-1/assessment.

the risks involved and to resolve any political and technical barriers that might be created from the implementation of this technology.

Not all renewables are beneficial and effective in developing a sustainable future; equally, not all conventional energies are outperformed by renewable energies. These factors demonstrate the need for a holistic prospect of a nexus, and the need for a diversified portfolio that will include both renewables and non-renewables. Decisions for achieving an optimal energy portfolio must be made at regional levels through consideration of individual resource availability in individual countries. Moreover, continuous electricity generation requires a set of services which are provided by hydropower.[60] By contrast, the variability of wind and solar powers should be compensated by backup technologies, or energy storage, such as pumped storage.[61] There is therefore a need for an energy mix, where instead of dominant reliance on one source of energy, a range of energy technologies with variable shares are selected to achieve the country's projected targets while ensuring energy security and minimum impacts are achieved. Not only will this allow a more sustainable approach to energy supply, but it would also minimise risk due to a diversified energy portfolio, which would spread the risk across a range of technologies. We should emphasise that this analysis is limited to electricity generation only, and it does not consider technical, political and feasibility constraints.

Bibliography

Akpan, U. F. and G. E. Akpan, 'The Contribution of Energy Consumption to Climate Change: A Feasible Policy Direction', *International Journal of Energy Economics and Policy* 2.1, 2012, pp. 21–33.

AQUASTAT, *AQUASTAT database*, 2016, http://www.fao.org/nr/water/aquastat/data/query/index.html?lang=en.

Barros, N. *et al*, 'Carbon emission from hydroelectric reservoirs linked to reservoir age and latitude', *Nature Geoscience* 4.9, 2011, pp. 593–6.

---

60 L. Gaudard and F. Romerio, 'Reprint of "The future of hydropower in Europe: Interconnecting climate, markets and policies"', *Environmental Science & Policy* 43, 2014, pp. 5–14.
61 El-Khayat, Barghouth, Mahmoud and Myrsalieva, 'Pan-Arab Renewable Energy Strategy 2030'; M. Guittet, M. Capezzali, L. Gaudard, F. Romerio-Giudici, F. Vuille and F. Avellan, 'Study of the drivers and asset management of pumped-storage power plants historical and geographical perspective', *Energy*, 2016, pp. 560–79.

Beaulieu, J., R. Smolensk, C. Nietch, A. Townsend-Small and M. Elovitz, 'High Methane Emissions from a Midlatitude Reservoir Draining an Agricultural Watershed', *Environmental Science and Technology* 48.19, 2016, pp. 11100–8.

Bond, A., A. Morrison-Saunders and J. Pope, 'Sustainability assessment: the state of the art', *Impact Assessment and Project Appraisal* 30.1, 2012, pp. 53–62.

Boyd, R., J. Cranston Turner and B. Ward, *Intended nationally determined contributions: what are the implications for greenhouse gas emissions in 2030?*, 2015, http://www.lse.ac.uk/GranthamInstitute/wp-content/uploads/2015/10/Boyd_Turner_and_Ward_policy_paper_October_2015.pdf.

Bridle, R., L. Kiston and P. Wooders, *Fossil-Fuel Subsidies; A Barrier to renewable energy in five Middle East and North African countries*, 2014, https://www.iisd.org/gsi/sites/default/files/fossil-fuel-subsidies-renewable-energy-middle-east-north-african-countri%20%20%20.pdf.

Bryden, J., L. Riahi and R. Zissler, *MENA Renewables Status Report*, 2013, http://www.ren21.net/Portals/0/documents/activities/Regional%20Reports/MENA_2013_lowres.pdf.

Burkhard, B., F. Kroll, S. Nedkov and F. Müller, 'Mapping ecosystem service supply, demand and budgets', *Ecological Indicators* 21, 2012, pp. 17–29.

Carbon Brief, *Paris 2015: Tracking country climate pledges*, 16 September 2015, https://www.carbonbrief.org/paris-2015-tracking-country-climate-pledges.

Churchman, C. W. and R, L. Ackoff, 'An Approximate Measure of Value', *Journal of the Operations Research Society of America* 2.2, 1954, pp. 172–87.

EEA, *Overview of electricity production and use in Europe*, 2015, https://www.eea.europa.eu/data-and-maps/indicators/overview-of-the-electricity-production-1/assessment.

EIA, *World energy demand and economc outlook*, 2016, https://www.eia.gov/forecasts/ieo/world.cfm.

El-Husseini, I., W. El-Sayed, T. Fayad and D. Zywietz, *A New Source of Power The Potential for Renewable Energy in the MENA Region*, 2010, http://www.strategyand.pwc.com/media/file/A_New_Source_of_Power-FINAL.pdf.

El-Khayat, M., A. Barghouth, M. Mahmoud and N. Myrsalieva, *Pan-Arab Renewable Energy Strategy 2030*, 2014, http://www.irena.org/DocumentDownloads/Publications/IRENA_Pan-Arab_Strategy_June%202014.pdf.

Fishburn, P. C., *Decision and Value Theory*, New York 1964.

FOA, *Land*, 2016, http://faostat.fao.org/beta/en/#data/RL.

Forester, J. W., 'System dynamics and the lessons of 35 years', *A Systems-Based Approach to Policymaking*, ed. K. B. de Greene, Boston 1993, pp. 199–240.

Gasparatos, A., 'Embedded value systems in sustainability assessment tools and their implications. Journal of Environmental Management', *Journal of Environmental Management* 91.8, 2010, pp. 1613–22.

Gaudard, L. and F. Romerio, 'Reprint of "The future of hydropower in Europe: Interconnecting climate, markets and policies"', *Environmental Science and Policy* 43, 2014, pp. 5–14.

Gaudard, L. *et al*, 'Climate change impacts on hydropower in the Swiss and Italian Alps', *Science of the Total Environment* 493, 2014, pp. 1211–21.

Gaudard, L., F. Avanzi and C. De Michelec, 'Seasonal aspects of the energy-water nexus: The case of a run-of-the-river hydropower plant', *Applied Energy*, 2017.

Gerbens-Leenes, P., A. Hoekstra and T. van der Meer, 'The water footprint of energy from biomass: A quantitative assessment and consequences of an increasing share of bio-energy in energy supply', *Ecological Economics* 68.4, 2009, pp. 1052–60.

Graham-Rowe, D., *Hydroelectric power's dirty secret revealed*, 2016, https://www.newscientist.com/article/dn7046-hydroelectric-powers-dirty-secret-revealed.

Guittet, M., M. Capezzali, L. Gaudard, F. Romerio-Giudici, F. Vuille and F. Avellan, 'Study of the drivers and asset management of pumped-storage power plants historical and geographical perspective', *Energy*, 2016, pp. 560–79.

Hadian, S. and K. Madani, 'A system of systems approach to energy sustainability assessment: Are all renewables really green?', *Ecological Indicators* 52, 2015, pp. 194–206.

Hadian, S., K. Madani, J. Gonzalezp, S. Mokhtari and A. Mirchi, 'Sustainable energy planning with respect to resource use efficiency: insights for the United States', *World Environmental and Water Resources Congress 2014*, Portland 2014, pp. 2066–77.

Hjorth, P. and K. Madani, 'Sustainability monitoring and assessment: new challenges require new thinking', *Journal of Water Resources Planning and Management* 140.2, 2014, pp. 133–5.

IEA, *Annual energy outlook 2015 with projections to 2040*, 2015, https://www.eia.gov/outlooks/aeo/pdf/0383(2015).pdf.

IEA, *Technology Roadmap 2035 2040 2045 2050 Wind energy*, 2013, https://
www.iea.org/publications/freepublications/publication/Wind_2013_
Roadmap.pdf.

IPCC, *IPCC Special Report on Renewable Energy Sources and Climate Change
Mitigation*, 2011, http://www.uncclearn.org/sites/default/files/inventory/
ipcc15.pdf.

Khan, N. Y., 'Multiple stressors and ecosystem-based management', *Aquatic
Ecosystem Health and Management* 10, 2007, pp. 259–67.

Kost, C. *et al*, *Levelized cost of electricity renewable energy technologies*, 2013,
https://www.ise.fraunhofer.de/content/dam/ise/en/documents/publications/
studies/Fraunhofer-ISE_LCOE_Renewable_Energy_technologies.pdf.

Madani, K. and S. Khatami, 'Water for Energy: Inconsistent Assessment
Standards and Inability to Judge Properly', *Current Sustainable/Renewable
Energy Reports* 2.1, 2015, pp. 10–6.

Magill, B., *Hydropower May Be Huge Source of Methane Emissions*, 2016,
http://www.climatecentral.org/news/hydropower-as-major-methane-
emitter-18246.

McDonald, R. I., J. Fargione, J. Kiesecker, W. M. Miller and J. Powell, 'Energy
sprawl or energy efficiency: climate policy impacts on natural habitat for the
United States of America', *PLoS One* 4.8, 2009, p. e6802.

Mekonnen, M., P. Gerbens-Leenes and A. Hoekstra, 'The consumptive water
footprint of electricity and heat: a global assessment', *Environmental
Science: Water Research & Technology*, 2015, pp. 285–97.

Mokhtari, S., K. Madani and N. B. Chang, 'Multi-Criteria Decision Making
under Uncertainty: Application to California's Sacramento-San Joaquin
Delta Problem', *World Environmental and Water Resources Congress 2012:
Crossing Boundaries*, Albuquerque 2012, pp. 2339–48.

OECD, *OECD Green Growth Studies*, 2011, https://www.oecd.org/greengrowth/
greening-energy/49157219.pdf.

OECD, *Renewable Energies in the Middle East and North Africa: Policies
to Support Private Investment*, 2013, http://www.keepeek.com/
Digital-Asset-Management/oecd/finance-and-investment/renewable-energies-
in-the-middle-east-and-north-africa_9789264183704-en#.WOQVA_krLIU.

Pouran, H., 'MENA, climate change ENA, climate change', *The Middle East in
London* 12.3, 2016, pp. 5–6.

Russell, J. A., 'Environmental Security and Regional Stability in the Persian
Gulf', *Middle East Policy* 16.4, 2009, pp. 90–101.

Sale, P. F. *et al*, 'The Growing Need for Sustainable Ecological Management of Marine Communities of the Persian Gulf', *A Journal of the Human Environment* 40.1, 2011, pp. 4–17.

Scherer, L. and S. Pfister, 'Hydropower's Biogenic Carbon Footprint', *PLOS ONE* 11.9, 2016, e0161947.

Sorrell, S., 'Reducing energy demand: A review of issues, challenges and approaches', *Renewable and Sustainable Energy Reviews*, 2015, pp. 74–82.

Tang, X., B. McLellan, S. Snowden, B. Zhang and M. Höök, 'Dilemmas for China: Energy, Economy and Environment', *Sustainability* 7.5, 2015, pp. 5508–20.

Tversky, A., 'Intransitivity of preferences', *Psychological Review* 76, 1969, pp. 31–48.

Wald, A., 'Statistical Decision Functions Which Minimize the Maximum RiskAnnals of Mathematics', *Annals of Mathematics* 46.2, 1945, pp. 265–80.

Weiser, M., *The hydropower paradox: is this energy as clean as it seems?*, *The Guardian* 6 November 2016, https://www.theguardian.com/sustainable-business/2016/nov/06/hydropower-hydroelectricity-methane-clean-climate-change-study.

World Bank, *A New Plan to Support Action on Climate Change in the Arab World*, 9 November 2015, http://www.worldbank.org/en/news/feature/2016/11/15/a-new-plan-to-support-action-on-climate-change-in-the-arab-world.

World Bank, *Bahrain*, 2016, https://data.worldbank.org/country/Bahrain.

World Bank, *CO_2 emissions*, 2016, http://data.worldbank.org/indicator/EN.ATM.CO2E.PC.

World Bank, *GDP per capita*, 2016, http://data.worldbank.org/indicator/NY.GDP.PCAP.PP.CD.

World Bank, *Middle East and North Africa – Adaptation to Climate Change in the Middle East and North Africa Region*, 2013, http://web.worldbank.org/WBSITE/EXTERNAL/COUNTRIES/MENAEXT/0,,contentMDK:21596766~pagePK:146736~piPK:146830~theSitePK:256299,00.html.

World Bank, *Middle East and North Africa Overview*, 2015, http://www.worldbank.org/en/region/mena/overview.

World Bank, *Qatar*, 2016, https://data.worldbank.org/country/qatar.

World Energy Council, *Comparison of energy systems using life cycle assessment*, 2004, https://www.worldenergy.org/publications/2004/comparison-of-energy- systems-using-life-cycle-assessment/.

World Nuclear Association, *Cooling Power Plants*, 2017, http://www.world-nuclear.org/information-library/current-and-future-generation/cooling-power-plants.aspx.

World Nuclear Association, *Safety of Nuclear Reactors – World Nuclear Association*, 2016, http://www.world-nuclear.org/information-library/safety-and-security/safety-of-plants/safety-of-nuclear-power-reactors.asp.

Yoon, K. P. and C, Hwang, *Multiple Attribute Decision Making: An Introduction*, California 1995.

12

The Energy Sector in Oman

Juman Al-Saqlawi, Niall Mac Dowell and Kaveh Madani

Introduction

Located in a region where over forty per cent of the world's oil and gas reserves lie, and following a similar pattern to that of its neighbours, Oman's economy has been reliant on crude oil export since the 1970's.[1] Aware of the dangers of dependence in oil, and with the discovery of natural gas in the 1980's, the Omani government resorted to using two main strategies: diversifying its economy and creating a sovereign wealth fund designed to provide the country with cash reserves at times of need.[2] Although successful, these strategies resulted in a domestic energy policy organised around the oil and gas sectors and led by the Ministry of Oil and Gas (MOG) and the Ministry of Finance (MOF).[3] With the unpredictability of fossil fuel prices and the global push towards CO_2 emission reduction,[4] and Oman's Ministry of Environment and Climate Affairs's (MECA) intention to achieve the nationally determined contribution (INDC) pledge of 2% emissions

---

1 EIA, *International Energy Statistics*, 2014, http://www.eia.gov/cfapps/ipdbproject/iedindex3.cfm?tid=3&pid=3&aid=6&cid=regions,&syid=2015&eyid=2015&unit=TCF; Knoema, *Cost of oil production by country*, 2014, http://knoema.com/vyronoe/cost-of-oil-production-by-country.
2 R. Shediac and H. Samman, *The Vital Role of Sovereign Wealth Funds in the GCC's Future*, Technical report, Booz & Co., 2015.
3 IRENA, *Sultanate of Oman, Renewables Readiness Assessment*, Technical report, International Renewable Energy Agency, 2014.
4 A. H. Al-Badi, A. Malik and A. Gastli, 'Sustainable energy usage in Oman; opportunities and barriers', *Renewable and Sustainable Energy Reviews* 15, 2011, pp. 3780–8; A. Kumar Sharma, 'Your email to Mr Khamis', MECA, 2013, personal communication; MECA and INDC, Technical report, United Nations Framework Convention on Climate Change, 2015.

reduction,[5] the sustainability of the current energy policy is questionable. Given the potential of solar energy as an alternative fuel and the lack of renewable based policies in Oman, identifying opportunities for its successful implementation can only be achieved through an initial understanding of the energy sector in Oman.[6] To this end, this chapter provides a review of the energy sector in Oman from home production and import of primary fuels to eventual final uses. The major stakeholders involved are identified and alternative primary fuels are discussed. Figure 20 is an energy flowchart for Oman based on IEA's data for the year 2013.[7] Based on this chart, the energy sector in Oman can be divided into three main sectors: the primary (supply) sector, the intermediary sector and the demand (end-use) sector, described in sections below. The contribution of these sectors to CO_2 emissions is depicted in Figure 21. Finally, any conclusions drawn from this analysis are discussed in the last section of the chapter.

The primary (supply) sector

There are two types of primary fuels used in Oman: oil (crude, natural gas liquids or NGL, and feedstock) and natural gas. These types of fuel are mainly produced domestically and only a small amount is imported from abroad.

Oil (crude, NGL and feedstocks)

In 2013, Oman produced an average of 941.9 thousand barrels per day, constituting approximately 1% of the world's oil production.[8] As evident in Figure 20,

---

5 M. Mattei, G. Notton, C. Cristofari, M. Muselli and P. Poggi, 'Calculation of the polycrystalline PV module temperature using a simple method of energy balance', *Renewable Energy* 31, 2006, pp. 553–67; 'Oman to play its part on climate change', *Times of Oman* 2015, http://timesofoman.com/article/73532.

6 A. Mokri, M. Aal Ali and M. Emziane, 'Solar energy in the United Arab Emirates: A review', *Renewable and Sustainable Energy Reviews* 28, 2013, pp. 340–75; R. T. Ogulata, 'Sectoral energy consumption in turkey', *Renewable and Sustainable Energy Reviews* 6, 2002, pp. 471–80; L. Raslavicius, 'Renewable energy sector in Belarus: A review', *Renewable and Sustainable Energy Reviews* 16, 2012, pp. 5399–413; O. Rauf, S. Wang, P. Yuan and J. Tan, 'An overview of energy status and development in Pakistan', *Renewable and Sustainable Energy Reviews* 48, 2015, pp. 892–931.

7 IEA, *Oman: Balances*, 2013, https://www.iea.org/statistics/statisticssearch/report/?count ry=Oman&product=balances&year=2014; J. Skea, P. Ekins and M. Winskel, *Energy 2050; Making the Transition to a Secure Low Carbon Energy System*, Earthscan 2011.

8 OECD, *Crude Oil Production*, 2013, https://data.oecd.org/energy/crude-oil-production. htm.

over 80% of the oil produced in Oman was exported, with over 95% of the oil exports destined for Asian countries – 60% to China.[9] This explains why 40% of the country's GDP is from oil exports and highlights the risky dependence of the country's economy on one client country.[10] The remaining 20% of the crude oil produced was domestically refined into oil products such as gasoline and jet fuel. Oman does not import crude oil; however, due to the geological composition and viscous nature of Oman's oil, 20% of Oman's natural gas has been used to increase oil production using various enhanced oil recovery (EOR) methods.[11] Consequently, oil production costs in Oman are the highest in the region, making solar energy an attractive possible alternative to natural gas for EOR.

There are currently 16 companies contributing to the exploitation and production of oil and natural gas in Oman. The Ministry of Oil and Gas (MOG) is the organisation responsible for developing and implementing plans, policies, regulations and laws governing the oil and gas sectors.[12] However, final approval on policy and investment rests with the Sultan of Oman.

Natural gas

On average, Oman produced 101.8 million m^3 natural gas per day in 2013. This constitutes less than 0.015% of the world's natural gas production.[13] Over 60% of the natural gas produced in Oman was consumed domestically, mainly in industry and power generation. This is due to the current policy of promoting industrial development in order to trigger activity and employment. As part of this policy, the gas provided for the industrial sector and power generators is sold at advantageous prices – 3 USD/mmBTU and 1.5 USD/mmBTU respectively. Although these prices are not lower than the United States's domestic gas price,[14] they are significantly lower than the world LNG export prices; which are on average 8

9 MOG, *Annual Report*, Technical report, Ministry of Oil and Gas, 2013.
10 NCSI, *Statistical Yearbook*, 2014; IEA, *Oman Energy and CO_2 Emissions Data*, 2013, http://ukdataservice.ac.uk/; World Bank, *Oman*, 2016, http://data.worldbank.org/country/oman; BBC, *Oman country profile*, 2013, http://www.bbc.co.uk/news/world-middle-east-14654150.
11 EIA, *Overview of Oman*, 2013, www.eia.gov/countries/cab.cfm?fips=MU.
12 MOG, *Brief History of the Oil and Gas Sector*, 2013, http://www.mog.gov.om/english/AboutUs/TheHistoryofOilGas/tabid/117/Default.aspx.
13 Enerdata, *Natural Gas Production*, 2013, https://yearbook.enerdata.net/natural-gas/world-natural-gas-production-statistics.html.
14 EIA, *Natural Gas*, 2017, https://www.eia.gov/naturalgas/weekly/#tabs-prices-2.

USD/mmBTU for the UK and Germany, and 13 USD/mmBTU for Japan.[15] This trend highlights the high opportunity cost of current policies and questions the sustainability of the current gas policy. The organisation responsible for the efficient management and delivery of natural gas to the relevant power plants and industries through pipelines is Oman Gas Company (OGC).[16]

In terms of exports, 36% of the natural gas produced was exported as liquefied natural gas (LNG), making the LNG sector the second major contributor to Oman's economy, constituting 12–15% of the GDP. These LNG exports are produced in two liquefaction facilities, Oman LNG and Qalhat LNG, located in the eastern region of the country, known as Al-Sharqiya. Together, they operate as a single entity called Oman LNG. It must be noted that due to the rising level of domestic demand for natural gas, Oman has cut LNG exports, resulting in an under-utilised LNG capacity where the gas liquefaction plant in Qalhat is operating at 2 million tons below capacity. At the moment, Oman only fulfils long-term LNG export contracts to Japan and Korea, where most of the country's LNG exports go to.

On the other hand, although Oman is not a major importer of natural gas, the country imported approximately 200 million ft³ per day in 2013 from Qatar via the Dolphin pipeline. This import is necessary to meet the rising level of domestic consumption, which is expected to substantially increase in the near future due to industry and power generation.[17] Therefore, the Omani government is developing the local gas fields, particularly the Khazan-Makarem field, in order to prepare them for production. The development of this field would increase the local production by three times and enhance the country's reserves overall. Additionally, all currently exported volumes of LNG are to be diverted away from foreign markets and sold to domestic consumers by 2024 when all long-term contracts are expected to terminate. Finally, there are plans for additional gas imports via a pipeline from Iran. If realised, this would be a 60 billion USD, 25-year supply deal.

---

15 BP, *BP Statistical Review of World Energy*, Technical report, British Petroleum, 2017.
16 OGC, *About Us*, 2013, www.oman-gas.com.om.
17 Global Research, *Oman Economic Overview*, Technical report, Global, 2011; IRENA, *IRENA Handbook on Renewable Energy Nationally Appropriate Mitigation Actions (NAMAs)*, Technical report, International Renewable Energy Agency, 2014.

Alternative primary fuels

Nuclear

Oman has no nuclear power plants and after the 2011 nuclear meltdown at the Fukushima Daiichi power plant in Japan, the country has chosen not to pursue a domestic atomic energy capability.[18]

Renewable energy

Being aware of the high opportunity cost of natural gas and the possible role of renewables in the country's future energy mix, several studies have assessed the potential of renewable energy resources for electricity production in Oman.[19]

   These studies all came with the conclusions that there is limited potential for electricity production from biogas, geothermal and wave, yet there are notable wind resources in the southern and eastern parts of Oman. Furthermore, it was found that the level of solar irradiance in Oman is amongst the highest in the world. This is clearly shown in Figure 22 which compares the average daily solar energy potential of Muscat with the rest of the world, calculated as the product of average daily irradiance and daylight hours.[20] From this chart it is clear that the available solar energy potential in Muscat is twice that of Berlin and London and is comparable to other 'sun-rich' cities such as Los Angeles, Madrid and La Paz. Furthermore, it was found that there is significant scope for developing solar energy

---

18 Global Security Newswire, *Oman opts not to Pursue Atomic Power*, 2012.
19 H. A. Kazem, 'Renewable energy in Oman: Status and future prospects', *Renewable and Sustainable Energy Reviews* 15, 2011, pp. 3465–9; COWI and Partners, *Study on Renewable Energy Resources, Oman*, Technical report, Authority of Electricity Regulation, 2008; A. S. S. Dorvlo and D. B. Ampratwum, 'Summary climatic data for solar technology development in Oman', *Renewable Energy* 14, 1998, pp. 255–62; A. S. S. Dorvlo and D. B. Ampratwum, 'Wind energy potential for Oman', *Renewable Energy* 26, 2002, pp. 333–8; J. A. Jervase, A. Al-Lawati and A. S. S. Dorvlo, 'Contour maps for sunshine ratio for Oman using radial basis function generated data', *Renewable Energy* 28, 2003, pp. 487–97; A. H. Al-Badi, A. Malik and A. Gastli, 'Assessment of renewable energy resources potential in Oman and identification of barrier to their significant utilization', *Renewable and Sustainable Energy Reviews* 13, pp. 2734–9; A. Gastli and Y. Charabi, 'Solar electricity prospects in Oman using GIS-based solar radiation maps', *Renewable and Sustainable Energy Reviews* 14, 2010, pp. 790–7; A. H. Al-Badi, M. H. Albadi, A. M. Al-Lawati and A. S. Malik, 'Economic perspective of PV electricity in Oman', *Energy* 36, 2011, pp. 226–32.
20 NASA, *NASA Surface Meteorology and Solar Energy-Irradiance*, 2017, https://eosweb. larc.nasa.gov/cgi-bin/sse/retscreen.cgi?email=skip@larc.nasa.gov/; NASA, *NASA Surface Meteorology and Solar Energy-Daylight Hours*, 2017, https://eosweb.larc.nasa.gov/cgi-bin/ sse/retscreen.cgi?email=skip@larc.nasa.gov/.

throughout Oman as depicted in Figure 23 where it is clear that the level of solar irradiance is highest in the northern and southern parts of the country where most of the electricity is supplied.[21] Given the high population density and the urban nature of the northern and southern regions of Oman,[22] the lack of land availability makes these regions more suitable for relatively small-scale solar projects. On the contrary, larger scale projects are more applicable in the central part of the country.

The intermediary sector

As shown in Figure 20, the primary fuels produced and imported into Oman are either used directly by end-users or converted into a different form of energy. The latter stage is mainly composed of two processes: oil refining and electricity generation. In oil refining, a number of oil products are produced and either domestically consumed or exported. On the other hand, most of the electricity generated is consumed domestically.

Oil products

To cater for Oman's local strategic demand of refined products, Oman Refinery Company (ORC) and Sohar Refinery Company (SRC) were established. These, in turn, were merged in 2007 to form Oman Oil Refineries and Petroleum Industries Company (ORPIC). The types of oil products produced by Oman's refineries are summarised in Figure 24 where it can be seen that the two main products are premium gasoline and gas oil (diesel), used in transport and electricity generation.[23] In Figure 20, it is clear that over 60% of the oil products produced are domestically consumed. The remaining 15%, composed mainly of regular gasoline, liquefied petroleum gas (LPG), kerosene and fuel oil, are exported. Additionally, Oman does import small volumes of refined petroleum products for use in the domestic market – 49% of which is diesel and 22% is premium gasoline. These products are imported mainly because of insufficient refining capacity, however there are plans to expand it.[24] Other imported oil products include benzene ingredients and methanol; which are not produced in Oman.

---

21 Y. Charabi and A. Gastli, 'GIS assessment of large CSP plant in Duqum, Oman', *Renewable and Sustainable Energy Reviews* 14, 2010, pp. 835–41; AER, *Annual report*, Technical report, Authority of Electricity Generation, 2014.
22 AER, *Existing Data Report*, Technical report, Authority of Electricity Generation, 2014.
23 NCSI, *Statistical Yearbook*, 2013.
24 'Oman oil refineries and petroleum industries starts work on Sohar refinery expansion

Electricity generation

In 2004, Sector Law, the law for the regulation and privatisation of the electricity and water sector, was issued.[25] This law implemented policies which included electricity sector restructuring, privatisation and regulation. As a result, the Authority of Electricity Regulation (AER), the Public Authority of Electricity and Water (PAEW), and Oman Power and Water Procurement Company (OPWP) were established. Operationally, the electricity sector in Oman comprises three separate and distinct markets: the Main Interconnected System (MIS), the Salalah Power System (SPS), and the Rural Areas Power System (RAPS), as shown in Figure 25. These markets serve different regions in Oman and there is no competition between them.[26]

MIS serves approximately 88% of the electricity customers in Oman while the remaining 9% are served by SPS. Both these systems use natural gas fired power plants, where roughly half are open cycle gas turbines (OCGT) and half are combined cycle gas turbines (CCGT).[27] Rural Areas Electric Company (RAECo) generates, transmits and distributes to only 2% of the electricity customers in the scattered rural areas of Oman using diesel fuelled facilities. This explains why over 97% of electricity generation in Oman is fuelled by natural gas. Transmission facilities in both MIS and SPS are provided for by a monopoly provider called Oman Electricity Transmission Company (OETC) using 400 kV, 220 kV and 132 kV lines. Distribution and supply facilities in MIS are provided by three licensed companies which have monopoly rights to distribute electricity within authorised areas. These are Muscat Electricity Distribution Company (MEDC), Majan Electricity Company and Mazoon Electricity Company. In SPS, distribution and supply falls under the jurisdiction of Dhofar Power Company (DPC).

In terms of types of consumers, the electricity markets in Oman supply electricity to seven main sectors as summarised in Figure 26 where electricity prices for end-users are identical in all parts of the country but vary by sector. In this chart it is evident that approximately 48% of the electricity produced goes to the

project', *Times of Oman* 2014, http://timesofoman.com/article/35245/Business/Oman-Oil-Refineries-and-Petroleum-Industries-starts-work-on-Sohar-refinery-expansion-project.
25 Oman Vibrant and Electric, *Worldfolio*, 2012, http://www.theworldfolio.com/interviews/john-cunneen-executive-director-and-qais-saud-al-zakwani-director-electricity-regulation/1852/; J. Cunneen, *Electricity Market Structure*, 2012, Power Point Presentation.
26 AER, *Annual Report*, Technical report, Authority of Electricity Regulation, 2011; A. Al-Badi, A. Malik, K. Al-Areimi and A. Al-Mamari, 'Power sector of Oman; today and tomorrow', *Renewable and Sustainable Energy Reviews* 13, 2009, pp. 2192–6.
27 OPWP, *7-Year Statement (2014–2020)*, Technical report, Oman Power and Water Procurement Company, 2014.

residential sector, making it the largest electricity consuming sector. However, it is interesting to note that the energy demand from one industrial customer at 4470 MWh per year is approximately equivalent to 260 residential customers (17 MWh per year). This implies that although the residential sector currently stands as the sector with the largest electricity demand, the addition of a few more industrial accounts could shift this situation, making the industrial sector the sector with the largest electricity demand.

In addition to an indirect subsidy thanks to the low gas prices, the electricity sector receives a direct subsidy from the Ministry of Finance (MOF) according to a mechanism described in the Sector Law. This factor brings electricity prices to very low levels, where in Oman they are nine times lower than in the UK and five times lower than in the US.[28] Table 1 summarises the direct subsidy received by each of the three electricity markets in Oman. This subsidy is dependent on the number of electricity customers. Although it is expected of MIS to receive the largest share of total financial subsidy, it is interesting to note that SPS and RAPS receive a significant amount of the subsidy despite the significantly smaller electricity generation provided by these markets. The reason for this is Oman's policy of identical electricity prices in all areas. Given that the geographical areas served by SPS and RAPS are less densely populated, the total supply costs are higher. Therefore, in order to keep electricity prices at the same level, consumer prices are heavily subsidised.

System	Financial Subsidy Provided (million OMR)	% of Total Financial Subsidy	% of Total Net Electricity Production
MIS	214.1	74.6	88.2
SPS	28.5	9.9	9.4
RAPS	44.5	15.5	2.4

Table 1: Final subsidy in million Omani Rials (OMR), percentage of total financial subsidy and percentage of total net electricity production by the three systems in Oman. This table shows that due to Oman's policy of identical electricity prices in all areas, geographical areas that are less densely populated and served by SPS and RAPS are heavily subsidised.

---

28 J. Krane, *Stability versus Sustainability: Energy Policy in the Gulf Monarchies*, Technical report, Cambridge University, 2013; EIA, *Residential Electricity Prices in Europe and the United States in 2013*, 2013, http://www.eia.gov/todayinenergy/detail.cfm?id=18851.

The demand (end-use) sector

There are four main end-users of energy in Oman: industry, transport, residential, and commercial and public services. These main end-users broadly fall under the responsibility of the Ministry of Commerce and Industry (MOCI), Ministry of Transport and Communications (MOTC) and Ministry of Housing, Electricity and Water (MHEW).[29] The total final energy consumption by the end-users is summarised in Figure 27 by fuel type.

Industry

The industrial sector is the largest consumer of energy in Oman, with 91% of its energy consumption coming directly from natural gas. In addition, it is a major consumer of electricity following the residential and commercial & public services sectors. This makes the industrial sector the largest emitter of CO_2 in Oman, contributing to 38% of total CO_2 emissions (Figure 21). Table 2 summarises the types of industries in Oman by disaggregating them into two levels as classified by International Standards of Industrial Classification (ISIC) codes.[30] Approximately 50% of natural gas consumption by the industrial sector came from metal industries although they only form 7% of total industrial investments and 1% of the total number of industrial establishments in Oman. This highlights the natural gas intensive nature of the metal industry, signifying the need to focus on this specific industry in order to reduce natural gas demand.

In terms of structure, there are currently eight industrial estates in Oman that are managed by the Public Establishment for Industrial Estates (PEIE).[31] In addition, there are three free zones: two in the south (Al-Mazunah and Salalah free zones) and one in the north (Sohar free zone). Finally, there is a special economic zone in the central part of the country (Al-Duqm) managed by the Special Economic Zone Authority (SEZA).

---

29 MOCI, *About Us*, 2014, http://www.mocioman.gov.om/?lang=en-US; MOTC, *About Us*, 2014, http://www.motc.gov.om/tabid/40/default.aspx; MOH, *About Ministry*, 2014, http://eservices.housing.gov.om/eng/Pages/Default.aspx; MOH, *FAQs*, 2015, https://eservices.housing.gov.om/eng/Pages/FAQs.aspx.
30 NCSI, *Statistical Yearbook*, 2012; S. C. Bhattacharyya and G. R. Timilsina, *Energy Demand Models for Policy Formulation*, Technical report, World Bank, 2009.
31 PEIE, *Estates*, 2013, http://www.peie.om.

First Level	Second Level
Mining and Quarrying	
Manufacturing	Food, beverages and tobacco
	Spinning, weaving, finishing textiles and leather
	Wood and wood products, including furniture
	Paper and paper products, printing and publishing
	Chemicals and chemical products, products of petroleum and coal
	Non-metallic mineral products
	Basic metal industries
	Fabricated metal products
Building and Construction	

Table 2: Disaggregation of the industrial sector in Oman
into two levels as classified by ISIC codes.

Transport

The second largest consumer of energy in Oman is the transport sector 100% of whose energy consumption comes from oil products, namely gasoline, since the main mode of domestic transport is 'road transport' (i.e. cars, motorcycles and trucks). Table 3 summarises the transport sector in Oman by disaggregating it into two categories: passenger transport and freight transport. Due to a combination of an increase in population and GDP per capita as well as new and improved road transport infrastructure,[32] the demand for transport fuel has quadrupled in the last ten years. This resulted in Oman's refining capacity being no longer able to meet the country's domestic demand for transportation fuel. Therefore, in addition to importing gasoline, Oman has a Gas-to-Liquids (GTL) programme, transforming natural gas into motor gasoline. With a diesel-fuelled national railway project planned for the near future,[33] and no other plans for alternative transport fuels,[34] the demand for oil-based transport fuel is expected to increase over the years.

---

32 WorldBank, *Oman Data*, 2012, http://data.worldbank.org; ROP, *Frequently Asked Questions*, 2014, http://www.rop.gov.om/english/onlineservices_faqs.asp.
33 A. E. James, *Oman's Railway Project to Start on a Fast Track*, 2013, http://www.timesofoman.com/News/Article-22632.aspx.
34 PAEW, *Solar Project*, 2013, http://www.omanpwp.com/What.aspx#85opwp&M=Menu17.

Need	Modes	Vehicles	Fuel Use
Public passenger transport	Road	Taxis	Gasoline
		Minibuses	Gasoline
		Intercity buses	Diesel
	Domestic air		
	Domestic water		
Private passenger transport	Road	Motorcycles	Gasoline
		Cars	Gasoline
Freight transport	Road	Pick-ups	Gasoline
		Light-trucks	Diesel
		Heavy trucks	Diesel
	Domestic water	Barges, ships	Diesel

Table 3: Disaggregation of the transport sector in Oman.

Residential

The residential sector is the largest consumer of electricity in Oman, where 86% of its total final energy consumption is fuelled by electricity while the remaining 14% comes from oil products – mainly butane and LPG for cooking purposes.[35] Over 80% of Oman's residential stock is located in the north of the country and therefore receives electricity through the main interconnected system (MIS). In terms of individual households, there are five main dwelling archetypes in Oman where over 80% are either villas, apartments or Arabic style houses. These houses are characterised by poor fabric performance where homes have little to no thermal insulation and single-glazed windows dominate.[36] Figure 28 outlines the end-use appliances used by the individual households in Oman where over 50% of energy demand is for cooling and air-conditioning purposes, indicating the importance of reducing cooling demand in order to reduce overall residential electricity demand. In fact, the electricity demand per household in Oman is amongst the highest in the world,[37] where it its eleven times higher than the UK, three times higher than the US, and comparable only to other countries in the region such as Kuwait and Qatar.

35 NCSI, *Households and Housing*, Technical report, National Centre of Statistics and Information, 2010.
36 T. Sweetnam, *Residential Energy Use in Oman: A Scoping Study*, Technical report, Passive Systems, 2014.
37 Enerdata, *Average Electricity Consumption per Electrified Household*, 2013, https://www.wec-indicators.enerdata.eu/household-electricity-use.html; RenewEconomy, *Average House Size by Country*, 2013, http://reneweconomy.com.au/2013/how-big-is-a-house-average-house-size-by-country-78685.

Commercial and public services

The commercial and public services sector is the smallest consumer of energy in Oman, yet it is the second largest consumer of electricity. All of its demand is met by electricity since this sector has similar end-use appliances as the residential sector (Figure 28), with very little or no cooking taking place.

Conclusion

Oman's strategy of diversifying its economy has shifted its reliance from one fossil fuel – oil – to another – natural gas. The fact that this strategy put a strain on the country's natural gas resources signifies a lack of scenario analysis in addressing some of Oman's long-term energy policies. Furthermore, within all of Oman's energy sectors, there is a common trend in the way in which the country tackles increased demand for energy; i.e. through increasing supply. However, there are various other ways in which demand could be reduced, such as increasing efficiency, demand-side management, influencing energy prices and providing alternatives. Examples of this include, LED lights, electric versus gasoline cars,[38] and the implementation of digital electric metres.[39] It is interesting to note that some of these various options are recognised in Oman's 2015 INDC submission. However, they are only defined in general terms, with no goals and detailed plans identifying the actions required to achieve these goals.

Although the current energy policy of providing gas for the industrial sector and power generators at advantageous prices has so far been successful in attracting investment and generating jobs, it results in significant financial losses for the government. Additionally, it does not encourage investors to choose more efficient technologies, nor does it encourage consumers to be more efficient in their power consumption. However, raising prices is politically challenging and requires a pragmatic approach which includes increased spending on education, health and social welfare. In Oman, low electricity prices cost the government over 700 million USD annually in direct subsidies. In addition to the subsidies, the fact that the electricity market serves as a regional monopoly does not help promote

---

38 Hybrid Cars, *Top 6 Plug-in Vehicle Adopting Countries – 2013*, 2013, http://www.hybridcars.com/top-6-plug-in-car-adopting-countries/7/.
39 TechnicalReview, *MEDC Launches Oman's First Prepaid Electricity Meter*, 2014, http://www.technicalreviewmiddleeast.com/power-a-water/power-generation/medc-launches-oman-s-first-prepaid-electricity-meter.

competition and reduce electricity prices.[40] Therefore, targeting the structure of the electricity market as well as the tariff is necessary for influencing consumer behaviour and demand, especially peak demand over which future electricity planning is determined.[41]

The country's decision not to use nuclear power means that the main other non-fossil fuel alternative for the power sector are renewables, mainly solar and wind. However, given the need for the flexibility to dispatch electricity at any given time, successful implementation of renewables is dependent on storage technologies, including the electricity grid. Since the residential sector is the largest consumer of electricity in Oman with over 50% of its demand coming from air-conditioning, renewables could be used to provide for this demand. This could be achieved by directly converting renewables to electricity or by solar thermal based technologies for use in water heating and cooling.[42] Given that houses in Oman are characterised by poor fabric performance, further focus must be placed on the architecture of homes as well as the implementation of insulation, which can be enforced through building standards. Implementing renewables would not only help to reduce consumption of natural gas and therefore CO_2 emissions, but it can be a driving factor for broader economic diversification. However, successful implementation of renewables in Oman is dependent on clear identification of barriers, some of which are summarised in Table 4,[43] as well as the implementation of policies, institutions and action plans designated to tackle such barriers. Finally, given that Oman's economy is highly reliant on oil exports to China, this signifies the need to diversify its oil export destinations. The fact that China is a world leader in solar technology[44] could prove beneficial for Oman and provide the opportunity to increase cooperation with China in developing this unused energy resource.

40 OFGEM, *The GB Electricity Retail Market*, 2015, https://www.ofgem.gov.uk/electricity/retail-market/gb-electricity-retail-market.
41 A. M. Al Shehri, *The Report: Saudi Arabia*, Oxford Business Group, 2010.
42 A. Zohar, M. Jelinek, A. Levy and I. Borde, 'The influence of the generator and bubble pump configuration on the performance of diffusion absorption refrigeration (DAR) system', *International Journal of Refrigeration*, 2008, pp. 962–9.
43 F. Beck and E. Martinot, 'Renewable energy policies and barriers', *Encyclopedia of Energy*, 2004, pp. 365–83.
44 A. Simon-Lewis, *How China is Leading the World in Solar Energy Production*, 2014, http://www.wired.co.uk/article/china-climate-change-policy-solar-production.

Barriers	Recommendations
Lack of institutions for renewables	Formulate an energy strategy which contains:
Role of current renewable institutions not clearly defined	(a) A renewable energy strategy/action plan
Obtaining permits for renewables is time consuming and unclear	(b) Plans in creating new institutions which should assist in permit attainment
There is an absence of targets	(c) Innovation in the financial sector
	(d) A target for renewable energy
	(e) Plans in developing expertise
	(f) Capacity building of developers, installers, business managers, financiers, government officials and regulators
Lack of expertise in renewables	Create training programs and improve education
Existing method of measuring solar/wind data is not reliable	Improve and create solar/wind mapping tools
Research on renewables is minimal and undefined	Additional and selective funding for research with focus on storage technologies is necessary
Grid structure potential to accommodate distributed generation is unknown	Assess grid structure and potential

Table 4: Summary of barriers to and recommendations for renewable
energy deployment in Oman as defined by IRENA.

Bibliography

'Oman oil refineries and petroleum industries starts work on Sohar refinery expansion project', *Times of Oman* 2014, http://timesofoman.com/ article/35245/Business/Oman-Oil-Refineries-and-Petroleum-Industries-starts-work-on-Sohar-refinery-expansion-project.

'Oman to play its part on climate change', *Times of Oman* 2015, http:// timesofoman.com/article/73532.

AER, *Annual Report*, Technical report, Authority of Electricity Generation, 2014.

AER, *Annual Report*, Technical report, Authority of Electricity Regulation, 2011.

AER, *Existing Data Report*, Technical report, Authority of Electricity Generation, 2014.

Al-Badi, A. H., A. Malik and A. Gastli, 'Assessment of renewable energy resources potential in Oman and identification of barrier to their significant utilization', *Renewable and Sustainable Energy Reviews* 13, 2009, pp. 2734–9.

Al-Badi, A. H., A. Malik and A. Gastli, 'Sustainable energy usage in Oman; opportunities and barriers', *Renewable and Sustainable Energy Reviews* 15, 2011, pp. 3780–8.

Al-Badi, A. H., M. H. Albadi, A. M. Al-Lawati and A. S. Malik, 'Economic perspective of PV electricity in Oman', *Energy* 36, 2011, pp. 226–32.

Al-Badi, A., A. Malik, K. Al-Areimi and A. Al-Mamari, 'Power sector of Oman; today and tomorrow', *Renewable and Sustainable Energy Reviews* 13, 2009, pp. 2192–6.

BBC, *Oman Country Profile*, 2013, http://www.bbc.co.uk/news/world-middle-east-14654150.

Beck, F. and E. Martinot, 'Renewable energy policies and barriers', *Encyclopedia of Energy*, 2004, pp. 365–83.

Bhattacharyya, S. C. and G. R. Timilsina, *Energy Demand Models for Policy Formulation*, Technical report, World Bank, 2009.

BP, *BP Statistical Review of World Energy*, Technical report, British Petroleum, 2017.

Charabi, Y. and A. Gastli, 'GIS assessment of large CSP plant in Duqum, Oman', *Renewable and Sustainable Energy Reviews* 14, 2010, pp. 835–41.

COWI and Partners, *Study on Renewable Energy Resources, Oman*, Technical report, Authority of Electricity Regulation, 2008.

Cunneen, J., *Electricity Market Structure*, 2012, Power Point Presentation.

Dorvlo, A. S. S. and D. B. Ampratwum, 'Summary climatic data for solar technology development in Oman', *Renewable Energy* 14, 1998, pp. 255–62.

Dorvlo, A. S. S. and D. B. Ampratwum, 'Wind energy potential for Oman', *Renewable Energy* 26, 2002, pp. 333–8.

EIA, *International Energy Statistics*, 2014, http://www.eia.gov/cfapps/ipdbproject/iedindex3.cfm?tid=3&pid=3&aid=6&cid=regions,&syid=2015&eyid=2015&unit=TCF.

EIA, *Natural Gas*, 2017, https://www.eia.gov/naturalgas/weekly/#tabs-prices-2.

EIA, *Overview of Oman*, 2013, www.eia.gov/countries/cab.cfm?fips=MU.

EIA, *Residential Electricity Prices in Europe and the United States in 2013*, 2013, http://www.eia.gov/todayinenergy/detail.cfm?id=18851.

Enerdata, *Average Electricity Consumption per Electrified Household*, 2013, https://www.wec-indicators.enerdata.eu/household-electricity-use.html.

Enerdata, *Natural Gas Production*, 2013, https://yearbook.enerdata.net/natural-gas/world-natural-gas-production-statistics.html.

Gastli, A. and Y. Charabi, 'Solar electricity prospects in Oman using GIS-based solar radiation maps', *Renewable and Sustainable Energy Reviews* 14, 2010, pp. 790–7.

Global Research, *Oman Economic Overview*, Technical report, Global, 2011.

Global Security Newswire, *Oman opts Not to Pursue Atomic Power*, 2012.

Hybrid Cars, *Top 6 Plug-in Vehicle Adopting Countries – 2013*, 2013, http://www.hybridcars.com/top-6-plug-in-car-adopting-countries/7/.

IEA, *Oman: Balances*, 2013, https://www.iea.org/statistics/statisticssearch/report/?country=Oman&product=balances&year=2014.

IEA, *Oman Energy and CO$_2$ Emissions Data*, 2013, http://ukdataservice.ac.uk/.

IRENA, *IRENA Handbook on Renewable Energy Nationally Appropriate Mitigation Actions (NAMAs)*, Technical report, International Renewable Energy Agency, 2014.

IRENA, *Sultanate of Oman, Renewables Readiness Assessment*, Technical report, International Renewable Energy Agency, 2014.

James, A. E., *Oman's Railway Project to Start on a Fast Track*, 2013, http://www.timesofoman.com/News/Article-22632.aspx.

Jervase, J. A., A. Al-Lawati and A. S. S. Dorvlo, 'Contour maps for sunshine ratio for Oman using radial basis function generated data', *Renewable Energy* 28, 2003, pp. 487–97.

Kazem, H. A., 'Renewable energy in Oman: Status and future prospects', *Renewable and Sustainable Energy Reviews* 15, 2011, pp. 3465–9.

Knoema, *Cost of Oil Production by Country*, 2014, http://knoema.com/vyronoe/cost-of-oil-production-by-country.

Krane, J., *Stability versus Sustainability: Energy Policy in the Gulf Monarchies*, Technical report, Cambridge University, 2013.

Kumar Sharma, A., 'Your email to Mr Khamis', MECA, 2013, personal communication.

Mattei, M., G. Notton, C. Cristofari, M. Muselli and P. Poggi, 'Calculation of the polycrystalline PV module temperature using a simple method of energy balance', *Renewable Energy* 31, 2006, pp. 553–67.

MECA and INDC, Technical report, United Nations Framework Convention on Climate Change, 2015.

MOCI, *About Us*, 2014, http://www.mocioman.gov.om/?lang=en-US.

MOG, *Annual Report*, Technical report, Ministry of Oil and Gas, 2013.

MOG, *Brief History of the Oil and Gas Sector*, 2013, http://www.mog.gov.om/english/AboutUs/TheHistoryofOilGas/tabid/117/Default.aspx.

MOH, *About Ministry*, 2014, http://eservices.housing.gov.om/eng/Pages/Default.aspx.

MOH, *FAQs*, 2015, https://eservices.housing.gov.om/eng/Pages/FAQs.aspx.

Mokri, A., M. Aal Ali and M. Emziane, 'Solar energy in the United Arab Emirates: A review', *Renewable and Sustainable Energy Reviews* 28, 2013, pp. 340–75.

MOTC, *About Us*, 2014, http://www.motc.gov.om/tabid/40/default.aspx.

NASA, *NASA Surface Meteorology and Solar Energy-Daylight Hours*, 2017, https://eosweb.larc.nasa.gov/cgi-bin/sse/retscreen.cgi?email=skip@larc.nasa.gov/.

NASA, *NASA Surface Meteorology and Solar Energy-Irradiance*, 2017, https://eosweb.larc.nasa.gov/cgi-bin/sse/retscreen.cgi?email=skip@larc.nasa.gov/.

NCSI, *Households and Housing*, Technical report, National Centre of Statistics and Information, 2010.

NCSI, *Statistical Yearbook*, 2012.

NCSI, *Statistical Yearbook*, 2013.

NCSI, *Statistical Yearbook*, 2014.

OECD, *Crude Oil Production*, 2013, https://data.oecd.org/energy/crude-oil-production.htm.

OFGEM, *The GB Electricity Retail Market*, 2015, https://www.ofgem.gov.uk/electricity/retail-market/gb-electricity-retail-market.

OGC, *About Us*, 2013, www.oman-gas.com.om.

Ogulata, R. T., 'Sectoral energy consumption in turkey', *Renewable and Sustainable Energy Reviews* 6, 2002, pp. 471–80.

Oman Vibrant and Electric, *Worldfolio*, 2012, http://www.theworldfolio.com/interviews/john-cunneen-executive-director-and-qais-saud-al-zakwani-director-electricity-regulation/1852/.

OPWP, *7-Year Statement (2014–2020)*, Technical report, Oman Power and Water Procurement Company, 2014.

PAEW, *Solar Project*, 2013, http://www.omanpwp.com/What.aspx#85opwp&M=Menu17.

PEIE, *Estates*, 2013, http://www.peie.om.

Raslavicius, L., 'Renewable energy sector in Belarus: A review', *Renewable and Sustainable Energy Reviews* 16, 2012, pp. 5399–413.

Rauf, O., S. Wang, P. Yuan and J. Tan, 'An overview of energy status and development in Pakistan', *Renewable and Sustainable Energy Reviews* 48, 2015, pp. 892–931.

RenewEconomy, *Average House Size by Country*, 2013, http://reneweconomy.com.au/2013/how-big-is-a-house-average-house-size-by-country-78685.

ROP, *Frequently Asked Questions*, 2014, http://www.rop.gov.om/english/onlineservices_faqs.asp.

Shediac, R. and H. Samman, *The Vital Role of Sovereign Wealth Funds in the GCC's Future*, Technical report, Booz & Co., 2015.

Al Shehri, A. M., *The Report: Saudi Arabia*, Oxford Business Group, 2010.

Simon-Lewis, A., *How China is Leading the World in Solar Energy Production*, 2014, http://www.wired.co.uk/article/china-climate-change-policy-solar-production.

Skea, J., P. Ekins and M. Winskel, *Energy 2050; Making the Transition to a Secure Low Carbon Energy System*, Earthscan 2011.

Sweetnam, T., *Residential Energy Use in Oman: A Scoping Study*, Technical report, Passive Systems, 2014.

TechnicalReview, *MEDC Launches Oman's First Prepaid Electricity Meter*, 2014, http://www.technicalreviewmiddleeast.com/power-a-water/power-generation/medc-launches-oman-s-first-prepaid-electricity-meter.

World Bank, *Oman*, 2016, http://data.worldbank.org/country/oman.

World Bank, *Oman Data*, 2012, http://data.worldbank.org.

Zohar, A., M. Jelinek, A. Levy and I. Borde, 'The influence of the generator and bubble pump configuration on the performance of diffusion absorption refrigeration (DAR) system', *International Journal of Refrigeration*, 2008, pp. 962–9.

Contributors

Iyad Abumoghli is a Senior Policy Advisor at the UN Environment in its headquarters in Nairobi. Previously, he held the position of Director and Regional Representative for the West Asia region.

Tony Allan is Emeritus Professor of Geography at SOAS University of London and King's College London. He is an internationally esteemed expert in water resources and the political economy of water policy and its reform. He was awarded the Stockholm Water Prize in 2008 for his revolutionary virtual water concept.

Marta Antonelli is a scientist at EAWAG, Swiss Federal Institute of Aquatic Science and Technology in Switzerland and the Euro-Mediterranean Centre on Climate Change (CMCC) in Italy.

Georgeta Vidican Auktor is Professor at the Nürnberg Institute of Technology Georg Simon Ohm and Research Fellow at the German Development Institute in Bonn.

María J. Beltrán holds a European PhD in Ecological Economics and Environmental Management. She is Adjunct Professor at the Economics Department, Pablo de Olavide University.

Matthew Broughton is a research associate at the United Nations Environment Programme Regional Office in Bahrain.

Mine Cinar is Director of the Center for International Business, and Professor of Economics at the Quinlan School of Business at Loyola University Chicago.

Philipp Dees is an energy economics researcher with a specific focus on the MENA region.

Ludovic Gaudard is a Postdoctoral Researcher at the Centre for Environmental Policy of Imperial College London. He holds a PhD in interdisciplinary studies in economics and environmental sciences.

Hassan Hakimian is Director of the London Middle East Institute and Reader in the Department of Economics at SOAS, University of London.

Nathalie Hilmi is a specialist in Macroeconomics and International Finance. In 2010, she joined the Centre Scientifique de Monaco as section head of environmental economics.

Helen Lackner is a Research Associate at the London Middle East Institute, SOAS, University of London.

Nancy Lindisfarne is a social anthropologist. She has done fieldworks in Iran, Afghanistan, Turkey and Syria.

Niall Mac Dowell leads the Clean Fossil and Bioenergy Research Group at Imperial College. He is a Reader in Energy and Environmental Technology and Policy at Imperial College London

Kaveh Madani is a Visiting Professor at Imperial College, a Henry Hart Rice Senior Fellow at Yale University, and a former Deputy Head of Iran's Department of Environment.

Maral Mahlooji is a PhD student at the Centre for Environmental Policy of Imperial College London.

Jonathan Neale is a writer and climate campaigner. He studied anthropology at LSE and did a PhD in social history at the University of Warwick.

Hamid Pouran is Research Associate at SOAS University of London and Lecturer in environmental technology at the University of Wolverhampton. He is Senior Member IEEE and Chair IEEE UK and Ireland Climate Change and Environmental Technology Special Interest Group (ETSIG).

Victor Planas-Bielsa is an applied mathematician and senior scientist at the Scientifique Center in Monaco.

Alain Safa is specialised in macroeconomics and international finance. He's a professor at the University of Nice Sophia-Antipolis and EDHEC Business School.

Safia Saouli is a doctoral researcher at Imperial College London's Centre for Environmental Policy. Her research focuses on developing a sustainable energy portfolio – integrating both renewable, conventional and unconventional types of energy – for the Middle East and North Africa region.

Juman Al-Saqlawi completed her PhD at the Centre for Environmental Policy, Imperial College London in 2017. The focus of her research was to further the understanding of the potential of implementing solar technologies in the Omani residential sector.

Tobias Zumbrägel is Chair of Middle Eastern Politics and Society at Friedrich-Alexander University Erlangen-Nuremberg, Germany.